PRINCE
PHILIP
REVEALED

Also by Ingrid Seward

By Royal Invitation
Royalty Revealed
Diana: An Intimate Portrait
Sarah, Duchess of York
Royal Children of the 20th Century
Prince Edward
The Last Great Edwardian Lady
The Queen and Di
William and Harry
William & Harry: The People's Princes
Diana: The Last Word
The Queen's Speech
My Husband & I

PRINCE PHILIP REVEALED

INGRID SEWARD

ATRIA PAPERBACK

New York   London   Toronto   Sydney   New Delhi

ATRIA
PAPERBACK

An Imprint of Simon & Schuster, Inc.
1230 Avenue of the Americas
New York, NY 10020

Copyright © 2020 by Ingrid Seward. All rights reserved.

All rights reserved, including the right to reproduce this book
or portions thereof in any form whatsoever. For information,
address Atria Books Subsidiary Rights Department,
1230 Avenue of the Americas, New York, NY 10020.

First Atria Paperback edition June 2021

ATRIA PAPERBACK and colophon are trademarks of Simon & Schuster, Inc.

For information about special discounts for bulk purchases,
please contact Simon & Schuster Special Sales at
1-866-506-1949 or business@simonandschuster.com.

The Simon & Schuster Speakers Bureau can bring authors to
your live event. For more information or to book an event,
contact the Simon & Schuster Speakers Bureau at 1-866-248-3049
or visit our website at www.simonspeakers.com.

Manufactured in the United States of America

1 3 5 7 9 10 8 6 4 2

Library of Congress Cataloging-in-Publication Data has been applied for.

ISBN 978-1-9821-2975-0
ISBN 978-1-9821-2976-7 (pbk)
ISBN 978-1-9821-2977-4 (ebook)

For Nicky and James

Contents

Contents

PRINCE
PHILIP
REVEALED

Prologue

I first met the Duke of Edinburgh in the late 1970s. He was in his mid-fifties and no longer the dashing polo-playing prince, simply a man in a suit. I was one of a group of girls involved in raising monies for a theater of which Prince Philip was a patron, and we went backstage afterward to meet him. He was charming, polite, and funny, and only now when looking back do I realize how wary he must have been of being photographed with a bunch of young girls.

The next time I met him was in Amman, in March 1984. I had moved on from PR and was working for *Majesty* magazine. He was with Queen Elizabeth on a state visit to the Hashemite Kingdom of Jordan as guests of King Hussein and Queen Noor. On the first afternoon there was a reception for the royal press corps, of which I was one, to meet Queen Elizabeth and Prince Philip—this was standard in those days.

As we walked into the British Embassy, all of us visiting media journalists and some of the heavy-hitting Middle East foreign correspondents lined up to shake hands as if we were at an old-fashioned wedding reception. I clearly remember the master of ceremonies calling out Ingrid Seward from Hanover Magazines, who then published *Majesty*. It was my first royal tour and I hadn't a clue what to do, so I just stuck around Michael Shea, Queen Elizabeth's press secretary, who told me where to stand and wait to be introduced to the Queen.

Before this happened I was approached by an equerry who said to me, "His Royal Highness the Duke of Edinburgh would like to meet you." I nodded vaguely, and before I could do anything, Prince Philip walked up to me and asked me in his crisp, dry voice if I was German. I suppose with a name like Ingrid and working for an organization called Hanover Magazines it was a possibility. As soon as I replied in the negative, he turned on his heel and walked away.

I was humiliated—I couldn't understand what I had done, but I later learned it was standard behavior for the duke. According to behavioral psychologists, people in a position of power such as Prince Philip frequently don't terminate a meeting properly. They just walk away if they are not interested. They know people only want to talk to them because of who they are, not as a real person, so they have no sensitivity toward the other individual's feelings.

Years later, when I was introduced to the duke again, this time by his then private secretary and friend Brian McGrath, at a small party in the grounds of Home Park during the Windsor Horse Show, he looked straight at me and walked away without uttering a word. Brian, looking flustered, came over to apologize, saying that the duke had thought I was from the *Daily Mirror* not *Majesty* magazine, which was why he had walked away. I met him again a few days later, when perhaps he had been briefed I was not from a tabloid newspaper, and we had what I imagined he would think was a civilized conversation about carriage driving. Realizing I was not the enemy, he was charm personified and put me in touch with his head groom, at that time David Muir. He had allowed David to take me out with his carriage ponies so I could see for myself what it was like.

I still couldn't quite believe it when I found myself sitting on the Balmoral tartan–covered box seat being driven from the Royal

Mews to the showground at Windsor with the Queen's four Fell ponies pulling us along. With Windsor Castle behind us, we clopped past the carefully trimmed lawns and flowering trees to Home Park and the nine-hole golf course where Prince Andrew used to practice his golf swing. We trotted beside the river Thames and the railway track on to the showground, where it was much rougher, and when a train roared past, the ponies quickened their pace, but they responded immediately when told to stop. I used the moment to ask David Muir about his boss.

"People that don't know the duke are intimidated by him," Muir admitted. "It can be like the parting of the Red Sea. As the duke walks up everyone stands back, but if you are honest with him, he is honest with you. He can spot a fake a mile away."

I have seen him dancing at the Squadron Ball at Cowes, expertly wrapped around Penny Romsey (now Countess Mountbatten of Burma) without a care about who would see them, so I presumed rightly or wrongly it was totally innocent. I have seen him being unpleasant and brusque, but I have also seen him lifting little children out of a crowd and over a barrier so they can give the Queen a posy. I have seen him feeding sugar lumps to his ponies after they have competed in a marathon.

With his intellectual rigor goes a great generosity of spirit. Practically everyone who has worked for him has unqualified affection for him, even though he continually shouts at them. He also has a capacity for intense dislike: of the press, his critics, and fools. His best relationships are those based on mutual respect such as he has for the Queen; his daughter, the Princess Royal; and his youngest son, the Earl of Wessex. He is also surprisingly unstuffy, although he has more blue blood running through his veins than his wife, the Queen.

According to Major General Sir Michael Hobbs, a former director of the Duke of Edinburgh Award who has worked with the duke since 1988: "He is reserved by nature and not a demonstrative man. He meets discomfort absolutely head-on and isn't worried by it. He is a loner, utterly happy within himself."

The duke claimed it was his mentor, Kurt Hahn, who persuaded him to become involved with the award: "Kurt Hahn came along one day and he sent for me and I went to see him at Brown's Hotel, where he always stayed, and he said, 'Boy, I want you to start an awards scheme.'

"I said, 'Thanks very much!' We had a badge scheme at Gordonstoun, and if you qualified throwing and running and jumping, you got a badge for it. I said, 'I can't start it, but if you put together a committee of the great and the good, I am perfectly happy to chair it, which is what happened.'"

Philip's relationship with Kurt Hahn was forged in the crucible of Gordonstoun School, where, under Hahn's tutorship, Philip developed his adult self. Because of his respect for Hahn, anything the elder man needed, Philip would consider very carefully. "His dream was that one day the award that bears his name wouldn't be necessary. It was a genuinely altruistic dream, and he believed and hoped it would become part of the development process of young people," said Michael Hobbs.

Philip likes a lot of people for specific parts of what they are, but he does not have many complete friends. Not surprisingly many of those he did have are dead, but Philip is pragmatic and doesn't dwell on the past or what might have been. As a high achiever himself, he expects the same from his friends when they are helping him, and yet when they disappoint him he is always fair. It was the same with his children.

In his youth his eldest son, the Prince of Wales, was frightened of him, and although they now have great respect for each other, it took years of misunderstanding. The late Diana Princess of Wales said he was an amusing dinner companion but she would never look to him for sympathy or go to him for help as opposed to advice or guidance, which he gave her. But at the end of her life she declared she hated him. In a conversation I had with her on the subject, she informed me she had warned her sons, William and Harry, never to shout at anyone who couldn't answer back the way their grandfather did.

As is often the case between younger and older generations, the duke's grandchildren find him easier than his children, in particular the Princess Royal's son, Peter Phillips, who has always been a particular favorite. According to a member of staff, as the duke became more cantankerous in his old age, the only one who could cheer him up was Peter, who used to love to go duck flighting with his grandfather, and they still play games together and tease each other.

His numerous physical impairments and auditory problems may have made him increasingly bad tempered, and according to research lowered testosterone also plays a part in making older men more irritable and moodier. Regardless, even in his late stage of life, Prince Philip still takes huge pleasure in defying convention. When the Queen was hosting a tea for President Donald Trump of the United States in July 2018, Prince Philip got himself into a helicopter to make the two-hundred-mile journey from Wood Farm in Sandringham to Romsey in Hampshire to stand at the font at Romsey Abbey as a godfather to six-month-old Inigo Hooper, his first cousin three times removed. Inigo, son of Lady Alexandra Hooper and her husband Tom, will one day inherit Broadlands, and ninety-seven-year-old Philip wanted to be there among the Mountbatten family, not at Windsor Castle with the US president.

Prince Philip continues to enjoy his life. He spends most of his time at the refurbished Wood Farm on the Sandringham estate, where if he has to do the occasional family get-together, he does it with good heart and a huge amount of the willpower he has always possessed. His determination to be at Prince Harry and Meghan Markle's wedding in May 2018, despite having a hip operation only six weeks beforehand, was an example of his fortitude. As always, he walked ramrod straight into the chapel and sat through the long service without displaying a flicker of discomfort. Although he didn't attend the reception afterward, he did turn up at Lady Gabriella Windsor's wedding to Tom Kingston when they married in May 2019, and he attended their reception at Frogmore House. At Christmastime he always hosts his staff party at Frogmore and refuses to change anything because of his age. The staff at Windsor has noted that since his car accident in January 2019, he has a renewed zest for life and has been far more cheerful, possibly because he feels he has been given a reprieve to get on with whatever remains of his life. He enjoys watching cooking programs on television, can still read, and enjoys the company of attractive women and intelligent conservation. He is surprisingly sensitive and has always been appalled by the stream of negative stories in the media about the royal family—his family—but he has always cautioned against suing the press except in a few instances. He knows it gives more coverage to a libel, plus it is an unpleasant and expensive process to go through.

Watching Fergie and Diana tearing apart what he considered sacrosanct—the institution of the monarchy—for their own ends made him very angry and hurt him considerably. It was only in 2019 that he would finally be reconciled with Fergie and be present at a lunch at Windsor Castle with the Queen, Fergie, and Andrew. They never touch on the past, as Philip sees no point in that, but he is able to be in Fergie's company without making her feel awkward. She is a good conversationalist and enjoys his continuing fascination with new things and ideas, which are sometimes a bit off-the-wall—but she can relate to them well. He once decided, for instance, it would be a good idea to introduce hawks into New York City to kill the vermin population that was a problem at the time.

Above all Prince Philip is loyal. He is loyal to his wife, the Queen, and the institution of the monarchy—which they have both given up so much to support—and it grieves him that the younger generation do not all appear to have the devotion to duty that has always been his byline. For him duty is at the center of everything. It is not a choice. It is one of life's givens and it is the framework from which all other things follow. Prince Philip has always operated within the framework that if you obey the rules, life will be so much easier. There will be no embarrassment and no one will step over the line and say things they later on regret. Although Philip finds comfort and security in structure, there is also a rebellious streak at the core of his character. He has always held the opinion that his way is the right way, and he does not enjoy being corrected if someone contradicts him.

"He is an alpha male playing a beta role, but he accepts that as it's his duty," said behavioral psychologist Dr. Peter Collett. "He buys into paying homage as it's playing the role, but outside of that he appears to find it difficult."

In 2016, the year of the Queen's ninetieth birthday, she was asked to present the trophies to the winner on Derby Day at Epsom for the first time in her reign. After the race the Queen took her place as the connections to the winning horse, Hazard, mounted the dais one by one to collect their trophies. First up was the winning owner, the Aga Khan, with whom the Queen could be seen discussing the race—she has extensive knowledge of the breeding of all the fancied runners. Next in line were the trainer Dermot Weld and the jockey Pat Smullen along with the stable lad who looked after the winning horse. Each man in turn received his trophy after a few words of congratulation from the Queen. Meanwhile ninety-four-year-old

Prince Philip was standing erect as always and off to one side of the Queen and the winning group. He was impeccably dressed in a morning suit with a gray top hat and a colorful green-and-maroon tie with a pearl-and-diamond anchor tiepin. He shook hands with each man as he mounted the dais, but took no part in the presentation ceremony. Despite the Queen's passion for horse racing, the duke has little interest in it himself and tried not to look bored by the proceedings. But the Derby is not a state occasion, so why did Philip make the trek down from the royal box to the presentation, only a week after his doctors ordered him to cancel his official engagements because of fears about his health? It was not an obligation.

It was his sense of duty. In all the years since the Queen's accession, Prince Philip's sense of duty has never wavered. He is always there. Two steps behind. His complex character is part of what makes him fascinating. "I often describe Prince Philip as a whirling comet with bits shooting off in different directions," recounted one of his female friends. "He is not a gentleman, because he doesn't put people at their ease when he can't be bothered, but he plays by the rules with his wife and family."

The Queen, who has been married to him for more than seventy years, has told us he doesn't take easily to compliments. He doesn't; he mistrusts their motives. He also objects to any details about his private life becoming public property. When Michael Fagan broke into the Queen's bedroom in 1982, the thing that worried Prince Philip the most was that the public would know their sleeping arrangements—they have separate interconnecting bedrooms like many aristocratic couples with different life schedules. The Queen switches off when the duke becomes difficult and walks away both physically and mentally. But although their marriage has been challenging at times, it has never been dull.

When he was still actively involved, the worst thing about royal life for Prince Philip was the official engagements that could be so personally restricting and stultifyingly boring. Philip is as well known for his gaffes as anything else, but most of them are couched not to be rude but to relieve the boredom. Occasionally a mishap relieves the tedium, and one of Philip's favorites occurred during a state banquet in May 1966, probably the only time anything has ever gone wrong on such an occasion.

The Queen was at the head of the table with Prince Philip next to her and the guest of honor, President Franz Jonas of Austria, on her right. The Archbishop of Canterbury was seated nearby, and opposite him sat a dame commander of the Order of the British Empire, who was also a brigadier in the army.

The brigadier, a well-proportioned lady, was wearing a black evening dress held in place by two thin shoulder straps. On the left side of the dress she wore medal ribbons. As a footman bent over to serve her vegetables, one of the buttons on his livery became entangled with the row of ribbons above her ample bosom. He tried to extricate himself while holding the salver of vegetables, which proved impossible. With difficulty he found a spot on the table to set down the dish, and with the help of the brigadier managed to untangle the button and strap.

Relieved but embarrassed and flustered, the footman bent to retrieve his vegetable dish and then another button became caught in the lady's other shoulder strap. Dismayed, she pulled away from the footman just as he pulled away from her. The strap snapped, closely followed by the other. In a panic she pushed herself back from the table and with the same movement pushed herself out of her dress. The archbishop stared at his plate while the Queen determinedly carried on her conversation with the president of Austria so he did not dare look toward the commotion. For once the rule that no one leaves the table before the Queen was broken and the lady hurriedly left in search of a couple of safety pins.

Prince Philip still repeats the story that tickled his well-developed sense of the ridiculous, although it might have been altered a little down the years of retelling.

The multifaceted, complex, humorous character that is Prince Philip has been fortunate enough to dedicate his spare time to the pursuit of knowledge, and to enjoy his life while doing so. During his last years he has refused to give in to illness or infirmity, realizing that to do so would deny him his final opportunity to understand what he had not understood before. He has used this time to read the books he always wanted to read but never had the time to do so and to go through the archives of his life so carefully filed by his loyal archivist. I don't think he has been afraid of death or afraid of life. His fear has been to leave things undone.

To the last he has remained a man of immense personal discipline and dedication to duty. Within the pages of this book I have attempted to explain who this man is and how he has managed to survive within his extraordinary life and make it actually worth living.

Chapter 1

ANCESTRY

As a young naval lieutenant based in Melbourne with the Pacific Fleet in 1944, Prince Philip of Greece and Denmark described himself as "a discredited Balkan prince of no particular merit or distinction." It was typical of his self-deprecating style of repartee. Far from being a minor Greek prince, Philip's royal antecedents connect him to the highest ranks of European royalty. His bloodlines provide direct links to British royalty, to the royal house of Denmark, to the grand dukes of Hesse in Germany, and to the Romanov imperial family in Russia.

At the beginning of the twentieth century, the convoluted family trees of the royal houses of Europe showed a high degree of intermarriage, with cousins marrying cousins. Princes and princesses never married commoners and large families were the norm. At the pinnacle reigned the most powerful queen in the world, Queen Victoria, who with her German husband, Prince Albert of Saxe-Coburg-Gotha, had nine children who went on to produce a total of forty-two grandchildren. Their marriages linked together the great powers of Great Britain, Germany, and Russia. France, albeit also a major power, was outside the circle of northern royal European marriages as it was principally Roman Catholic and without a royal family.

The other great European dynasty was that of King Christian IX of Denmark, who reigned from 1863 to 1906. At the outbreak of the First World War in 1914, the grandchildren of Queen Victoria and King Christian IX together occupied the thrones of Denmark, Greece, Norway, Germany, Romania, Russia, and Great Britain.

The Queen and Prince Philip are third cousins because both are great-great-grandchildren of Queen Victoria. The Queen is a direct descendant of Queen Victoria's eldest son, Prince Albert Edward, later King Edward VII. Philip is a direct descendant of Queen Victoria's second daughter, Princess Alice, the grandmother of Philip's mother, who was also called Alice. King Christian IX's daughter Queen Alexandra, who was the wife of King Edward VII, and his son William, who was later King George I of Greece, were brother and sister, linking Philip's father Andrew (King George I's son) to King George V of England (King Edward VII's son) as first cousins.

Christian IX was chosen as heir to the Danish throne when the senior line of succession became extinct. He was the first Danish monarch of the House of Glucksburg. As a young man he had sought the hand of Queen Victoria but was rejected in favor of Prince Albert. He married Princess Louise of Hesse-Cassel, and with his German wife they had six children. Every father wants to see his children marry well, especially so if a royal family is involved. Few could have done quite as well as King Christian IX of Denmark. He was the father of a British queen, a Russian tsarina, and two European kings. It was the ambitious Queen Louise who successfully schemed to get their children married to scions of Europe's royal and princely houses. Their second-eldest daughter, Dagmar, became Maria Feodorovna when she married the future Tsar Alexander III, Emperor of Russia and King of Poland. Their eldest daughter, Alexandra, married the Prince of Wales in 1863 and became Queen of England when Edward VII acceded on the death of Queen Victoria. Another daughter, Thyra, married the heir to the throne of Hanover.

After he was crowned king, Christian IX organized a family gathering that was held every other year at the Fredensborg Palace north of Copenhagen. So great were the numbers attending from across Europe that several three-hundred-place-setting dinner services were commissioned from the Royal Copenhagen porcelain factory. The grandchildren who played games together in the extensive grounds included the future Tsar Nicholas II of Russia and three future kings: George V of the United Kingdom, Haakon of Norway, and Constantine I of Greece. Although coming from a country with a population of less than 2.5 million, such was the influence of the Danish family among the royal houses of Europe that King Christian IX became known as "the father-in-law of Europe."

King Christian IX was created a Knight of the Garter in 1865, and his descendants have continued close links with the British royal family ever since. At the time of her coronation, both Queen Elizabeth and Philip—Christian IX's great-grandson—were awarded the Order of the Elephant, Denmark's highest-ranked Order of Chivalry.

Christian's eldest son, Frederick, succeeded him as King of Denmark, while his younger son William became King George I of Greece at seventeen years old—the latter would be Philip's grandfather. William was a reluctant monarch who did not want to abandon his career in the Danish navy and spoke not one word of Greek. The great powers of Europe—England, France, and Russia—had signed the London Protocol of 1830, which declared Greece an independent state and stated that a hereditary sovereign for Greece should be chosen from outside the country. Otto, a Bavarian prince, was selected as the first King of Greece, but he became unpopular and was deposed in 1862. William was subsequently chosen because it was thought that having a Danish king of Greece would avoid upsetting the balance of power in Europe. On March 30, 1863, the Greek National Assembly elected him King of the Hellenes, under the regnal name of George I. He soon became a popular monarch, learning to speak Greek in a matter of months and making himself available to the Greek people with weekly audiences.

George went to stay with his sister, the tsarina, in Russia for the purpose of finding a wife. When visiting the tsar's younger brother, the Grand Duke Constantine, he fell for his fifteen-year-old daughter, Olga. They were married shortly after Olga's sixteenth birthday, at the Winter Palace in St. Petersburg in 1867. Together they had seven children, of whom Philip's father Andreas, commonly called Andrew, was last but one. Philip's paternal grandmother, Olga, was the niece of Tsar Nicholas II. After fifty years on the throne, George I was assassinated in Thessaloniki in 1913 while taking his daily stroll among his people.

Entry number 449 in the Corfu Register of Births shows that on May 28, 1921, a son was born to Prince Andrew of Greece, son of King George I of Greece, and Princess Alice, daughter of Prince Louis (Ludwig) of Battenberg. The baby was baptized in the Greek Orthodox Church as "Philippos." It was not until two years later, when Greece adopted the Gregorian calendar, that the date of birth was changed to June 10, which is Philip's official birthday. His full title was Prince Philip of Greece and Denmark, but at school he insisted that he was just plain Philip. The royal family into which Philip was born a prince on his father's side was not Greek in origin. It was a branch of the House of Glucksburg descended directly from the kings of Denmark. Until Philip took British nationality in 1947, he called himself "Philip of Greece." When he became a British citizen, he renounced his foreign title of prince and became Lieutenant Philip Mountbatten RN. On the eve of his wedding he was created

His Royal Highness Duke of Edinburgh, Earl of Merioneth and Baron Greenwich. He would not become a prince again until ten years later, when the Queen elevated him to "the style and dignity of a Prince of the United Kingdom."

Although born in Greece, a country he was to leave while still an infant, Philip's connection to that country was tenuous to say the least. His mother, Princess Alice, had never been in Greece until she married Prince Andrew, and she had no Greek blood relatives. Alice was a Battenberg with close connections to the British royal family. She was born at Windsor Castle in the presence of Queen Victoria in 1885. Her mother, Victoria, was one of Queen Victoria's granddaughters and would become a huge influence on Philip when he was a schoolboy in England. After she was widowed, Philip's grandmother Victoria often traveled with him to Germany in the school holidays to visit her granddaughters who lived there. Alice's father was Louis of Battenberg, later 1st Marquess of Milford Haven, whose family home was in Darmstadt.

Louis may have been born German, but he joined the British Navy at the age of fourteen and became a naturalized British subject. He rose to be First Sea Lord. When the First World War broke out, Louis sent a signal to all the British warships: "Commence hostilities against Germany." However, Louis had married Princess Victoria of Hesse and by Rhine, and being a Grand Duke of Hesse himself, he was considered to be too German to be head of the Royal Navy in wartime. In 1914, anti-German sentiment was running high in England; Dachshunds were kicked in the street and Beethoven's and Wagner's music was considered unfit for British ears. After forty-six years in the Royal Navy, Prince Louis was persuaded to write to the First Lord of the Admiralty, Winston Churchill. as follows:

"I have lately been driven to the painful conclusion that at this juncture my birth and parentage have the effect of impairing in some respects my usefulness on the Board of Admiralty. I feel it to be my duty as a loyal subject of His Majesty to resign the office of First Sea Lord hoping thereby to facilitate the task of administration of the great Service to which I have devoted my life."

For his troubles he was created the 1st Marquess of Milford Haven. Three years later, in 1917, King George V felt compelled to change the family name from Saxe-Coburg-Gotha to the House of Windsor. At the same time Battenberg was anglicized to become Mountbatten. Louis's younger son, also called Louis but known to all as Dickie, was a naval cadet who vowed to avenge his father's humiliation. He too became First Sea Lord and rose to even greater heights as the last viceroy in India and supreme commander of the Allied forces in South East Asia in the Second World War. As well as being Philip's uncle, Dickie became a close friend and had a great influence on Philip's future.

In her childhood, Philip's mother, Alice, was brought up in England and became a favorite of Queen Victoria, who wrote to her frequently. Alice would stay at the royal residences of Osborne on the Isle of Wight, Balmoral, and Windsor Castle for weeks at a time while her father was stationed with the navy in Malta. When Queen Victoria died, Alice was sixteen and considered a great beauty, so much so that the Prince of Wales remarked, "No throne is too good for her."

Alice was born profoundly deaf but became an expert lip-reader proficient in several languages. In 1902, she was staying at Buckingham Place for the coronation of King Edward VII when she met Andrew, then a handsome young cavalry officer in the Greek army, and fell in love.

When it was announced in 1903 that Prince Andrew of Greece and Princess Alice of Battenberg had become engaged, the Prince and Princess of Wales, later King George V and Queen Mary, gave an engagement party at Marlborough House that was attended by King Edward VII. Alice and Andrew's closeness to the British royal family would prove a vital factor in their lives some twenty years later, when the intervention of King George V saved Andrew from execution.

The marriage took place in 1903 in Darmstadt; the week-long celebrations paid for by Tsar Nicholas II were lavish and attended by the greatest ever assembly of European royalty to gather in one place, including Queen Alexandra of England. The tsar arrived in the luxurious imperial train, bringing with him the Russian Imperial Choir and an entourage of grand dukes and duchesses and a retinue of servants. There were three separate wedding ceremonies, at one of which Alice gave the wrong answers to the priest's questions—she could not read his lips, which were obscured by his flowing beard. The lavish celebrations continued for a week. Alice's uncle Ernie, Grand Duke of Hesse, put up the guests in his two palaces in Darmstadt. Ernie's cousin the Grand Duchess of Mecklenburg-Strelitz complained about the expense and extent of the celebrations, saying "there is no reason for it, a Battenberg, daughter of an illegitimate father, Andrew a fourth son of a newly baked king."

It is true that Andrew's father was a new king, but Prince Louis was not illegitimate. He was the son of a commoner, Julie Hauke, later the first Princess of Battenberg. When in 1947 Dickie Mountbatten published his family tree, establishing the Battenbergs and their ancestors as one of the oldest and most chivalrous families in Europe, he had to acknowledge that his grandfather Alexander, son of the Grand Duke of Hesse, broke with tradition and married a lady-in-waiting at the Imperial Russian Court.

After the wedding Alice moved to Greece to live with Andrew in his family home in the royal compound at Tatoi outside Athens.

They also had a home in Corfu named Mon Repos, where Alice brought up her four daughters before Philip was born some seven years their junior. Andrew and Alice were relatively poor as he had only his Greek army pay and Alice came with no great dowry, but Philip's background was not as impecunious as has been made out. In their home in Corfu, his parents employed an English couple as housekeeper and houseman, an English nanny called Emily Roose, and several maids and gardeners. They also had the means to travel all over Europe whenever the need arose. Philip and his nanny were taken to London with his family twice before he was two years old, firstly for the funeral of Prince Louis, the Marquess of Milford Haven, and then in 1922 for the wedding of his uncle Dickie Mountbatten to the hugely wealthy heiress Edwina Ashley. The Prince of Wales, later King Edward VII, was Dickie's best man.

Andrew was a career soldier and had gone to an officers' training school in Athens at the age of fourteen. He had risen to the rank of lieutenant general when disaster struck in 1922. Andrew was engaged fighting the Turks in Asia Minor. After the Greek army was destroyed at Smyrna and millions of Greeks became refugees, Andrew and several fellow officers were court-martialed for their part in the debacle. Andrew was sentenced to death on the grounds of disobeying an order in battle. However, his life was saved by the intervention of King George V, who ordered a gunboat to be sent to Crete. Andrew's sentence was reduced to banishment from Greece and loss of citizenship. Philip was still a baby when he and his family were evacuated from Greece in the British gunboat *Calypso*.

As *Calypso* sailed out of Phaleron Bay toward the Italian port of Brindisi via Corfu, the intense sense of relief that Andrew had felt at escaping the firing squad soon evaporated as the realization of the dreadful situation in which he now found himself dawned upon him. He had dedicated his life to the Greek army as a professional soldier only to suffer the disgrace of being stripped of his rank and nationality and sent into permanent exile. Years later he asserted in his memoirs that he had been made a scapegoat to cover up the incompetence of the Greek high command. He was facing an uncertain future with no career, few assets, and a young family of five children to look after. Being the proud man that he was, it was difficult for him to accept the reality that, in order to survive, he would have to go begging to his brothers, of which two had married wives with great fortunes.

The family's first stop was in London, where Andrew was able to thank the King for saving his life and his family. Andrew never recovered from the ignominy of being drummed out of the Greek army. After eight years of living in Paris, the family home broke up in 1930 when all four of his daughters married, his wife was committed to a sanatorium, and Philip went away to boarding school in England. Andrew drifted round Europe, occasionally staying with one of his daughters in Germany. Apart from a brief return to Greece in 1935, when the monarchy was restored, he spent his remaining years in Monte Carlo. After the occupation of France by the Germans, Andrew was stranded in Monte Carlo, unable to get a visa to travel anywhere. He lived with his mistress, Comtesse Andrée de la Bigne, until he died in 1944 at the age of sixty-two. Philip never saw his father again during the last five years of Andrew's enforced stay in Monte Carlo.

Alice spent several years being treated for mental illness in Switzerland before she started to recover in 1936. During this period she did not see Philip for five years. Her recovery became complete when in 1937 her daughter Cecile died in an air crash along with her husband and three children. It seems that the shock of their deaths brought Alice to her senses. She had become extremely religious and devoted the rest of her life to helping those in need. She moved back to Athens and remained there throughout the war. The Greek people suffered terribly during the German occupation, with all food being requisitioned for German troops. Many thousands of Greeks died of starvation. Alice organized soup kitchens for the starving children and risked her life by hiding a Jewish family from the Germans, for which she was posthumously awarded Israel's highest honor, Righteous Among the Nations. Philip and his sister Sophie traveled to Jerusalem in 1994 to receive the award. In the last years of her life, Alice returned to England and lived in a suite of rooms at Buckingham Palace as the guest of Queen Elizabeth.

When bloodlines are considered, Philip is a true-blue mix of German, Danish, and Russian blood. His grandmother Victoria married Louis of Battenberg, grandson of the Grand Duke of Hesse-Darmstadt, and German blood flows down from Christian IX's wife, Louise of Hesse-Cassel, and Queen Victoria's husband, Prince Albert of Saxe-Coburg-Gotha. It was no coincidence that Philip's four older sisters all married German aristocrats. When Philip, then a first lieutenant in the Royal Navy, was first interviewed for the British press, in the naval dockyard in Newcastle, his interviewer Olga Franklin described him as having "the looks of a typical prince of a Hans Andersen fairy tale." She put his blond hair and blue eyes down to his great-grandfather King Christian IX of Denmark. Throughout his life Philip displayed the characteristics of his Northern European bloodlines, not those of the hot-blooded emotional Greeks and other Mediterranean peoples.

Philip's connections to Russia should not be overlooked. His grandfather King George I of Greece married the Grand Duchess Olga, giving Philip a Russian grandmother; King George's sister Dagmar married Tsar Alexander III; Philip's two aunts Marie and Alexandra both married Russian grand dukes; his uncle Nicholas married Grand Duchess Elena of Russia; and his great-aunt Alix

(Princess Alexandra of Hesse) married Tsar Nicholas II, both of whom were executed along with their children at Ekaterinburg in 1918. Philip's great-aunt Ella, who was the widow of Grand Duke Serge and the inspiration for Alice's life of service to others, suffered a horrible death in 1918. Along with five other members of the Russian imperial family, the Romanovs, she was thrown down a mineshaft and left to die. There was a close connection between the Romanovs and Darmstadt in Germany. The Russian church in Darmstadt, St. Mary Magdalene Chapel, is named in honor of the patron saint of Tsar Nicholas's mother and was built of Russian stone on Russian soil transported to Darmstadt by train. The Russian imperial family and court used the church during regular visits to the tsarina's brother Ernst Ludwig, who was Uncle Ernie to Alice.

This family closeness explains why Philip cared enough to help solve a mystery. In the 1990s, Philip allowed British and Russian researchers to test his DNA in order to identify remains suspected to be those of Tsarina Alexandra and three of her children killed in 1918. As Alexandra's great-nephew, he would share some of her DNA and the bodies were identified. The test was repeated with the same result when the two other children's remains were found.

In 1957, Philip was asked in an interview if he would like to visit the Soviet Union. He replied, "I would like to go to Russia very much—although the bastards murdered half my family." All was apparently forgiven in 1994, when Philip joined the Queen on a state visit to Russia at the invitation of President Boris Yeltsin. The couple stayed at the Kremlin and on the Royal Yacht *Britannia* in St. Petersburg during their four-day visit, which began on October 17. In a link with history, Philip and the Queen sat in the tsars' box at the Bolshoi Theatre on their first night to watch a performance of *Giselle*. They also spent two days in St. Petersburg visiting the Hermitage Museum and the palatial quarters of the tsars.

*

Philip's bloodlines are apparent from his appearance and demeanor as well as the strength of character that he has displayed throughout his life. His blond hair and deep blue eyes hint at his Nordic Viking roots, while his self-discipline, iron will, and work ethic can be attributed to his German ancestry. The duke's abundant sense of humor is Anglo-Saxon at its roots, but it is distinctly Russian not to display emotion in public, something that Philip has done only extremely rarely.

Chapter 2

EARLY INFLUENCES

A myth has been perpetuated by a series of biographers that Prince Philip's early life was unsettled and unhappy. He has been variously described as "the product of a broken home," "having a traumatic life of high drama and financial insecurity," "the man who survived a disruptive, itinerant childhood full of drama and personal tragedy," and having had a "turbulent early life." Yet, when questioned by his biographer Basil Boothroyd on the subject, Philip said, "I don't think it necessarily was particularly unhappy, it wasn't all that unsettled."

According to UNICEF, early childhood—the period that spans up to eight years of age—is critical for cognitive, social, emotional, and physical development. During these years, a child's newly developing brain is highly plastic and responsive to change as billions of integrated neural circuits are established through the interaction of genetics, environment, and experience. Optimal brain development requires a stimulating environment, adequate nutrients, and social interaction with attentive carers. The first five years of a child's life are fundamentally important. They are the foundation that shapes children's future health, happiness, growth, development, and learning achievement at school, in the family and community, and in life in general. Those closest to Philip in the early years were his parents, Andrew and Alice, and his nanny, Emily Roose.

Therefore the major influences in Philip's formative years are his family and his school. He was born into a large, loving, and happy family, and after four daughters his parents were delighted to have a son at last. His four older sisters adored him and spoiled him. "He had such unbelievable charm," his youngest sister, Sophie, recalled.

Philip knew nothing of the forced exodus from Corfu, since it took place while he was still a baby, and on arrival from Corfu the family stayed in London for a short time with Philip's grandmother Princess Victoria at Kensington Palace. In January 1923, Andrew and Alice sailed for New York at the invitation of Andrew's brother Christopher and his American wife, Nancy, the extremely rich widow of a tinplate tycoon. Their two elder daughters stayed with Victoria in London while Philip and his two other sisters were sent to stay with their uncle George and his wife, Marie Bonaparte, in Paris. Marie had inherited a fortune from her mother's family, who were the founders of the Monte Carlo Casino. After two months in the United States, Andrew and Alice sailed back to Europe on the Cunard liner *Aquitania* and settled in St. Cloud, a leafy suburb about six miles from the center of Paris.

The 1920s in Paris were known as *Les Années Folles*, meaning "The Crazy Years." Also known as the Roaring Twenties, the decade was a time noted for artistic expression. Paris was famed for high fashion: the International Exposition of 1925 featured more than seventy Parisian fashion designers, and it was in the midst of this period that the Paris-based Coco Chanel introduced the "little black dress." The artists Picasso, Modigliani, Brancusi, and Chagall all frequented the same Parisian cafes, and Paris was also the center of a vibrant music scene with the arrival of jazz and the Charleston from America. The high value of the dollar made Paris an attractive and economical place for Americans to reside. The authors Ernest Hemingway, F. Scott Fitzgerald, and Henry Miller had taken up residence in Paris. Hemingway's book *A Moveable Feast* described Paris and his favorite haunts in the 1920s. The cafes were also frequented by émigrés and large numbers of white Russians who had escaped the Bolshevik revolution in 1917; these included grand dukes and duchesses who were Andrew's distant cousins and had been guests at his wedding in Darmstadt. Andrew would travel into Paris from St. Cloud daily to meet with fellow exiles to discuss politics and plan coups, which never took place. Many Russian émigrés believed that their mission was to preserve the pre-revolutionary Russian culture and way of life while living abroad. The Ballets Russes had established itself in Paris under Sergei Diaghilev, later transferring to Monte Carlo around the same time that Andrew moved there himself.

Andrew's bighearted brother George provided him and his family with their new home in St. Cloud, which was one of several properties he owned there. It was not far from the Bois de Boulogne, which in those days was an extensive public park. In addition to Philip and his four older sisters, the household comprised a number of servants including Andrew's valet, Alice's maid, and Philip's nanny, Emily Roose, known to all as "Roosie." Marie Bonaparte provided for the household expenses as neither Andrew nor Alice had paid employment in Paris. Alice worked as a volunteer in a charity shop selling Greek products for the benefit of less well-off fellow refugees. She was in receipt of a small allowance from her brother George Milford Haven and had inherited one tenth of the estate owned by her father, who was the 1st Marquess of Milford Haven on his death in 1921. However, the estate's value was largely wiped out by German hyperinflation in the 1920s as the family seat and lands were in Germany near Darmstadt.

As a disgraced former officer in the Greek army, Andrew was unemployable. However, thanks to the generosity of his brothers, he was not forced to lower himself to the status of a Paris taxi driver as many of his Russian relatives had been. His finances were helped considerably when in 1923 Christopher's wife, Nancy, died from cancer and left a sum of money to go toward school fees for Andrew's children and other expenses. Financial help also came from Alice's brother, Dickie Mountbatten, whose wife, Edwina, had inherited a vast fortune from her grandfather Sir Ernest Cassel, one of the wealthiest men of his day and a good friend of King Edward VII. Andrew managed to retain ownership of Mon Repos, the former family home in Corfu, in spite of the attempts of successive Greek governments to seize it. He eventually sold it in 1937. While they did not have a palace with liveried footmen, Andrew and his family lived comfortably enough with a retinue of servants and were certainly not quite as impoverished as has been suggested. Throughout his life Andrew was never without a valet to look after him and always remained dapper and well dressed.

By the time the family moved to St. Cloud, the four daughters were largely old enough to manage without the attentions of a nanny. Roosie had initially been employed by Alice in 1904 for all of her children, and she was present at Philip's birth when the family doctor decreed that the most suitable place for the delivery was the dining-room table at Mon Repos. (Some say it was the kitchen table, but when you visit Mon Repos you see it has a plaque in the dining room.) Philip now became thirty-two-year-old Roosie's main charge. She was loving and kind, but she was also strict and instilled in him an all-important sense of Englishness that stayed with him for the rest of his life.

Roosie was there for the official registration of Philip's birth, along with the Queen Mother Olga of Greece as his godmother, when he was given the name Philippos in the registry of births. A formal christening followed in the Orthodox Church in Corfu city. Cheering crowds lined the streets leading to the church, where a band played and the city officials watched the baby being immersed in the font. Later, when the family was forced to flee Corfu and the warship *Calypso* picked up eighteen-month-old Philip and his four sisters, it was Nanny Roose who helped with the evacuation and again when they arrived in Brindisi in Italy.

"Brindisi was a ghastly place," Princess Sophie, Philip's last surviving sister, recalled. She described it as the worst town she had ever been in. "It was a terrible business. My sisters, who were seventeen and sixteen, had to get everything ready [for the evacuation]." When they were put ashore in Brindisi, nothing seemed to matter after the terribly rough journey by sea. They allowed Philip to clamber around the floor of the train during the journey to Rome and then to Paris, making himself black from head to toe. "Leave him alone," Roosie advised his mother when Alice tried to restrain him. "A divine person, much nicer than all the other nannies, we adored her," Philip's sister Sophie said when describing Roosie.

Roosie, who had trained as a nurse at St. Thomas's Hospital in London, was the daughter of a bootmaker in Plymouth. Prior to her engagement by Alice, she had been in the service of English ladies and gentlemen, with her last employer being Royal Naval Commander Herbert Savory. Roosie believed in all things English and had English food, medicines, and baby clothes sent over from London for Philip. It was through her that the King's English became Philip's first language, and she even taught him English nursery rhymes. Philip later recalled, "We spoke English at home but then the conversation would go into French. Then it went into German on occasions. If you couldn't think of a word in one language, you tended to go off in another."

"Nobody's allowed to spank me but my own nanny," Philip once informed his friend when his friend's nanny was about to discipline Philip for breaking a vase. Roosie's word was final, and if there was any discipline to be done, she did it. From what little is known about Nanny Roose, who was born in 1872, she was a warm and loving person.

According to child psychologists, a child's concept of himself between the ages of two and four is based on what the most important people in his life think of him, and self-confidence can be created or it can be crushed. In Philip's case it appears to have been created. The very early behavior of mothers or nannies toward their children is important in regards to the child's ability to form later human relationships, which Philip managed admirably. Studies show that the shape of the personality and the direction their lives will take are all laid down in the first six or seven years and cannot be fundamentally changed. Therefore a nanny's power to do good or evil, to warp or straighten or to build or destroy, was virtually unlimited. Far from being neglectful, Philip's early years were remarkable for their security and love, received after the fashion of the time—from the arms of the nanny.

Philip remained in touch with Roosie after she retired to South Africa when Philip was seven. It was a sad parting, but Roosie needed to live in a warm climate on account of her severe arthritis. In typical nanny fashion, Roosie maintained a correspondence from South Africa with both Philip and his eldest sister, Cecile. In March 1932, she wrote to Cecile, "It is still summer here and twelve pineapples for a shilling. It makes me long to send some to Philip, he told me once, he loved me nearly as much as pineapple."

In another letter to Cecile she wrote, "Philip gave me pleasure again; another letter full of fun. Did I remember while I told him to get up quick Easter morning and while I was out of the room he dressed and got into bed again—when I got back and found him in bed I began to scold, then out Philip jumped already dressed! Then the fun to laugh at me. He wrote rather large, said not to tire my eyes, bless him." Evidently Philip inherited a love of practical jokes from his father, who according to Philip's cousin Princess Alexandra turned everything into a joke. Philip himself said of his father and uncles, "anything could happen when you got a few of them together. It was like the Marx Brothers." Roosie died in 1933 in Simon's Town near Cape Town. The inscription on her tombstone reads, "Emily L. Roose. In loving and deeply grateful remembrance of 25 years devoted friendship and service. From Prince and Princess Andrew of Greece and their children Margarita, Theodora, Cecile, Sophie and Philip."

The family traveled extensively throughout Europe by train to stay with relations, many of whom had managed to retain royal estates and lived in style. By the time he was four years old, Philip had been taken to London four times, sometimes with his mother and sisters, but always accompanied by Roosie. Then as now, anyone who had the means to do so left the heat of Paris in July and August, and Philip's family were no different. Princess Alexandra writes of holidays spent at the Panker estate on the Baltic coast, the summer residence of the Landgrave of Hesse, and remembered how Philip loved swimming in the sea. "It was always Philip," Alexandra said, "who ventured out of his depth" or "who rounded up other boys encountered on the beach and organized an intensive castle building brigade." He was also given a box Brownie camera and took up photography, which remained a lifetime hobby.

Several holidays were spent by Philip and his two younger sisters and sometimes with Alice at the palatial villa near Le Touquet that belonged to the Foufounis family, wealthy Greek émigrés. It was there that Philip, at the age of five, struck up a close friendship with Hélène Foufounis, one that was to endure for many years. In the UK, Hélène was known as the cabaret singer Helen Cordet from her television appearances. Madame Foufounis became so fond of Philip that she said, "I loved him as my own." Philip also spent holidays in England with his grandmother Victoria at Kensington Palace.

Before the First World War, regal children were brought up largely by nurses, governesses, and nannies; fathers did not play a hands-on role. Philip and Andrew had a much closer relationship than many fathers and sons of the period, at least until Philip was eight and the family unit dispersed. Philip's sisters Margarita and Sophie recalled, "Andrew and Philip had a great fondness for each other" and "they used to laugh together like mad." In her biography of Philip, his cousin Alexandra wrote that Andrew "always treated Philip with the same indulgent raillery. I heard him joking with my cousin [Philip] sometimes on his athletic prowess or youthful escapades, but as Philip's papa he would give him advice whenever it was sought, with a gentle gravity. Philip adored his father and looking back I can see physical resemblances." Alexandra also said that Andrew explained to Philip the real importance of being a prince. "To be a prince one had to excel like a prince . . . a prince in fact must always prove himself." Philip heeded his father's words and throughout his life sought to excel at everything he tackled.

Philip maintained that in the early years at St. Cloud, his uncles on his father's side had a greater influence than has been generally recognized. He said, "I grew up very much more with my father's family than I did with my mother's and I think they are quite interesting people. They're the sort of people who haven't been heard of much." When the family was in residence in Paris, "Big George," as Philip's uncle was called, who lived nearby, gave a lunch party every Sunday. Uncle George was especially fond of children and came over each evening to kiss Philip good night and make sure he said his prayers. Christmas was very much a family affair, and Roosie remembered putting out stockings for all the children, even though the older ones were by then quite grown up.

The family was international and spoke in several different languages, mainly German, and Philip's four sisters all went on to marry German aristocrats. Although Alice was brought up in England, her father, Prince Louis of Battenberg, had never lost his German accent even after a lifetime in the Royal Navy, and he maintained a family home in Darmstadt. Furthermore, as is common with the deaf, her English speech was not crystal clear, although she always spoke English to Philip and used the sign language that he had been taught.

When six-year-old Philip was at his first school, The Elms, his mother's mental illness began to manifest itself. Initially it took the form of an obsessive religious fervor, which may have passed unnoticed by Philip, at least until he was eight years old. In 1928, Alice was still well enough to take her daughter Cecile, then seventeen years old, to stay with Victoria at Kensington Palace for the London season. Together they went to a number of balls and to Cowes for the regatta week. Cecile then went to stay with King George V and Queen Mary in Scotland at Balmoral Castle. Philip spent the summer holidays with Roosie and two of his sisters at Sinaia in the Carpathian Mountains, staying with Queen Helen of Romania. Philip's cousin Alexandra remembered their "nannies all cheerfully sitting down to tea with bowls of caviar." Philip was allowed no such extravagance. He was trained, Alexandra said, "to save and economize better than other children, so much so he acquired a reputation for being mean."

Alice returned home in October to St. Cloud, in time for her and Andrew to celebrate their silver wedding anniversary, but as Roosie was away during the family parties that marked the occasion, Alice slept with Philip in his nursery. In a letter to Miss Edwards, another member of the staff, she wrote, "Philip is always very good with me." During the winter Alice busied herself with translating Andrew's book *Towards Disaster* from Greek into English. The book was little more than Andrew's defense of his actions that caused his dismissal from the Greek army and banishment into exile. It is thought that the exertion of the work caused her mental state to deteriorate further.

By mid-1929, the deterioration of her health began to cause the family concern. She became obsessed with religious mysticism. At this time eight-year-old Philip must have become aware that all was not well with his mother. At Christmas, Alice, feeling depressed and exhausted, booked herself and her maid into a hotel in Grasse on the Côte d'Azur. Andrew, Philip, and his sisters spent Christmas together in St. Cloud. Early in the new year, Alice was admitted as a voluntary patient to a sanatorium at Lake Tegel near Berlin. While she was there, her daughter Cecile announced her engagement to her cousin Prince George Donatus of Hesse. Alice discharged herself from Tegel in April and returned to the family in St. Cloud. Andrew persuaded his mother-in-law, Princess Victoria, to come to St. Cloud as Alice's behavior was becoming more and more strange. Victoria took control of the situation, and on May 2, 1930, she had Alice admitted to the Bellevue clinic in Kreutzlingen in Switzerland. This marked the end of family life at St. Cloud and the start of a new chapter in Philip's life. In June, Philip spent his ninth birthday at Schloss Wolfsgarten, the country retreat of "Uncle Ernie," the Grand Duke of Hesse, where the family gathered to celebrate both Cecile's engagement and sixteen-year-old Sophie's engagement to Prince Christophe of Hesse. Cecile wrote to Alice: "Philip is quite blissful. Uncle Ernie gave him a new bicycle for his birthday. He rushes around on it all day. In the evening from the moment he has finished his bath till he goes to bed he plays his beloved gramophone which you gave him. He got really lovely presents this year. He is very good and does just what he is told."

Not long after afterward, Andrew closed down the house in St. Cloud. All four daughters were by now living in Germany, Alice was in the sanatorium in Switzerland and Philip was sent away to school in England in September. Alice eventually made a full recovery and spent the rest of her life dressed as a nun while she tended to the poor and sick in Athens.

From the age of eight onward, it was Alice's family in England who became the main influences in Philip's life, initially Uncle George Milford Haven, who acted in loco parentis until his premature death in 1938, when Uncle Dickie Mountbatten took over. Philip's maternal grandmother, Princess Victoria, the 1st Marquess of Milford Haven's widow, was a constant presence—albeit it a somewhat strict one—in Philip's life. She lived in an apartment at Kensington Palace, where Philip kept his school trunk and often stayed during the half-term holidays. Philip described her apartment as "a sort of base where I kept things." He became very attached to his grandmother, who often traveled with him to Germany in the holidays to stay with one of her granddaughters. Philip said later, "I suppose that my grandmother had a greater influence on my character than either of her sons [George and Dickie]." In a letter to his headmaster at Cheam, written from HMS *Magpie* in Malta on November 2, 1950, he wrote: "She was much more to me than Grandmother as I lived for many years in her house and she was for a long time responsible for my schooling. She had an iron will and she never weakened in any way."

Andrew had decided that he wanted Philip to continue his education in England, and on the advice of Alice's brother George Milford Haven he settled on Cheam School. Not only had George been at Cheam himself, but he also had a son David at Cheam two years older than Philip, who was to become Philip's great friend and best man at his wedding. In the short school holidays, Philip lived with George at Lynden Manor, a country house near Maidenhead. George had seen naval action in the First World War at Jutland and Heligoland. Philip never tired of hearing George's stories of the Battle of Jutland, when his ship's guns glowed red-hot for continual firing as three sister ships blew up from direct hits. George had a brilliant mathematical and inventive mind. He designed and built working steam engines and devised a number of labor-saving devices. It was here that the seeds of Philip's interest in science and engineering were sown. He too in later life often looked for such improvements, at Buckingham Palace and on the royal estates. George was married to Nada, the fun-loving bohemian former Russian countess whose extravagance caused George to leave the navy in 1930 to pursue a career in business. It was George and Princess Victoria, Philip's maternal grandmother, who took care of the school fees at Cheam, and George who put in appearances on sports days and at prize-giving ceremonies.

George was a director of a number of companies, including Marks & Spencer and Electrolux, of which Sir Harold Wernher was chairman. His wife was Lady Zia Wernher, the sister of Nada Milford Haven. When questioned on the subject of influence, Philip said, "I have been thinking about this influence business and you can certainly add Harold Wernher to the list." Philip often stayed with the Wernhers during the 1930s, at Thorpe Lubenham Hall, their farmhouse in Leicestershire. The Wernhers were extremely rich and maintained a full retinue of servants, including a butler and footmen. Philip became close friends with the Wernhers' three children. Their daughter Gina, who later was a trustee of the Duke of Edinburgh's award scheme, said that Philip often had good discussions with her father. Many years later the Wernhers' grand-daughter Sasha Duchess of Abercorn became a close confidante of Prince Philip.

Over the next few years Philip occasionally saw his father in the summer holidays and sometimes at Christmas, when they stayed with one or another of Philip's married sisters in Germany. Alice was unable to come to any of the weddings, but Andrew was ever present to give his daughters away, and Philip was allowed out of school to go to all four of the weddings, acting as train bearer for Cecile, the first to be married. He traveled over for the weddings from London with his grandmother Victoria.

To be sent away to boarding school at the age of nine like Philip was commonplace among the monied classes in England; in fact eight was the more usual entry age. In the era before long-distance air travel became the norm, many boys did not see their parents from year to year because their fathers were ruling the far-flung corners of the British Empire that reached around the globe. Philip's case was different in that he did not see his mother for five years, from 1932 until 1937, and he saw less and less of his father. Later in life he played down the effect that this had on him, saying: "The family broke up. My mother was ill, my sisters were married and my father was in the south of France. I just had to get on with it. You do. One does."

It did have the effect of making him emotionally stronger, self-sufficient, and able to deal with whatever life had in store for him without showing his heart on his sleeve. A few years later he dealt with two family tragedies within a few months with little outward display of emotion, namely the deaths of George Milford Haven from cancer in April 1938 and the air crash that killed his sister Cecile, her husband, Don, and their children in 1937.

If the loss of one sister was to have a tragic impact on Philip, another of his sisters, Theodora, had a positive one. She had married her second cousin, Berthold Margrave of Baden, in 1931, and although there was a great age difference Berthold became close to Philip. "He taught me to drive and fish for trout with a dry fly and must have had a major influence on my character," said Philip. Philip's sister Sophie said, Philip "liked all of his brothers-in-law and got on very well with them . . . he would have lengthy and serious talks with them. He was so interested in everything and was always very keen to learn and understand things."

However, this family link was to have an even greater significance for Philip. Berthold was the son of Max von Baden, the last chancellor of Germany before the end of the First World War. Max's secretary was a German Jew, Kurt Hahn, who also wrote his speeches. Hahn was not initially an educator, but under the auspices of Max von Baden in 1920 he became the first headmaster of the Schule Schloss boarding school in Salem, which was intended to help educate a new German intellectual elite. Hahn would become one of the major influences in Philip's life.

Philip had met Hahn a year earlier when staying with Theodora during the school holidays. He said there was an air about Hahn that commanded instant wariness and respect. Hahn, who was later made CBE, was instrumental in the setting up of the Duke of Edinburgh Awards scheme and the Outward Bound organization, both of which encouraged young people to help themselves get on in life. Of the Awards scheme Philip said: "I would never have started it but for Hahn, certainly not. He suggested I ought to do it, and I fought against it for quite a long time. Because you know what the British are like about that sort of thing."

Hitler took power in January 1933, and within months Hahn had been arrested for speaking out against the Nazis and had to leave the country. He fled Germany and opened a new school in Scotland called Gordonstoun in 1934, at which Philip became one of the very first pupils that year. Hahn was held in such respect that he was able to recruit an eminent first board of governors at Gordonstoun that included the headmaster of Eton and the Archbishop of York. By then Andrew was based in Monaco and only came to London occasionally. He told Victoria that he wanted Philip to finish his education at Gordonstoun and then sit the entrance examination for the Royal Navy.

After the death of George Milford Haven his brother, Dickie Mountbatten, took over the role of Philip's surrogate father. Andrew wrote to Dickie, "Do I beg you take charge of Philip's upbringing." It was rather late in the day as Philip was already almost seventeen years old when George died. As a child, Philip occasionally saw Dickie at family gatherings and they got along well. In 1938, Dickie wrote to his wife, Edwina: "Philip was here all last week doing his entrance exams for the navy. He has his meals with us and he really is killingly funny. I like him very much." This is a clear indication that Dickie was only then getting to know Philip.

Dickie, who had no son of his own, was extremely ambitious and keen to expunge what he considered a slur on his family name when his father was forced to resign as first sea lord in 1914 and to anglicize the family name from Battenberg to Mountbatten three years later as it was considered too German. He was determined to get to the top in the navy, as his father had before him. Dickie was influential in encouraging Philip to join the Royal Navy and arranged for him to have extra coaching before sitting the entrance examination to the Royal Naval College, Dartmouth.

Although many have claimed that Mountbatten was the most significant influence in Philip's life and development, this is an overstatement. While there is no doubt that Dickie was able to use his influence in getting Philip various postings in the navy and in progressing Philip's romance with Princess Elizabeth, the degree of influence he had on molding Philip the man is questionable. Philip himself said: "Mountbatten certainly had an influence on the course of my life, but not so much on my ideas and attitudes. I suspect he tried too hard to make himself a son out of me." And on another occasion he remarked: "One impression I think needs to be corrected is that the whole of my life has been spent here [in the UK] and that I was brought up by Lord Mountbatten, neither of which is true." As Dickie was away much of the time on active duty in the navy, the amount of time they could spend together was limited. What did rub off on Philip was Dickie's drive to succeed and will to win. Years later, after Philip had married Princess Elizabeth and been posted to Malta, the two men became close friends. It was in Malta that Dickie introduced Philip to polo, which became his main sporting interest.

The principles of hard work, self-discipline, and helping others to which Philip stayed true throughout his life were instilled initially by his mother, Alice, who was described by her daughter Sophie as having an iron will, and then by his years at Gordonstoun under the auspices of Kurt Hahn. From his father Philip acquired his sense of fun and humor. His sister Sophie said: "My father died in 1944. He was so like him. Philip had the same mannerisms, movements, way of standing, walking and laughing—the colossal sense of humor, really seeing the funny side of things always, and making everybody else laugh."

That was Philip. His sensitivity came from his mother and nanny, his sense of the ridiculous from his father. His dogged determination, his resilience, his courage, and his sense of duty were character traits he developed during his wide-ranging education. In later life it enabled him to become committed to the concept of the monarchy. He saw duty as at the center of everything in his life, as it was his framework from which all other things followed. Of course, he rebelled against it, as that too was part of his character, and when there was room for negotiation there was always room for conflict, but he always returned to the framework set down by his rigid personal rules decided upon early in his life. Be the best. Don't give in. Accept challenges and meet them; succeed by your own ability, not by good fortune. Others might attribute Philip's achievements to preferment, which impelled him to be incontrovertibly the best so he was succeeding not by his marital good fortune but by his own strength of character.

Chapter 3

EDUCATION

"I would like as many boys as possible to enjoy their schooldays as much as I did," Prince Philip told his 1970s biographer, Basil Boothroyd. Mr. Boothroyd, who has been described as "a *Punch* contributor and a stylish sycophant," published his amusing portrait of Prince Philip in 1971 and through a series of interviews, letters, and wry observations pinpointed Philip's feelings on his early life.

Although Philip's education was not notable for its classroom success, each of the four schools he attended between the age of six in Paris and when he entered the Royal Naval College, Dartmouth, at eighteen had one thing in common: they were all fee-paying private schools. Philip was one of the privileged elite that comprise roughly 5 percent of the population educated by the independent sector rather than the large majority educated in state schools. Both Cheam School, which Philip entered at nine, and later Gordonstoun were boys-only boarding schools where uniforms, rules, strict discipline, and stiff punishment were all part of a life, which suited Philip as it gave him the structure he had lacked in his somewhat nomadic childhood. Living away from home was the norm and holidays were short. Life was competitive both in getting into the school sports teams and in getting to the top of the class in lessons. In all these respects school life had much in common with the Royal Navy. With this grounding Philip was well prepared for his later time with the Queen and her court. He found comfort and security in the structure of its royal protocol and conventions, its formality and the wearing of uniform required by the consort on state and military occasions.

When he was six years old, Philip was enrolled at the MacJannet American School in St. Cloud, which was known as The Elms on account of the huge trees that shaded the school. Donald Mac-Jannet, an American First World War pilot who had studied at the Sorbonne, founded the school in 1924 principally for young Americans living in Paris. His views on education had much in common with those of Kurt Hahn, who was later to become such an influence on Philip. MacJannet believed in teaching the values of tolerance, enlightenment, and cultural understanding. He promoted the ideals of hard work and discipline paired with exposure to foreign cultures and mutual respect. As well as many Americans, there were boys of several other nationalities in the school during Philip's three years there, and two of Philip's best friends were the sons of the Chinese ambassador in Paris. Philip's other friends during his three years at The Elms included his cousins Prince Jacques and Princess Anne of Bourbon-Parma, who went on to marry King Michael of Romania. MacJannet described Philip as "rugged, boisterous but always remarkably polite. Full of energy and got along well with other children."

Initially Philip was teased for insisting that he had no surname and was "just Philip," which later became Philip of Greece, a name he used for many years even though his Danish passport was inscribed with his full triple-barreled surname. A photograph that has appeared in a number of biographies shows Philip with a few of his contemporaries at The Elms practicing archery. One of the pupils shown standing next to Philip in the photograph is Alan Reeves, who went on to become an American consular official. In his old age Alan Reeves gave a detailed account of life at The Elms for the benefit of the MacJannet Foundation. In this Alan described Philip as "a half-Greek classmate of noble birth who lacked a surname: the future Prince Philip, whose impoverished mother was sometimes seen darning her son's socks, notwithstanding her status as the sister of Britain's Lord Mountbatten."

Alan described Donald MacJannet as being a tough taskmaster. If a boy misbehaved, one standard punishment was to make the boy run a gauntlet of his fellow students while they whipped him with their belts. Another ordeal, as Reeves recalled, was mealtimes in the main building. "I remember the luncheons too well, as they were terrible," he said. He recoils at the memory of "bitter cooked endive." Many years later, he said, "I was told MacJannet did it deliberately to toughen us up."

One result of the majority of students being American was that Philip learned to play baseball before he played cricket. The school survived until the Second World War broke out, when, according to Alan Reeves, "the Germans burned the buildings to the ground." In his subsequent career in government and politics, Reeves was known in Washington, DC, as "the straight"—that is, a straightforward and honest man in a customarily devious profession. He attributes much of that reputation to his time at The Elms. "That experience helped shape me," he said.

In MacJannet's biography *Schoolmaster of Kings*, he said Philip's mother suggested that Philip should be encouraged to work off his energy by playing games and learning "Anglo-Saxon ideas of courage, fair play and resistance." She said she envisaged him ending up in an English-speaking country, perhaps America, so she wanted him to learn good English and to develop English characteristics.

Alice made him do extra Greek prep three evenings a week and asked the school to set him daily exercises for the holidays. It is said that he often arrived at school half an hour early at nanny Emily Roose's urgings, and he would fill in the time cleaning blackboards, filling inkwells, straightening up the classroom furniture, picking up wastepaper, and watering the plants. Roosie instilled in Philip a dedication to duty. The school fees for The Elms were met by Andrew's brother Christopher, who had married an American heiress with homes in New York, Palm Springs, and Paris.

When Alice's health deteriorated in May 1930 and Andrew decided to relinquish his parental responsibilities and shut up the family home in St. Cloud, another boarding school had to be found for Philip. Unsettling as it must have been for young Philip, he later described his time at The Elms as "three of the happiest years of my life."

His father, Andrew, wanted to send his son to school in England, thinking it would be far better than the harsh Greek military alternative that he had experienced as a youth. Although Andrew doted on his only son and spoiled him—his sisters described him as their "overindulged little brother"—he was not up to looking after such a bumptious, extroverted little boy and felt that his uncle George Milford Haven would do a far better job. Milford Haven had himself been to England's oldest preparatory school, Cheam, and his son, David Earl of Medina, two years older than Philip, was also there. The headmaster, the Reverend Harold Taylor, was a former naval chaplain, and for the period, when harsh discipline and a spartan regime for young boys was de rigueur, the school of seventy boys was relatively friendly. Philip was popular because he was good at games, although he had a quick temper and could avoid being bullied as he was able to give as good as he got.

The headmaster's son, Jimmy Taylor, was a boarder at Cheam at the same time as Philip, and in 2008 he published an account of what life at Cheam School was like in 1930. Philip provided a short introduction in which he said that it brought back many half-forgotten memories as well as many vivid ones. He went on to say:

"I had not anticipated that the fact that I was a Prince of Greece would arouse such curiosity among all the other boys when I first arrived. Thankfully this subsided fairly quickly when they discovered I was not a freak." Mistakenly, he said he started at Cheam as a seven-year-old; a rare error on his part, as it is a fact that he went there as a new boy when he was nine.

Cheam was a preparatory school in a large house on extensive grounds with a staff of twenty-two to look after seventy boys between the ages of eight and thirteen. Several of the staff spent their entire working lives at the school, including Jane, the dormitory maid for sixty years, who used to clean out the boys' ears with carbolic soap on communal bath nights. Although the Taylors were not well off, and the headmaster struggled with the school's finances to keep the fees at £55 per term, the staff included a butler, a footman, and an under-footman who served the family meals in the private dining room during school holidays. This was a sign of the times. All the households in which Philip stayed while growing up maintained a retinue of servants.

Life at Cheam was fairly austere, with hard beds and cold baths. There was no heating in the dormitories and the windows were left open all year round. A tooth mug of water left on a windowsill would freeze overnight. School food was plain, with the same dish being served on the same day every week. The evening meal consisted of bread and dripping and a cup of cocoa. New boys had to be kitted out with a summer suit, a winter knickerbocker suit, and an Eton suit for Sundays, plus whites for cricket and tennis and a school cap and blazer. As the school outfitters was Harrods, it was an expensive process and for Philip a far cry from the darned socks and patched trousers of his days at The Elms.

Derby Day was a half holiday at Cheam School, and the whole school would line up in the High Street to cheer King George V and Queen Mary as they passed through Cheam in their Daimler limousine on the way from Windsor to Epsom racecourse. Their majesties would wave as they passed by, but it is unlikely that they recognized their cousin's son Philip with his shock of white-blond hair among the crowd.

Corporal punishment was meted out with regularity. A sound beating on the buttocks was the standard punishment. The headmaster used a bamboo cane for offenses in the school such as pillow fights after lights-out in the dormitories. The assistant masters applied the slipper for offenses or bad work in class. Any boy not paying attention was likely to be hit by a well-aimed piece of chalk sent flying forcefully across the classroom. As a clergyman, the headmaster held morning service for the whole school in the chapel every morning and three services on Sunday, a day when no games were allowed.

Philip's academic record at Cheam was unexceptional, but he did win prizes for mathematics and French, a language in which he was fluent. He excelled at sports, winning the diving and high jump competitions, and his 1932 school report noted that he was an improved cricketer all round and very lively in the field. Later in life Mr. Taylor said: "Philip got himself into all the usual schoolboy scrapes. I had to cane him more than once. When he was twelve my wife and I said of him that he would make a really good king, thinking then of him as King of Greece, not as a husband of Princess Elizabeth. He has the two qualities most needed in a king—leadership and personality."

Philip remained friendly with the Reverend Taylor and

corresponded with him regularly long after he left Cheam and was sent to the school at Salem. Some of Philip's letters to Taylor are typewritten, and in one sent from his new school, dated October 7, 1933, when he was twelve, he wrote: "We are not very far from Salem about an hour with a bicycle thus I can go and see my sister when I want to. There are lots of very nice boys here as therewere [*sic*] at Cheam, and I made friends with a lot of them."

At the end of Philip's introduction to Jimmy Taylor's book on life at Cheam in the 1930s, Philip wrote: "Life has changed dramatically since those far-off days but I suspect that the process of growing up is not all that different today. Every child has to make the passage to adulthood by learning what life is all about. I count myself lucky to have begun the process at Cheam under the guidance of HMS Taylor."

George Milford Haven lived at Lynden Manor in Holyport, some twenty miles from London. It was a thirteenth-century beamed manor house surrounded by a moat and set in acres of fine gardens, and it became Philip's home from home while he was at Cheam. George was married to the colorful Russian Nadejda, the great-great-granddaughter of the Russian poet Alexander Pushkin. She was, as her niece Myra Butter has remembered, "off the wall, the best fun. Completely different, very bohemian." She later became notorious for her affair with Gloria Vanderbilt, who regularly stayed at Lynden when Philip was there. Nada, as she was known, and George were sophisticated lovers of life, and nothing fazed them. They also had an extensive collection of pornographic books kept in a library, which no doubt Philip got his hands on and showed to his friends as children are apt to do. Philip had experienced grand German castles with liveried footmen serving at table, but this was different, and for an independent young boy, the fun he must have had would have alleviated much of the sadness of missing his own parents.

Through Nada's sister Zia, who was married to Sir Harold Wernher, Philip got to know the Wernher family and often stayed with them at their country house Thorpe Lubenham Hall near Market Harborough. He became close to the children Alex, Gina, and Myra (now Lady Butter). Myra remembers him as "a very good-looking young Viking" who was "frightfully neat and tidy with his room and used to fold his grey flannel trousers under the mattress because that pressed them." His closest friend however was George's son David, Philip's cousin, who years later was best man at his wedding.

Another of Philip's friends, Princess Alexandra of Greece, was sent to Heathfield School, a boarding school for girls, at the same time that Philip went to Cheam. She hated boarding school just as much as Philip enjoyed it, and she corresponded with Philip regularly. Alexandra, in her biography of Philip, tells of the time he and David, having cycled down to Dover, a distance of more than one hundred miles, were too saddle-sore to cycle back. They stowed away on a grain barge in Dover Harbor, bound for the London Docks, and spent two nights sleeping on sacks of grain in the hold. On another occasion, Philip broke a tooth in a clash in a game of hockey with David.

Between December 1930 and August 1931, within a year of Philip starting at Cheam, all four of his sisters got married in Germany. Remarkably, each of them married titled German aristocrats with landed estates and palatial homes. The girls had been based at St. Cloud in Paris, and with their mother Alice under treatment in a sanatorium, it is not known who played the role of matchmaker.

The first to marry was Sophie, the youngest, who married her handsome second cousin once removed, Prince Christophe of Hesse, shortly after her sixteenth birthday. She had fallen for "Chri," as he was called, who was thirteen years her senior, while staying with her aunt Irene on the Baltic coast. They were married on December 15, 1930, at Schloss Friedrichshof, a palace belonging to Christophe's mother, the Landgravine of Hesse, which is now a luxury hotel. Inside and out it looks remarkably like a larger version of Sandringham House, with a carved rising staircase, long corridors, and ornate plasterwork on the ceilings. At the time Friedrichshof, which was originally intended for summer use, had every kind of modern luxury including central heating and electric light. When Philip got to know Chri later, he described him as "a very gentle person" and, in spite of his active service with the Luftwaffe, "kind and had a good sense of humour. So, he was actually the complete opposite of what you would expect."

Having traveled from England during the Christmas holidays with his grandmother Victoria, he attended the wedding with his three other sisters and his father, Andrew. After the wedding, Philip's grandmother took him to see his mother at the sanatorium in order to tell her about the wedding, which she had not felt well enough to attend, and they stayed at a nearby hotel. Victoria reported that all went well, but Alice confided to Victoria that she did not think she had long to live. Two days after the wedding, Philip sent a misspelled typewritten letter from Nues Palais Darmstadt to his headmaster at Cheam, Mr. Taylor. "The wedding was most beautiful," he wrote, and "another sister is going to be maraid soon. You will find two more letters like this so Do not be afraid. I can not write much more because Iwill be late. Best wishes from, Philip."

A month later, the next sister to get married was eighteen-year-old Cecile, to her cousin Donatus of Hesse, the son and heir of the Grand Duke of Hesse, who was known to the family as Uncle Ernie and had two palaces in Darmstadt. The people of the town of Darmstadt lined the streets to the church and cheered the bride and bridegroom as they passed. Philip was allowed to leave Cheam for a few days to attend the wedding and was brought back to England by his uncle Dickie Mountbatten.

In the Easter holidays, Philip traveled to Germany again with his grandmother for the wedding of his eldest sister, twenty-six-year-old Margarita, to Prince Gottfried of Hohenlohe-Langenburg, a great-grandson of Queen Victoria. They married in Schloss Weiker-sheim, a seventeenth-century palace with an ornate knights' hall and statue-filled gardens. Gottfried was heir to Schloss Langenburg, a palace with more rooms than Buckingham Palace. Andrew again performed his duties as father of the bride, walking her down the aisle and giving her away, and Alice, who did not attend any of her daughters' weddings, was nowhere to be seen. History does not relate who paid for the lavish receptions for each of Philip's sisters' weddings but it was certainly beyond Andrew's means.

In the summer of 1931, twenty-five-year-old Theodora, the last of Philip's four sisters, married Berthold Margrave of Baden, a title that goes back to the tenth century. Berthold's family seat was Schloss Salem, a former Cistercian monastery on the shores of Lake Bodensee, where in 1920 his father, Max von Baden, the last imperial chancellor of Germany, had founded a school with the assistance of his secretary Kurt Hahn. Prince Max said of Salem School: "I am proud of the fact that there is nothing original here. We have cribbed from everywhere, from the English public schools, from Goethe, from Plato and from the Boy Scouts." It was this combination of ideals that Kurt Hahn successfully forged into a new concept of schooling.

After the wedding in the spa town of Baden-Baden, Philip, his grandmother Victoria, and his father, Andrew, stayed at Wolfsgar-ten, Uncle Ernie's country estate, which was originally a hunting lodge. For many years, all visitors to Wolfsgarten have signed the visitors' book by scratching their names on the windowpanes with a diamond-tipped pen. Philip's name appears both as "Philip" in 1931 and, much later, after his marriage, when Philip used to visit his German cousins, as "Herzog von Edinburg"—the German for "Duke of Edinburgh." As Alice was again too ill to attend Theodora's wedding, Philip was taken to visit her at the sanatorium in Kreutzlingen. This visit was not a success, and it must have been disturbing for Philip, because his mother was prone to violent mood swings. It was the last time Philip was to see her for five years.

Philip first met Kurt Hahn when staying at Schloss Salem for Theodora's wedding. In the summer of 1933, when Hahn was forced to flee Germany, Philip left Cheam at the age of twelve, a year younger than usual, in order to continue his education at his brother-in-law's school at Salem. It was not what Philip wanted, and it must have been a great wrench for him to leave before his last year. He was already in the cricket Second XI team and would undoubtedly have made the First XI had he been allowed to stay on. He clearly missed Cheam, writing a typewritten letter in October 1933 to Mr. Taylor: "I hope you will have a good football team this year as last. . . . Please give my wishes to the school and all the masters."

Just before Christmas, he wrote to Taylor again, this time in his own hand, which he complained " 'quite akes' with writing so many Xmas letters." It was Theodora who managed to persuade George Milford Haven and Andrew that Philip should leave Cheam. She and his new German brothers-in-law believed Germany was the right place for Philip to continue his education, and he would be able to have a home with Theodora at Salem. The persecution of Hahn and other Jews was not seen as an issue. At least two of Philip's brothers-in-law would become confirmed Nazis.

Kurt Hahn's educational philosophy was based on respect for adolescents, whom he believed to possess an innate decency and moral sense, but who were, he believed, corrupted by society as they aged. He believed that education could prevent this corruption, if students were given opportunities for personal leadership and to see the results of their own actions. He advocated "experiential" learning—putting young people in situations to challenge them mentally and physically. Pupils had to go for a run before breakfast, drank milk at mealtimes, did forty-five minutes of athletics during their mid-morning break, and, after lunch, lay flat on their backs for forty-five minutes while a teacher or older pupil read aloud to them. They also helped with the upkeep of the school.

On Saturdays, the boys formed "guilds" of explorers, farmers, and artists, which Hahn said gave their eyes a "gleam." Hahn said he wanted to prevent the erosion of children's "inherent spiritual-ity." He was deeply influenced by Plato's thoughts. He also pro-moted concern and compassion for others, the willingness to accept responsibility, and concern and tenacity in pursuit of the truth.

Hahn began his fierce criticism of the Nazi regime after Hitler's storm troopers killed a young Communist in the presence of his mother. When he spoke out against the storm troopers, who had re-ceived no punishment, Hahn spoke against Hitler publicly. He asked the students, faculty, and alumni of the Salem School to choose be-tween Salem and Hitler. As a result of his conduct and the fact that he was a Jew, he was imprisoned in 1933, a few months before Philip arrived at the school. After an appeal by the British prime minister, Ramsay MacDonald, among others, Hahn was released, and in July 1933 he was forced to leave Germany and moved to Britain.

By the time Philip arrived, there were 420 pupils at Salem and it was considered one of the leading schools in Europe. Hitler had been made Chancellor of Germany in January 1933 and the Nazis opened the first concentration camp at Dachau later that year. Hein-rich Himmler, as police president of Munich, officially described the camp as "the first concentration camp for political prisoners." By the time Philip arrived, Theodora's husband Berthold was struggling to prevent the Nazis from taking over the school. The German pupils were forced to sign up with the Hitler Youth, but Philip was exempt as a foreigner. Some teachers joined the SS storm troopers, and Philip complained that there was a lot of "ghastly foot-slogging."

A few boys tried to stick it out against the Nazi takeover of the school, and one such boy was caught and had his head shaved by the Hitler Youth. Philip gave the boy his Cheam Second XI cricket cap to cover his head. In due course, the Nazis took over the administration of the school. Berthold protested at the Nazi takeover of the school but was powerless to stop it. In contrast to Berthold's struggle against the Nazis, one of Philip's other brothers-in-law, Christophe, was a committed Nazi and had become an officer in the SS. He later joined the Luftwaffe and was killed in an air crash in action in 1943.

Philip was too young to have much of a political opinion, but he mocked the Nazi salute, which he likened to the raised arm of a boy in class at Cheam asking if he could be excused to go to the lavatory. He lived with his sister Theodora and brother-in-law Berthold at Schloss Salem, which made him an outsider from the rest of the pupils, who were boarders in a wing at the school. For someone who looked back on his school days as very happy times, Philip did not particularly enjoy his time at Salem.

It was to Philip's great relief that after two terms it was decided that he should return to Britain to continue his schooling. As Theodora explained: "We thought it better for him and also for us." His father, who was in France, had been consulted, and the obvious choice was that Philip should follow Kurt Hahn to the new school he had founded in Scotland, Gordonstoun.

Through a local landowner that he had known in his days at Oxford, Hahn had found a suitable property in Scotland for his new school on the Morayshire coast, between the town of Elgin and the Moray Firth. It was a dilapidated mansion set in some five hundred acres (eight hundred hectares) where Hahn established his new Salem. When Philip arrived in September 1934, the school was in its second term and Philip was one of only twenty-seven pupils. In such a small group Philip was to get to know and admire Hahn at close quarters.

Hahn's appearance was somewhat intimidating. As a result of undergoing brain surgery, he had become extremely sensitive to sunlight and avoided it at all costs. Hahn therefore prepared for the outdoors with a large wide-brimmed hat and sunglasses more akin to a motorcyclist's goggles. He also wrapped himself in an enormous cloak in order to shield all parts of his body from the sun.

It was his view that boys should be kept busy at all times with a wide variety of activities, particularly in the great outdoors, to avoid the danger of being afflicted by the five decays of youth. He named these as the decay of fitness, decay of initiative and enterprise, decay of care and skill, decay of self-discipline, and decay of compassion. All boys had to take part in every kind of activity, from housework to lifesaving, from climbing to construction—Philip was given the job of building a pigsty, which remains at Gordonstoun to this day.

Hahn regarded seafaring as an essential element in the curriculum and considered the Moray Firth as one of his best teaching aides. Philip spent much time in the port at Elgin working on small boats and sailing the school's own schooner, *Prince Louis*, named after his grandfather. He went on a number of longer trips, including across the North Sea to Norway and down the west coast of Scotland. He had better sea legs than his contemporaries and as a result found himself in charge of the galley in rough weather, which sowed the seeds of a lifelong interest in cooking. Captain Lewty, the master in charge of sailing, wrote in Philip's report: "He proved himself to be a cheerful shipmate and very conscientious in carrying out both major and minor duties. He is not afraid of dirty and arduous work. He is one of the most efficient members of the Seamanship Guild."

Gordonstoun school uniform included short trousers, even for the older boys, to expose the legs to the elements. Hahn also espoused cold baths, early morning runs, lifesaving exercises, and mountain climbing. Later in life, Philip commented on the supposedly harsh outdoor life. He said: "It's somehow got the reputation of being a spartan, tough, rigorous and generally body-bending sort of organisation. In fact, it isn't at all and never has been. It's a misunderstanding of what it is all about. I think it rationalises the whole of the physical activities . . . instead of this obsession with games we in fact had a great many more activities." Philip played hockey and cricket, although initially the school was too small to have teams to compete against other schools. By the time Philip left, the number of boys had grown to 135 and Philip had risen to become captain of the hockey and cricket teams as well as guardian, the school name for head boy.

In 1937, Philip suffered a family tragedy when Cecile, her husband, Don, and her children died in an air crash just outside Ostend in Belgium. They were flying to London for the wedding of Uncle Ernie's son Lu Hesse to Margaret Geddes. Their plane crashed into a factory chimney in thick fog. At the time Lu was working at the German Embassy in London as secretary to von Ribbentrop, the German ambassador in London. Philip had been extremely close to his sister Cecile—she was the closest to him in age. Hahn had to call Philip into his study at Gordonstoun to break the news of the disaster. Hahn recorded that Philip, only sixteen at the time, took it like a man. The funeral took place in Darmstadt, which was hung with giant swastika banners, and the populace gave Nazi salutes as the cortège passed by. Philip can be seen in photographs walking beside his brother-in-law Christophe, who is in SS uniform with other family members dressed as Brownshirts. Philip in a civilian suit looks very out of place among the military uniforms.

The following April, Philip experienced another tragedy when, after some months of illness, George Milford Haven died of bone marrow cancer at the age of forty-five. George had been a father figure to Philip since his days at Cheam, and his death caused Philip great sadness, but his contemporaries at Gordonstoun said he kept his feelings to himself. Experiencing so many traumas in early life can result in what psychologists call a "highly defended personality," which would account for his ability to deal with his personal disasters without any outward sign of emotions. However, George's death would have a profound effect on Philip's life as Lynden Manor was no longer home from home, and George's younger brother, Dickie Mountbatten, took over the role of father figure. In his diary Dickie described George as "the sweetest natured, most charming, most able, most brilliant, entirely lovable brother anyone ever had."

Hahn's verdict of Philip was that his best was first class, but that his second best was not good enough. In a school report he said: "Prince Philip's leadership qualities are most noticeable though marred at times by impatience and intolerance. In dealing with younger boys Philip has a natural power of command and his sense of humour and a rapid understanding of human nature have proved a great help to him in tasks of leadership."

Looking back years later, Hahn wrote: "When Philip first came to Gordonstoun his most remarkable trait was his undefeatable spirit. He felt the emotions of both joy and sadness deeply, and the way he looked and the way he moved indicated what he felt. That even applied to the minor disappointments inevitable in a schoolboy's life. His laughter was heard everywhere. In his schoolwork he showed lively intelligence. In community life, once he had made a task his own, he showed meticulous attention to detail and pride of workmanship which was never content with mediocre results."

Philip spent his last term at Gordonstoun preparing for the entry examination to the Royal Naval College, Dartmouth, where according to Hahn "the exacting demands of great service would enable him to do justice to himself." While staying in Cheltenham, Dickie Mountbatten arranged for Philip to receive additional coaching with a Mr. Mercer, who specialized in coaching boys for Dartmouth.

The majority of entrants to Dartmouth came via other naval schools such as Osborne, therefore they had several years prior training in naval matters. As war was looming, Winston Churchill introduced a fast-track entry system for boys like Philip who had been to traditional public schools. These special entrants lived in temporary huts away from the main building. Philip did extremely well at Dartmouth, coming out ahead of those with a traditional naval schooling to win the award of the King's Dirk for best cadet of his year. His only failing seems to have been his difficulty in spelling correctly. This is apparent in his letters to his old headmaster and in his midshipman's log, where "buoys" appears as "bouys" and "except" as "exept." War was declared on September 3, 1939, but that did not quite end Philip's education. Years later, when he was a married man, Philip was enrolled in a course of advanced seamanship for officers at the Royal Naval College, Greenwich. For several months he spent weekdays at Greenwich, returning home at weekends.

Prince Philip may not have been a great academic, but he certainly took plenty from his schooling, and the importance of this period colored his thoughts for the rest of his life. For him the emphasis would never be on academic learning, but on what education brought to the individual in terms of character.

Among the many offices that Philip took on after leaving the Royal Navy were the chancellorships of several universities, Edinburgh and Cambridge among them. In the course of the many addresses and after-dinner speeches he has given, one theme stands out—that it is the building of character rather than academic learning that is the most important element in education. In his speech on installation as chancellor of Edinburgh University, after making Kurt Hahn an honorary doctor of law, Philip set out his personal views on teaching and learning when he said:

"Life in school should be so ordered that is in a real sense a preparation for life in a larger community; it is out of classroom hours and away from home that many of the practical lessons of life are taught and learned. The schools therefore have this further duty to teach the young to live as members of the community with all that implies in learning to give and take and play their part in a common life."

In the same speech Philip went on to praise teachers and to talk about schools in general. He said that every school had its own characteristics and that it was a blessing that schools should be different and each one unique. It is unfortunate that when it came to his own children, he did not take that into account, in sending Prince Charles to Gordonstoun, for which he was clearly unsuited and where he was very unhappy. When it comes to schooling it is certainly not the case that one size fits all.

Philip returned to his pet theme in 1957, addressing the Outward Bound Trust, another of Kurt Hahn's creations for helping young people to learn through adventures in the outdoors. Philip said: "For some reason it is perfectly respectable to teach history and mathematics, electronics and engineering, but any attempt to develop character and the whole man tends to be viewed with suspicion. All the more remarkable because the great men of history have all had an exceptional strength of character."

Again in 1978, when talking about moral standards, he said: "The problem with moral standards is a great deal more difficult and their importance within the education process is frequently overlooked. Yet the experience of every civilisation has been that the general standards of honesty, integrity, compassion, manners and personal behaviour which are acquired during the education process are far more significant than the standards of academic achievement."

For Philip academic excellence takes second place to the development of character. The Duke of Edinburgh Awards scheme, Outward Bound schools, the National Association of Boys' Clubs, all of which he promoted constantly, are character-building concerns.

As Philip said, "I am one of those ignorant bums that never went to a university, and a fat lot of harm it did me."

With the book-learning part of his education now over, Philip moved into the Royal Navy, and it was here that his character would fully emerge in a way that would even impress the young princess.

Chapter 4

THE ROYAL NAVY AND
THE COURTSHIP

High on a hill above the town of Dartmouth in Devon, in South West England, Britannia Royal Naval College—often referred to as Royal Naval College, Dartmouth—has been training Royal Naval officers since 1863. In May 1939, Philip started life as a Dartmouth cadet shortly before his eighteenth birthday, having taken the entrance examination after leaving Gordonstoun. This was a relatively advanced age to enter because many of the cadets had spent several years as junior cadets prior to taking the entrance exam. In the circumstances Philip did reasonably well, coming sixteenth out of thirty entrants. He entered as "Prince Philip" as Dartmouth was no stranger to royalty, with King George V, King Edward VIII, and King George VI all having been naval cadets there.

Not long after Philip entered Dartmouth, King George VI and Queen Elizabeth paid a visit to the naval college, having earlier inspected the naval fleet at Weymouth. On July 22, 1939, the Royal Yacht *Victoria and Albert* anchored in the mouth of the river Dart.

On board with the King and Queen were their two daughters Princess Elizabeth and Princess Margaret; also in attendance in his capacity as aide-de-camp to the King was Dickie Mountbatten. It was on this occasion that Philip first publicly and knowingly met his future bride, Princess Elizabeth, although they had both been present on several royal occasions. When Philip was thirteen and the princess was eight, they both attended the 1934 wedding of Philip's cousin Princess Marina, later Duchess of Kent, and Elizabeth's uncle, Prince George, Duke of Kent.

It is not known what Philip thought of the young Princess Elizabeth at this meeting at Dartmouth. But it is clear that the princess fell for Philip at once on that pivotal weekend. King George VI's official biographer, Sir John Wheeler-Bennett said, "This was the man with whom Princess Elizabeth had been in love from their first meeting." Later, when Elizabeth had acceded to the throne, she read the proofs of the book prior to its publication and changed not one word of this statement. In a letter written in 1947 to author Betty Shew, who was compiling the book *Royal Wedding* as a souvenir of the marriage, the young princess agreed to share details of her relationship with her naval officer fiancé. In a letter written in ink on headed notepaper from Balmoral Castle she wrote:

"The first time I remember meeting Philip was at the Royal Naval College, Dartmouth, in July 1939, just before the war. (We may have met before at the Coronation, or the Duchess of Kent's wedding, but I don't remember). I was 13 years of age and he was 18 and a cadet just due to leave. He joined the navy at the outbreak of war, and I only saw him very occasionally when he was on leave—I suppose about twice in three years.

"Then when his uncle and aunt, Lord and Lady Mountbatten, were away he spent various weekends away with us at Windsor. Then he went to the Pacific and Far East for two years as everyone there will know."

The visit of the two princesses to the naval college was somewhat curtailed due to an outbreak of chickenpox and mumps among the cadets. They were restricted to the house of the officer in charge of the college, Admiral Sir Frederick Dalrymple-Hamilton. It seems likely that Dickie Mountbatten suggested that of all the cadets Philip should be given the unenviable job of entertaining two young girls while the King and Queen carried out their formal inspection of the college. Not only were Philip and the princesses distant cousins, but Philip was well known as a friend of the royal family through his mother, Princess Alice.

The account of that day is found in the memoirs of the princesses' governess Miss Marion Crawford. To "Crawfie" are attributed the remarks made by Princess Elizabeth about Philip, such as "how good he is" after a game of croquet and "how high he can jump" as he leaped over the net on the tennis court. The following day Philip, at the suggestion of Uncle Dickie, was invited to lunch on the royal yacht, where he again entertained the princesses. When the royal yacht set sail, it was escorted downriver by a number of Dartmouth cadets in small boats, rowing as hard as they could, and among them was Philip in a rowing boat on his own. As all the other small craft dropped away, Philip was the only one who followed the *Victoria and Albert* into the open sea, watched by the King and Princess Elizabeth from the yacht's stern. It was only when the captain with his megaphone ordered Philip to turn back that he gave up.

Philip's recollection of that first encounter was somewhat vague. He told his biographer Basil Boothroyd, "Well, we'd met at Dartmouth, and as far as I was concerned it was a very amusing experience, going on board the yacht and meeting them, and that sort of thing, and that was that." When asked at what time did he decide that he was going to marry Princess Elizabeth, he said, "Well, certainly not at Dartmouth." Philip continued, "During the war I once or twice spent Christmas at Windsor because I'd nowhere particular to go. . . . I thought not all that much about it. . . . We used to correspond occasionally . . . it isn't so extraordinary to be on kind of family relationship terms with somebody. You don't necessarily have to think about marriage."

The facts are rather different from Philip's disingenuous recollection of events. Dickie Mountbatten was a master strategist, as is evidenced by his great success as a supreme commander of the Allied forces in South East Asia during the Second World War. He was also extremely ambitious. Sometime after the Dartmouth meeting, he hatched a plot to marry a Mountbatten into the British royal family, and Philip was part of his plan from the outset.

Philip left Dartmouth with the King's Dirk, the prize for the best cadet of his year, but when war broke out a few weeks later he was faced with a problem. As a foreign national it was not possible to progress up the ranks in the Royal Navy, and he could not apply for British citizenship as the naturalization department in Britain had been suspended for the duration of the war. After Uncle Dickie pulled some strings, the Admiralty gave permission for Philip to continue his career in the navy. As a Greek citizen he was technically a neutral, until Greece joined forces with the Allies a year later when the opportunistic Italians invaded Greece, on Philip's nineteenth birthday.

Philip's first posting as midshipman, in February 1940, was to the battleship HMS *Ramillies*, which was in the Mediterranean Fleet with Vice Admiral Tom Baillie-Grohman as captain. Baillie-Grohman was an ardent diarist and note taker, and some twenty volumes of his papers are stored at the Royal Naval College, Greenwich. As was his practice with all new midshipmen, Baillie-Grohman had an interview with Philip as soon as he came on board. In the course of the conversation it is recorded that Philip said that his uncle Dickie Mountbatten (who had requested

Baillie-Grohman to accept Philip on his ship) had ideas for him and thought Philip could marry Princess Elizabeth. Philip added that he often wrote to Elizabeth. Baillie-Grohman advised Philip not to say a word of this to any of his shipmates. As Philip was then eighteen and Elizabeth only thirteen, marriage would have been a distant prospect, but this was at a time when royal marriages were often discussed and arranged when the parties were young.

We can only surmise that Elizabeth instigated the correspondence by writing to Philip to thank him for looking after her and her sister at Dartmouth—something any well-brought-up girl would do. It seems that this correspondence went on throughout the war. His cousin Princess Alexandra, in her biography of Philip, recounted that she met him when he was on shore leave in Cape Town in 1941 and said Philip was busy writing a letter. When she asked, "Who to?" Philip replied, "Lilibet—Princess Elizabeth of England."

HMS *Ramillies* was an old battleship launched in 1916 that was given the job of escorting transports of Australian vessels and troops to Europe. When shore leave in Australia came up, Baillie-Grohman, being mindful of Mountbatten's plans for Philip, arranged for him to stay on a sheep station hundreds of miles into the interior, rather than be exposed to the nightlife of Sydney, where all kinds of girl trouble were possible.

Meanwhile Philip's real interest was the navy. As a midshipman he was required to keep a log in which, in the words of the Admiralty, "midshipmen are to record in their own language all matters of interest or importance in the work that is carried out . . . in their ship."

The object of keeping the journal was to train midshipmen in the power of observation, the power of expression, and the habit of orderliness. Philip's log runs from his posting to HMS *Ramillies* in February 1940 until June 1941, when he returned to England to sit for his sublieutenant's course and examination in Plymouth. As well as containing keenly observed descriptions of all action seen by Philip on the four ships where he served as a midshipman, the log is full of technical drawings, colored maps, charts, and diagrams. His depictions of such items as the electro-hydraulic steering gear, the Weymouth Cooke Sextant Rangefinder, and assorted cringles, shackles, and thrust blocks give an early indication of Philip's life-long interest in engineering and technology. The handwritten log was put on display in an exhibition celebrating his ninetieth birth-day in Windsor Castle Drawings Gallery. It shows an eye for detail and excellent powers of draftsmanship.

In his log Philip records that HMS *Ramillies* was not a comfort-able assignment. The sleeping quarters were so cramped and airless, he wrote: "Nobody ever turns in. The most popular sleeping quar-ters are in the gun room where the midshipmen sleep in two arm-chairs, two sofas and on the table. It is very hot at night." In April 1940 Philip was transferred to HMS *Kent*, a flagship with heavy armament. "The ventilation is so much better," he wrote, "that it is quite possible to stay below decks in comfort." When HMS *Kent* put in at Durban for a refit, the crew enjoyed liberal hospitality from the locals, so much so that Philip wrote in his log on leaving, "Many hearts were left behind in Durban." Whether his was one of them is not recorded. One of Philip's contemporaries noted that he avoided any serious emotional entanglements, something echoed by Philip's close friend Mike Parker a couple of years later. Could it be that he was heeding Mountbatten's advice and staying out of any trouble that might thwart the plan to gain the hand of Princess Elizabeth in marriage?

After a short posting to a shore station in Colombo, where Philip found little to do aside from catching fish for the captain's table, he was transferred to a third ship, which he recorded somewhat sarcastically in his log: "A few minutes after one o'clock on Sunday

October 1st 1940 I walked aboard Her Majesty's ship HMS *Shropshire*, the third ship in eight months to receive this singular honour." Three months later he was moved yet again, this time to HMS *Valiant*, a newly modernized battleship where he would at last see the action that he longed for. Within three days of his joining the ship it was involved in the bombardment of Bardia in Libya, which he described as a very spectacular affair. After this encounter Philip took some shore leave in Greece, where he spent some days with his royal relations. He was also reunited with his mother, Alice, whom he had not seen for five years. Although Greece was under serious threat from the advancing Germans, Alice refused to leave Athens, where she was determined to see out the war. As two of her sons-in-law were high-ranking German officers, this was not as foolish a decision as it might have appeared.

On HMS *Valiant*, Philip was put in charge of searchlight control, a vital post since the Italian navy was seeking to escape from Cape Matapan under cover of darkness. His account in his log starts: "My orders were that if any ship illuminated a target I was to switch on and illuminate it for the rest of the fleet." He continued, "Remembering the torpedo-howling attack which we witnessed on Crete, anti-aircraft action stations were closed up just before sunset . . . reconnaissance aircraft had found three Italian cruisers steaming eastwards in the neighbourhood of Crete . . . the enemy's shooting was getting rather too accurate . . . the midship light picked out an enemy cruiser and lit her up as if it were broad daylight." He went on to illuminate another cruiser, which was destroyed in seconds like the first one. For his actions in the Battle of Cape Matapan, Philip was mentioned in dispatches by Admiral Cunningham, and they were reported in the captain's log: "The successful and continuous illumination of the enemy greatly contributed to the devastating results achieved in the gun action . . . and thanks to his alertness and appreciation of the situation we were able to sink in five minutes two 8-inch-gun Italian cruisers." For his actions King George II of Greece awarded Philip the Greek War Cross.

If Philip was too busy with his career and the war to think about marriage, there were others for whom it was a subject of interest. Sir Henry "Chips" Channon, the MP and renowned diarist, found himself in Greece in 1941 at the same time Philip was enjoying some shore leave in Athens. One entry in his diary reads, "There is Prince Andrew, who philanders on the riviera while his son Prince Philip serves in our navy." The entry of January 21, 1941, refers to "an enjoyable Greek cocktail party. Prince Philip of Greece was there. He is extraordinarily handsome. . . . He is to be our Prince Consort and that is why he is serving in our navy, but I deplore such a marriage. He and Princess Elizabeth are too interrelated." His information came from Philip's aunt Princess Nicholas of Greece, the mother of Marina, Duchess of Kent.

Whether or not Philip was aware of what was being discussed behind his back is not known. We do know that at some point during the war Philip and Princess Elizabeth exchanged photographs. Philip kept hers in a battered leather frame in his cabin on board HMS *Whelp*, and she kept his on her dressing table in Windsor Castle. Surely such an exchange would not have taken place without mutual expressions of love. Princess Elizabeth could not have been more than eighteen years old at the time. It was well known among the crew that letters to and from the princess came through the post rooms of Philip's ships with regularity.

Philip saw more action on HMS *Valiant* in the Battle of Crete in May 1941. Things were not going well for the Allies in the Mediterranean. *Valiant* had been ordered to intercept German landings on Crete and in doing so came under heavy attack from Stuka dive-bombers. Philip's log reads: "We were bombed from a high level by a large number of small bombs . . . came whistling down landing very close all down the port side. It was only sometime later I discovered we had been hit twice on the quarterdeck. . . . There were only four casualties (three dead, one wounded)." While this action was taking place, Dickie Mountbatten's destroyer HMS *Kelly*, of which he was captain, was sunk in another part of the Mediterranean. Of the ship's company of 264, only 128 were rescued, among whom was Mountbatten. Had he gone down with his ship, Philip's life might well have turned out rather differently. After his rescue Mountbatten was landed in Alexandria, minus his uniform and covered in fuel oil. HMS *Valiant* was also in Alexandria being patched up after the Battle of Crete. Dickie was surprised to be met by Philip, who roared with laughter at his uncle's unfortunate appearance, as he was always so meticulous about his apparel.

In June 1941, Philip was to return to England to take his sublieutenant's examination. His troopship was routed via Nova Scotia to pick up some Canadian troops. On the way back the ship put into Puerto Rico to refuel, which is where the Chinese stokers decided to jump ship and disappear. Philip and the other three midshipmen on board had no choice but to descend into the boiler room to shovel coal into the furnaces. For this duty Philip received a certificate as a "boiler trimmer."

Philip passed his examination with distinction and in June 1942 was posted to HMS *Wallace*, where he was promoted four months later. At the age of twenty-one he was one of the youngest seconds in command in the Royal Navy. It was HMS *Wallace*'s job to escort convoys down the east coast of Britain from Rosyth to Sheerness, which was a dangerous duty as the convoys were under constant attention from German U-boats and torpedo boats, and the waters were heavily mined. Philip was a strict disciplinarian and was determined that his ship should be the finest in the squadron. It soon became apparent to him that there was another destroyer whose first lieutenant had the same idea. This was Lt. Michael Parker of HMS *Lauderdale*, which was often berthed next to HMS *Wallace* at their base in Rosyth. What started out as a fiercely competitive relationship, built on a desire for excellence, developed into a close friendship that was to last many years. Parker recalled later: "We were highly competitive. We both wanted to show that we had the most efficient, cleanest and best ships and ship's company in the navy."

Being based in Rosyth meant that Philip could take his shore leave in the UK. He sometimes stayed with his cousin Marina Duchess of Kent at Coppins, her house in Iver, Buckinghamshire. In 1943, she gave a small private party at which Philip danced for the first time with Princess Elizabeth. He was also on several occasions a guest at Windsor Castle, where he entertained the King with navy yarns. "I'd call in and have a meal," as Philip put it to his biographer Boothroyd.

In June 1943, HMS *Wallace* was sent to the Mediterranean to assist in the Allied landings of troops in Sicily. It was during this time that Philip conjured up a plan to throw overboard a wooden raft with smoke floats attached to create the illusion of debris ablaze on the water, a ruse that undoubtedly saved his ship and the lives of the crew.

Harry Hargreaves, one of the crew, recalled the terrifying events of that night. "It was obvious that we were the target and the German bombers would not stop until we had suffered a fatal hit. It was for all the world like being blindfolded and trying to evade an enemy whose only problem was getting his aim right. There was no doubt in anyone's mind that a direct hit was inevitable. It was less than five minutes after the aircraft had departed and—if the previous space in time was approximately the same—we had about twenty minutes to come up with something. We couldn't steam far in that time, not even far enough to make the aircraft think we had moved."

Hargreaves continued: "The first lieutenant [Philip] went into hurried conversation with the captain, and the next thing a wooden raft was being put together on deck. Within five minutes they launched a raft over the side—at each end was fastened a smoke float. When it hit the water the smoke floats were activated and billowing clouds of smoke interspersed with small bursts of flame gave a convincing imitation of flaming debris in the water. The captain ordered full ahead and we steamed away from the raft for a good five minutes and then he ordered the engines stopped. The tell-tale wake subsided and we lay there quietly . . . until we heard aircraft engines approaching. The sound of the aircraft grew louder until I thought it was directly overhead and I screwed up my shoulders in anticipation of the bombs. The next thing was the scream of the bombs, but at some distance. The ruse had worked and the aircraft was bombing the raft. I suppose he was under the impression that he had hit us in his last attack and was now finishing the job."

Hargreaves said later: "Prince Philip saved our lives that night. I suppose there might have been a few survivors, but certainly the ship would have been sunk. He was always very courageous and resourceful and thought very quickly."

In 1943, Philip was invited to stay at Windsor Castle at Christmas, but because he had flu he was unable to attend the dance the King had organized for his daughters. However, he was able to come to their pantomime and stay for the rest of the weekend. To raise funds for charity during the war and keep everyone entertained, the King had devised the idea of staging a pantomime every Christmas, and that year it was *Aladdin*, with the two princesses in the starring roles. According to Crawfie, the pantomime went off well, with Philip laughing in all the right places. Philip's cousin David Milford Haven then joined him, and they stayed for a week enjoying dinner parties, film shows, and dancing round the gramophone. According to Crawfie, Princess Elizabeth had told her Philip was "the one." Crawfie also said, "There was a sparkle about her that none of us had ever seen before."

Philip had seen all four of his sisters marry German noblemen with landed estates and fully staffed palatial homes. He would be very aware that he could not expect to inherit anything from his father other than a few personal effects. Princess Elizabeth would one day be one of the richest women in the world. Few young men would not have had their heads turned by the prospect of marrying a beautiful young heiress who would one day be a queen. The fact that she had fallen deeply in love with Philip at first sight was something that even Mountbatten could not have foreseen.

In the spring of 1944, Philip was posted to Newcastle-upon-Tyne, where the new destroyer HMS *Whelp* was in the process of being commissioned for service. He was to spend the rest of the war as HMS *Whelp*'s first lieutenant. While the ship was still at the shipyard, a journalist tracked down Philip and was surprised to find the prince living in a small hotel and traveling by bus daily to the shipyard. No mention however was made of Princess Elizabeth. During this period Philip had the opportunity of getting to know her rather better. In a letter written by Princess Elizabeth, which was auctioned in 2016, she wrote: "I only saw him very occasionally when he was on leave—I suppose about twice in three years . . . [in 1944] he spent various weekends away with us at Windsor. Then he went to the Pacific and Far East for two years." By August 1944, HMS *Whelp* was ready to join the destroyer flotilla assigned to the eastern fleet in the fight against Japan. At the same time, the war in Europe had turned in favor of the Allies following the successful

D-Day invasion. En route to the Suez Canal, *Whelp* put in at Alexandria a few days before Mountbatten arrived in Cairo.

Philip and Lord Killearn, the British ambassador, met Mountbatten at Cairo aerodrome. Mountbatten was another who kept a regular diary. On August 24, 1944, he wrote that he'd had long discussions with Philip and then with King George of Greece in the British Embassy gardens. His diary entry records that he had "very satisfactory discussions" on the subject of the possible marriage between Philip and Princess Elizabeth, which would have necessitated Philip giving up his Greek citizenship.

In December 1944, Philip's father, Andrew, died of a heart attack in Monte Carlo, cut off from his entire family by the war even though his daughter Sophie had tried to get permission from the German authorities to let her visit. As *Whelp* was engaged in attacks on Japanese oil refineries, there was no question of Philip being able to go to the funeral. Mike Parker said later that Philip really loved his father and that his death at the age of sixty-two came as a great shock to him. After the war ended, Philip and Parker traveled together to Monte Carlo to collect Andrew's personal effects from his mistress. "We were sitting in the Hotel de Paris," Parker recalled, "waiting for her, with a cocktail each and in came this woman with blue glasses. I'd never seen glasses like that. And as she entered she smiled at the doorman and said 'Evenin Charles.' I'll always remember that." According to Parker, Doris—as she called herself—and Prince Philip got along "from the first," and he left them alone to reminisce about Andrew and his love of animals, his humor, and, of course, his lack of funds. Apart from old suits, some cuff links, and a pair of silver-backed hairbrushes, Andrew left nothing but debts and memories. In 1946, he was conveyed by a Greek cruiser to Athens, where he was finally buried in the gardens of the royal palace at Tatoi.

*

In May 1945, Philip spent several months in Australia while HMS *Whelp* was being refitted. Mike Parker was also stationed at the same Australian base with his ship HMS *Wessex*. Together they enjoyed a round of parties with Mike's family and friends at which there was no shortage of attractive young girls. According to his cousin Alexandra's biography, Philip "hit feminine hearts with terrific impact" and yet he "fought a series of delaying actions all aimed at one objective: non-involvement." As his friend Mike Parker put it: "There were armfuls of girls but nothing happened—nothing serious. . . . We were young, we had fun, we had a few drinks, we might have gone dancing and that was it. . . . Philip was actually quite reserved. He didn't give away a lot. There have been books and articles galore saying he played the field. I don't believe it. People say we were screwing around like nobody's business. Well, we weren't."

By this time Princess Elizabeth had her own suite of rooms at Buckingham Palace and her own staff. In 1945, she joined the Auxiliary Territorial Service at her own insistence, at the age of eighteen, as a subaltern, becoming the first female member of the royal family to join the armed services as a full-time active member. By the end of the war she had reached the rank of junior commander, having completed her course at No. 1 Mechanical Training Centre of the ATS and passing as a fully qualified driver. She famously celebrated VE day by slipping out of Buckingham Palace wearing her ATS uniform in the company of several Guards officers. She had grown up considerably since the days of the *Aladdin* pantomime at Windsor.

After the refit in Australia, HMS *Whelp* was on the way to take part in the planned invasion of Japan when atom bombs were dropped on Hiroshima and Nagasaki, precipitating the unconditional surrender of Japan. Philip was one of the British officers to witness the formal signing of the instrument of surrender on

September 2, 1945, which took place on board the aircraft carrier USS *Missouri* in Tokyo Bay.

With the war ended, Philip's last voyage was to bring prisoners of war back to England. Having disembarked in January 1946, Philip's next job was to oversee the decommissioning of HMS *Whelp*. A few months later Philip was posted to an officers' training college at Corsham to lecture petty officers on seamanship. Times were tough in England immediately after the war, with both fuel and food being rationed. The winter of 1946–47 was exceptionally bitter, with the Thames freezing over at Windsor. Philip had to lecture his students by candlelight, wearing his navy greatcoat to keep warm.

In her letter to Betty Shew, the princess explained how their romance progressed: "We first started seeing more of each other when Philip went for a two-year job to the RN Petty Officers' school at Corsham—before that we hardly knew each other. He'd spend weekends with us, and when the school was closed, he spent six weeks at Balmoral—it was great luck his getting a shore job first then! We both love dancing—we have danced at Circo's and Quaglino's as well as at parties."

Philip began making frequent trips to Buckingham Palace, racing to London about one hundred miles away in his little MG sports car, in order to dine with Princess Elizabeth at Buckingham Palace, with Princess Margaret ever present as a chaperone. "Philip enjoys driving and does it fast!" the princess wrote to Betty Shew. "He has his own tiny MG of which he is very proud of—he has taken me about in it, once up to London, which was great fun, only it was like sitting on the road, and the wheels are almost as high as one's head." When in London, he stayed at the Mountbattens' house in Chester Street, where he was looked after by Dickie's valet John Dean. In his literary portrait of Philip, Dean remarked on how little clothing

Philip possessed. Dean used to darn Philip's socks and wash his only good shirt overnight when Philip came to stay. Dean noticed that Philip always traveled with his framed photograph of Elizabeth.

In the summer of 1946, Philip was invited to stay with the royal family at Balmoral, where days were spent deerstalking and shooting grouse. It was here that at some point Philip proposed marriage to Elizabeth. Philip's recollection of precisely how it came about is quite vague. He later told Basil Boothroyd: "I suppose one thing led to another. I suppose I began to think about it seriously, oh, let me think now, when I got back in '46 and went to Balmoral. It was probably then that we, that it became, you know, that we began to think about it seriously, and even talk about it."

It wasn't the most enthusiastic description of a marriage proposal, but Philip is not the sort of person to give into gushing detail, and to him it was a private matter and was going to remain that way, hence his reserve about discussing it at all. It was also an extremely serious decision. Despite Philip's impoverished circumstances, he had been accepted as one of the family and, far from being thought unsuitable, was considered easily the most "eligible" candidate for the hand of the future queen.

The King, whose consent was required under the Royal Marriage Act, gave his agreement, but he insisted that the engagement be kept secret at least until after the royal family returned from a tour of South Africa that would keep Elizabeth out of the country from February to April 1947. The King reasoned that it would give the princess another six months to make sure that her mind was certain in her choice. Rumors of an impending announcement appeared in several national newspapers, and in September 1946 Buckingham Palace issued a statement firmly denying the rumors. In any event there were several hurdles to overcome.

Philip was a prince of Greece. Mountbatten's attempts to get his naturalization as a British citizen pushed through had been thwarted for the time being for diplomatic reasons. It was considered by the government that the Greek political situation should settle before Philip could apply for naturalization. After the war there was uncertainty as to whether the Greek monarchy would be restored. As Philip was a prince of Greece, it was considered that his naturalization might be perceived as a lack of confidence in the Greek monarchy. The problem was resolved when in 1946 a plebiscite voted for the restoration of the monarchy. Although a navy man with a distinguished war record, Philip was also a foreigner with German family connections. Mountbatten took steps to smooth the way forward. He took Philip to the House of Commons to meet a group of younger members of Parliament. To counter what he saw—with some justification—as a vendetta against his family from Lord Beaverbrook's Express Newspapers, Mountbatten invited the editors of the *Daily Express* and *Sunday Express* to drinks at his house in Chester Street to meet Philip and to sound out the editors on the subject of Philip becoming a British citizen. He took the trouble to explain that Philip's desire to be British went back to his early days in the Royal Navy and had nothing to do with the rumors of an impending engagement.

All went well, and when Philip's naturalization eventually came through in March 1947, there was no adverse comment in the press. The question of a name for Philip had to be resolved once he had renounced his foreign titles and was no longer Prince Philip of Greece and Denmark. The College of Heralds came up with the name Oldcastle, which was acceptable to Philip, but Dickie Mountbatten got his way when Philip became Lt. Philip Mountbatten RN.

Philip felt that his flamboyant uncle was being overzealous in promoting the engagement and asked him to back off. According to Mountbatten's biographer Philip Ziegler, Philip wrote to Mountbatten in these terms: "Please, I beg of you not too much advice in an affair of the heart or I shall be forced to do the wooing by proxy. . . . I am not being rude but it is apparent that you like the idea of being General Manager of this little show, and I am rather afraid that she [Princess Elizabeth] might not take to the idea quite as docilely as I do. It is true I know what is good for me, but don't forget she has not had you as uncle loco parentis, counsellor and friend as long as I have." It was fortuitous that Mountbatten left the English shores to become the last Viceroy of India in March 1947. He was able to leave content in the knowledge that his long-term plan had come to fruition. Not only was his nephew about to become officially engaged to Princess Elizabeth, but the name Mountbatten would now be linked to the British crown.

Mountbatten would not have it all his own way. After the death of King George VI in 1952, Dickie was heard boasting at dinner that the House of Mountbatten was now the royal family in Britain. Prince Ernst August of Hanover was at the dinner and did not like what he heard. He reported the conversation to Queen Mary, who was furious. She said that her husband, King George V, had changed the family name from Saxe-Coburg-Gotha to Windsor for all time. Queen Mary contacted Prime Minister Winston Churchill, who informed the new Queen that the royal house must be called the House of Windsor. Philip had tried to make a case for the House of Edinburgh but was rebuffed. He was furious, complaining, "I am nothing better than an amoeba."

Three months after the royal party returned from South Africa, a court circular was issued from Buckingham Palace on July 9, 1947: "It is with the greatest pleasure that the King and Queen announce the betrothal of their dearly beloved daughter the Princess Elizabeth to Lieutenant Philip Mountbatten R.N. son of the late Prince Andrew of Greece and Princess Andrew (Princess Alice of Battenberg), to which union the King has gladly given his consent."

*

For such a self-contained person who had lived much of his life in privileged obscurity, Philip was about to see all of that change. Suddenly he became an object of unwelcome interest. Disliking criticism, it irritated Philip that the press should have such strident opinions on his personal life. It was the beginning of his lifelong battle with the media and the end of his private life.

Chapter 5

"INCREDIBLY HAPPY, JUST GORGEOUS"

When Philip became officially engaged to Princess Elizabeth on July 10, 1947, his entire worldly goods fitted into several suitcases. He had no hidden wealth, no property, and no bequests. He survived on his naval lieutenant's pay of £11 a week, which is about £427 ($536) in today's money. According to his valet, John Dean, who joined him in 1947, he didn't even own a pair of decent hairbrushes—although he had his father's ivory-handled shaving brush and his gold signet ring. He had three naval uniforms, a couple of lounge suits—one salvaged from his father's possessions, which he had altered and wore for a number of years—a blazer and flannels, evening dress lent by Mountbatten, and a shooting suit.

The clothes had been useful during the summer at Balmoral in August 1947, the first summer of Philip's formal induction to the royal family. Not everyone was as enamored by Philip as his fiancée clearly was, and even the princess's private secretary, Jock Colville, who was part of the sporting party, was puzzled by the relationship between the couple. He could see she was clearly in love with her fiancé but wondered if Philip was quite so smitten or had simply "hit the jackpot." Regardless of what anyone else thought, Elizabeth was delighted that at last the secret she had kept to herself and her immediate family for so long was finally in the open.

As Philip was marrying a future monarch, the engagement ring he chose needed to be a significant piece. His mother, Princess Alice, came to his rescue and gave him one of the tiaras that she had received as a wedding present half a century earlier. It was a diamond-and-aquamarine tiara given to Alice by Tsar Nicholas II and Tsarina Alexandra of Russia. Alexandra was Alice's aunt; Nicholas was a first cousin of the groom, Prince Andrew. The tiara also came with an accompanying suite of jewels.

The tiara was dismantled to make the three-carat solitaire with five smaller diamonds on either side set in platinum. Philip designed it himself with jeweler Philip Antrobus. Several of those diamonds were used to make the ring as well as Elizabeth's wedding present, a beautiful diamond bracelet. When Philip brought the engagement ring to Buckingham Palace on July 9, 1947, to present it to his fiancée, they then went to show the King and Queen. The ring was a little too large, and the princess pointed out it would have to go back to the jewelers, but added anxiously, "We don't have to wait until it's right, do we?" She wrote to Betty Shew later admitting she didn't know the "history of the stone, except that it is a fine old cutting."

At least Philip didn't have the expense of a wedding ring, as the people of Wales supplied a nugget of Welsh gold from which the ring was made. She never takes it off and inside the ring is an inscription. No one knows what it says, other than the engraver, the Queen, and her husband.

King George VI knew he would have to be cautious about the budget for the wedding and the monies awarded to his daughter and her cash-strapped future husband. The postwar era was very tough, and the country had suffered one of the snowiest winters of the twentieth century, followed by floods and nationwide power cuts. Although the war had ended two years previously, all basic foods were rationed, as were clothes, coal, furniture, and petrol. Between the announcement of the engagement in July 1947 and the wedding in November, things worsened for many people; the meat ration was reduced, and potatoes became scarce as a result of the poor harvest. Austerity was very much the order of the day.

Initially, to save expense, the wedding was going to be held privately in St. George's Chapel, Windsor, but the government decided that it should be a public occasion to lighten up the war-weary country and give its people something to celebrate. The cost of the monarchy, then as now, had to be justified. The ruling Labour Party government were wary of the wedding appearing too extravagant and were reticent about any allowances for the prince on his marriage. As he frequently did, Mountbatten acted as a go-between, writing to Labour MP Tom Driberg in July 1947 to explain the situation:

"You can rest assured," he wrote, "that he [Philip] understands this problem and indeed he spoke to me about it when I was at home in May. I am sure he is entirely on the side of cutting down the display of the wedding and his own personal feelings are against receiving any civil list for the very reasons which you give. I have however persuaded him that it is essential he should take something. [Philip] has virtually no money beyond his pay; his tiny little two-seater made a big hole in his private fortune and except when travelling on an officer's warrant he usually goes Third Class by train. As a future Prince Consort however, I think you will agree that Third Class travel would be regarded as a stunt and a sixpenny tip to a porter as stingy. . . . It really amounts to this; you either have got to give up the Monarchy or give the wretched people who have to carry out the functions of the Crown enough money to be able to do it with the same dignity at least as the Prime Minister or the Lord Mayor of London is afforded."

The Labour government was surprisingly sympathetic and granted £50,000 for the princess on her marriage and £10,000 for her husband, with the proviso that the King surrender £100,000 savings made on the civil list during the economies of the war years as a contribution.

Despite the additional expense accorded to the royal family in a time when most of their subjects had very little, the young couple were extremely popular, as witnessed by Mabell Airlie, Queen Mary's lady of the bedchamber, at their first public appearance at a garden party at Buckingham Palace.

"When I looked at Princess Elizabeth, flushed and radiant with happiness I was again reminded of Queen Victoria," Lady Airlie recalled in her memoirs. "Although the Queen had been old, plain and fat when I had seen her and this girl was young, pretty and slim she had the same air of majesty."

"Prince Philip shook hands rather shyly," Lady Airlie noted as she watched him work the crowd. "I noticed that his uniform was shabby—it has that usual after the war look—and I liked him for not having got a new one for the occasion as many men would have done, to make an impression." (Philip always hated ostentation, and he would have considered a new uniform quite unnecessary and showy.) "Observing him I thought he had far more character than most people would imagine, I wondered whether he would be capable of helping Princess Elizabeth someday, as the Prince Consort had helped Victoria. I felt he would, although I should not live to see it."

"They've wasted no time," King Peter of Yugoslavia observed at the same garden party, adding "It's rather like throwing him to the lions."

Queen Wilhelmina of the Netherlands likened Philip's situation to "entering the royal cage." And she told him so.

"A royal consort should entirely sink his own individual existence in that of his wife," Prince Albert, Queen Victoria's consort, had said. But Philip was never going to be a consort. He had always been his own person and wanted to continue to be so, which made it far more difficult. He loathed the attention everything he did caused. One night, on his way back from Corsham, his black-and-green sports car skidded off the road and hit a tree. He was unhurt except for a twisted knee, but it was only a month before the wedding, and the registration HDK 99 was easily recognizable. The press found out and used it as headlines:

"Philip: Take it Easy" (*Sunday Pictorial*). "Lt Philip Hurt in Car Crash" (*Daily Mail*). The press got a bit sterner after the marriage, with another "crash" in February 1948. It only dented the wing of a taxi at Hyde Park Corner, but this time Princess Elizabeth was with him.

In the midst of all the unwanted attention, Philip desperately needed a degree of private life and somewhere to disappear. The King had given the couple an old grace and favor house, Sunninghill, as an engagement present. It was close to London and Windsor, but it had been used by the army during the war and was in a state of dilapidation. The controversy about how much it would cost to repair was still raging when one night in August it mysteriously caught fire and was burned to the ground. (Forty years later the site was used to build the Duke and Duchess of York's new home, which also eventually fell into disrepair, when the couple split up, and was eventually sold and pulled down.)

Philip was used to being homeless, and after the engagement until the day of his marriage, he lived in his grandmother the Dowager Marchioness of Milford Haven's Kensington Palace home with the Third Marquess of Milford Haven, his best man to be, David. To keep Philip company, David moved from the Chelsea house he shared with his girlfriend to be in an adjoining bedroom on the top floor. It was somewhat spartan for a palace, with bare floorboards that creaked. Irritatingly for the two young men, their rooms could only be reached by an uncarpeted stairway that alerted Philip's grandmother whenever they came home late, which was frequently. In order to avoid waking her, they would sometimes creep onto the roof and enter via one of the top casement windows, which was easy enough to do.

In London the royal wedding was a great excuse to shake off the years of austerity, and the ladies of the court took their jewels out of their safes, found their best frocks, and partied. Two nights before the wedding, in the royal tradition, a grand ball was given by the King and Queen at Buckingham Palace. The royal estates provided the fare: the finest wines were brought up from the cellars and the silver plate, crystal, and porcelain were taken out of their boxes and prepared. Old Queen Mary was in sparkling form. "When Winston Churchill went up to greet her, she held out both her hands to him, which I have never seen her do before," Lady Airlie recalled.

"It was obvious that the marriage of the Princess, who was both a dearly loved granddaughter and the future Sovereign, delighted her," Lady Airlie said. "In the short time since she had grown to know about him really well, Prince Philip had won both her liking and her approbation. She told me that when a member of the royal family had said to her that the only thing which could be brought against him was that he had been to a crank school with the theories of complete social equality where the boys were taught to mix with all and sundry and that it would remain to be seen whether the effects of this training would be useful or baleful to the King's son-in-law, she had replied decisively—'useful.'"

According to Mabell Airlie, Queen Mary was far broader minded than was popularly supposed. However, she did draw the line at at least one of the fifteen hundred wedding presents sent to Elizabeth and Philip, which was a loincloth knitted by Gandhi. She was deeply shocked by such an indelicate gift being on public display. "What a horrible thing," she exclaimed.

Philip, who was standing nearby, failed to see why she was so distressed and said, "I don't think it's horrible. Gandhi is a wonderful man; a very great man." Queen Mary apparently chose to keep silent, but later Princess Margaret had the foresight to hide the loincloth behind some other gifts when Queen Mary made a return visit the next day.

Not only was the cost of the wedding a sensitive issue, but so was the choice of guests. Anti-German feeling was still strong: although the war had been over for some thirty months, the country was still ravaged by its damage and everything was in short supply. King George VI certainly did not want to emphasize how many of both his and the bridegroom's relations had strong German connections, most notably Philip's three remaining sisters, all of whom had married German nobility.

"We had just been through a war," Mike Parker said by way of explanation, "and Germans were Germans."

"I think Philip understood," recalled Pamela Mountbatten, Philip's cousin, but his sisters certainly didn't. For years afterward they'd say, "Why weren't we allowed to come to your wedding?" They weren't exactly "storm troopers."

From his father's seven brothers and sisters, all but one had died, but Philip's favorite, Uncle George, came from France with his wife, Marie Bonaparte, and their daughter, Eugenie, alongside various cousins. The final guest list included six kings and seven queens and was the largest gathering of royalty, regnant and exiled, anyone could remember. One other notable absentee was the Duke of Windsor, the princess's uncle, of whom she was still very fond, but her mother refused to receive his wife, Wallis Simpson, and it would have been inappropriate to have one without the other.

On the eve of the wedding, King George VI had admitted Lieutenant Mountbatten RN to the royal family by making him a Knight Companion of the Order of the Garter and authorizing him to use the appellation of Royal Highness, which he had surrendered on his naturalization as a British subject. The King also granted him Baron Greenwich, Earl of Merioneth, and the Dukedom of Edinburgh. The titles were only announced on the morning of the wedding, with the announcement of the Garter, which meant they were too late for printing in the order of service for the wedding. It simply said, "Lieutenant Philip Mountbatten RN."

In the months leading up to the wedding there had been many times Philip wished that he could indeed remain Philip Mountbatten RN. The enormity of what he was taking on had unnerved even him. He was not a fool and, unlike his future wife, did not compartmentalize things and then hope they might simply fade away. He faced up to his problems and dealt with them, but psychologically he felt estranged as the frenetic wedding preparations went on all around him. He seemed to have lost his own identity and instead been included as part of his fiancée's, which made him uncomfortable. Since he had been a teenager, he had been responsible for himself, and he was not used to having to put someone else first, especially someone as notable as his fiancée. His natural instinct was to rail against it and be aggressive, but he knew he couldn't hurt the princess's feelings, and she would never understand his distressing inner turmoil.

He had distractions, of course, and one of his escape routes was his introduction to what was called the Thursday Club. In 1947, a couple of newspaper editors, the royal photographer Baron Nahum, and the actor James Robertson Justice formed a group that met every Thursday in London for lunch. They chose Wheeler's seafood restaurant in Old Compton Street, Soho, where the club owner, Bernard Walsh, gave them a private upstairs room for their lunchtime revelries.

Philip's friend Baron, who had been "discovered" as a photographer by Mountbatten in 1935, introduced him to the club. The introduction of the duke and his friend David Milford Haven to the group of writers and artists, actors and editors gave it a cachet it hadn't had before. There was no protocol: the Duke of Edinburgh was simply Philip, and the innocent but bawdy fun suited his unrefined brand of humor.

On one occasion Philip and Milford Haven waged a bet with Baron that he could not photograph a cuckoo coming out of the clock at exactly 3 p.m. Baron poised himself with his camera by the clock, waiting for the cuckoo to pop out, but on the stroke of three Philip and Milford Haven threw two smoke bombs into the fireplace. There was a huge bang and the room filled with soot from the chimney. Larry Adler, another member, remembered being told that there happened to be some police outside, who heard the explosion and rushed upstairs to find out what was going on.

"It took a lot of explaining," Adler recalled, "and even more diplomacy to keep the incident out of the papers."

Philip has always valued discretion above all else, and although persistent murmurings of romantic liaisons surrounded him even at this stage, the young naval lieutenant ignored them. He had always enjoyed female company as much as he enjoyed his merry band of male friends, and having been brought up with four elder sisters, he had a natural empathy with women. What he really disliked was what he considered the idiocy of the royal household hidebound by archaic rules and traditions that made no sense to him at that time.

Mountbatten's former chief of staff, General Sir Frederick "Boy" Browning, who was married to the novelist Daphne du Maurier and was to become the princess's comptroller, sensed Philip's apprehension about his future and suggested he get away for a few days, take leave from Corsham Naval Base, where he was currently employed. Boy Browning proposed Philip go for a weekend to Menabilly, the home his wife leased in Fowey, Cornwall. It was remote and beautiful and no one would think of looking for him there. Above all it was peaceful and he would have the entertaining company of Browning's wife, who was hugely successful and had recently published her eighth novel.

Daphne du Maurier was waiting on the local station platform when Philip arrived to greet him. She was his senior by a number of years and was an intelligent companion and sympathetic listener. An understanding arose between them, which despite the well-publicized rumors of an affair was not sexual but was emotionally intimate. She was beautiful and had a male kind of energy that Philip liked. At Menabilly they went for long walks down the steep path to the cove and private beach, where in summer months Daphne would sunbathe topless. At the end of the weekend, with the wedding looming, Philip said, "I don't want to go back, I want to stay here with you." She replied, "Not on your life. For a start I am fourteen years older than you. Second, I am married and third, your country needs you. Get on that train."

Although Philip's official stag night was at the Dorchester Hotel the night before the wedding, his friends from the Thursday Club, headed by photographer Baron, decided to cheer him on with an unofficial party at the Belgravia restaurant the Belfry, in Halkin Street, a week beforehand. The building had once been a church, and the twenty-five-strong male-only group, including his best man David Milford Haven, dined in the beamed Belfry. A twenty-five-person seating plan and menu shows guests from the world of literature, the arts, and journalism and reveals they feasted on foie gras, turtle soup, mixed grill, and crêpes Suzette. The menu, designed by Philip's friend the artist Felix Topolski, simply said, "Dinner to Distant Country member, Lieut. Philip Mountbatten, Royal Navy," and underneath, "Who is to be married on 20th November 1947."

David Milford Haven, for reasons not entirely clear but no doubt for financial gain, chose to write an article for the *Daily Mail* about the evening. It was harmless and it was well after the event, but it was a betrayal in Philip's eyes and it ruined their friendship. Milford Haven wrote, "We celebrated the passing of one or more good fellows into the state of matrimony with all the traditional rites and customs," and continued, "while the brandy circulated and the cigar smoke grew thicker than the speech of the raconteurs." The party went on until the small hours before the group spilled out into the early-November morning.

"The following day I think both Prince Philip and I staying together at Kensington Palace, felt the need for a slight stabiliser. Unfortunately, we were due to meet a high member of the church that morning and after careful consultation we only consumed only one glass of light sherry apiece after breakfast. We felt by midmorning the effects of this tonic would have dispersed the results of the night before. But I think the venerable gentleman guessed. He allowed us to remain seated during most of the time we were with him and I for one, was profoundly grateful for his understanding."

The "official" stag party the night before the wedding was organized by Mike Parker with the help of Marjorie Lee, the former public relations officer at the Dorchester Hotel. "There were only twelve in the party, all in naval uniform and it was during the evening the press discovered they were at the hotel." Marjorie remembered, "They asked if they could get pictures, so when the sweet had been served, I popped inside to ask the head waiter if I could have a word with Lord Mountbatten, as he was in charge."

Mountbatten agreed and Marjorie took the photographers upstairs to get the pictures. Philip then had the bright idea of taking a picture of them. Getting hold of the *Daily Mirror* camera, he took some pictures, while Mike Parker took another camera and did the same. With the cameras in their possession, Philip and Parker then pulled out and smashed the flashbulbs on the floor, thus rendering the cameras useless but doing no lasting damage.

Marjorie Lee remembers how once the press had gone Philip wanted to go to the kitchens to thank the chef. Amid much laughter they got hold of a luggage trolley and wheeled him perched on the top of the trolley into the service lift and thence to the suite of kitchens. If the chef, Jean Baptiste Virlogeux, was surprised, he didn't show it, and in an insouciance only known to the French, he acted as if princes appeared on trolleys in his kitchen every day. Philip sat on the trolley, speaking in French, which was his second language, and told the astonished chef how much they had enjoyed the meal.

"It was a great night," Parker recalled. "Everyone was in naval evening dress. Mountbatten was the senior guest, alongside David Milford Haven and the captains and first lieutenants of the 27th Destroyer Flotilla. It was a very happy occasion. It was an evening of comrades. Philip was an orphan of sorts and we were family."

There are no personal recollections from Philip of the wedding day on November 20, but in his memoirs his valet, John Dean, recalled the events as he remembered them. At seven o'clock in the morning he tapped on the newly ennobled duke's door in Kensington Palace and entered with a cup of tea. "He woke at once and was plainly in great form, extremely cheerful and no way nervous," Dean recalled. "There had been a wedding rehearsal the previous day so we all knew exactly what we had to do and the split-second timings of the day's arrangements were clear in my mind."

After Philip breakfasted on coffee and toast and had dressed, the valet gingerly handed him his sword as the final touch to his attire for the day. "It was not a full-dress uniform, but the kind in which you expect to see a naval officer when you meet him in the street. The sword which I handled so gingerly as I gave it to him, was not his own; like all the new generation navy he did not possess one. It had belonged to his grandfather, Prince Louis of Battenberg."

"How the duke resisted the temptation to light a cigarette I do not know," Dean recalled. "He had given up the habit, as from the previous night and did not complain." Having been a heavy smoker for years, Philip decided to give it up on his way back to Kensington Palace the night before the wedding and has never touched a cigarette since. This was not the case for David Milford Haven, who was dying for a smoke and was obliged to hide his best man's outfit under a raincoat and cycle to Kensington High Street to buy a packet.

Patricia Mountbatten, Prince Philip's first cousin, paid an early morning call to him at Kensington Palace. "I saw him just after breakfast that morning," she told Philip's biographer Gyles Brandreth. "We were alone together—we were cousins and we knew each other very well—and I said something about what an exciting day it was and suddenly, he said to me, 'Am I being very brave or very foolish?'"

"He was apprehensive," she explained. "Not about marrying Princess Elizabeth, but about what marriage would mean for him. He was giving up a great deal. In many ways nothing was going to change for her. Everything was going to change for him."

When Milford Haven returned from his quest for cigarettes, each man downed a gin and tonic to toast the last moments of Philip's bachelorhood. Outside the door of the Kensington Palace apartment, a small crowd had gathered to see the bridegroom leave. "Among them was Miss Pye," said John Dean, "who had been with the Dowager Marchioness of Milford Haven's grandmother for fifty years and was her personal maid. She had known the Duke since he was a baby and he called her 'Piecrust.' The Duke shook hands with Piecrust, with the palace sweep and other old retainers. Grinning he ordered coffee for the shivering newspaper reporters assigned to see him start."

When the duke and Milford Haven finally left for Westminster Abbey at 11:15 a.m., they realized they were wearing identical peaked caps. David had the bigger head, and if for some reason Philip picked up the wrong one it would have fallen over his eyes, so they made an ink mark inside David's so they could tell one from another. These tiny details of etiquette kept them calm and gave them something to laugh about.

Patricia Mountbatten's younger sister Pamela was one of the bridesmaids, and in her memoirs she had some touching personal recollections of the day.

"Being one of the tallest, I was in the last pair of bridesmaids in the procession with Princess Margaret and Princess Alexandra at the front. In the rehearsal we had all been warned not to step on the tomb of the unknown warrior, but one of the little pages, Prince Michael of Kent, stepped right on it."

"The train was very heavy," Prince Michael remembered many years later. "Going around corners and not treading on it was complicated from what I remember."

"The service was very moving and as Princess Elizabeth and the newly created Duke of Edinburgh said their vows, the crowd outside could hear every word through the loudspeakers," Patricia Mountbatten said. "Once the service was over, a fanfare of trumpets and a rousing organ voluntary accompanied our procession back down the aisle. We followed through the ecstatic crowds back to the palace, closely followed by the King and Queen and most of the royalty of Europe."

Back at the palace the bridesmaids sat down to watch the huge group of royalty being bossed around by photographer Baron as he tried to get them still enough to take his shots. Pamela recalled that the light was terrible and they kept talking and moving. "Freddie of Greece kept chatting to Juliana of the Netherlands irrespective of instructions; the long bird of paradise feathers on my mother's hat obscured several people behind her and Grandmama—no fan of group photographs—positioned herself firmly at the edge of the group leaving a little space between her and her neighbour, hoping she might be left out of the picture."

After the photographs were over the bridesmaids and pages went out onto the balcony to join the others.

"We were met by an incredible sight," Pamela remembers. "The police had been holding everyone back around the Victoria Memorial, but when we came out, they let them go and we could see—and hear—a sea of people surging forward. Every time the newlyweds waved, the volume of cheering increased. We were later told that while they were waiting the crowd had been singing 'All the Nice Girls Love a Sailor.' "

A few days later, when she was back in Athens, Philip's mother, who had been his only close family member present at the abbey, wrote to her son: "How wonderfully everything went off and I was comforted to see the truly happy expression on your face and to feel your decision was right from every point of view."

It is doubtful if her son had confided any doubts he might have had about his future to his deaf mother, but knowing her son she would have understood the potential difficulties of putting "such a bird in such a cage." Alice also wrote a twenty-page description of the wedding itself that she sent on to Philip's absent sisters.

The first part of the honeymoon at Broadlands, the Mountbattens' Hampshire estate, was not an outstanding success. The princess was accompanied by her dog, the corgi Susan, as well as her maid, Bobo

MacDonald, who was extremely protective of her young mistress and had little time for Philip.

As the Mountbattens had returned to India, the royal couple were supposed to be alone, but the duke's valet, John Dean, was shocked to see the hundreds of onlookers who continually appeared around and about the estate trying to get a glimpse of the young couple. The press was also out in force, with photographers so anxious to get a picture that they placed ladders against the abbey's walls to look through the windows as the newlyweds attended Sunday worship. It was not the most satisfactory situation, but after a week they moved to the privacy of Birkhall on the Balmoral estate and were left to their own devices. The imposing L-shaped harl-coated house with the gushing sound of the river Muick outside and the crackling of wood fires inside was sublimely romantic. At the time there was heavy snow and the house boasted log fires in every room, even the bedroom.

"It's heaven up here," Elizabeth wrote to her mother. "Philip is reading full length on the sofa, (he had a cold) Susan is stretched out before the fire, Rummy is fast asleep in his box by the fire, and I am busy writing this in one of the armchairs near the fire (you see how important the fire is!)." Even Philip's valet, John Dean, and Princess Elizabeth's maid, Bobo, were getting along, and although Philip had not expected to find Bobo at her mistress's side at all times, even when she was in the bathroom, he realized he was going to have to learn to put up with it.

Back in London, without a home to go to, there was little choice except for Philip to move in with his in-laws. He was given a bedroom in the princess's apartment, with a sitting room in between her room and his. One of the first things he did was to shift the furniture to make it more comfortable and less formal. He had a trained observer's eye from many hours spent at watch on board various ships and knew exactly how furnishings or pictures would look their best. They were not entirely without privacy since the King had given them the use of Windlesham Moor, a five-bedroom house nestled in leafy suburbia off the Bagshot–Sunningdale road as a weekend home. It was the nearest thing to a normal home that the princess had ever lived in, and it was the first real home Philip had been able to call his own. He took huge pleasure in arranging furniture and wedding presents and hanging pictures and wanted to pay for everything, but he couldn't afford the necessary staff, so Princess Elizabeth sneakily recruited a couple from Buckingham Palace and paid them herself. Eileen Parker, whom I interviewed many years later, recalled a weekend at Windlesham.

"There were extensive grounds and Prince Philip, who was mad about cricket in those days, had created a pitch there. He and Mike who was his friend as well as his equerry, would either practise at the nets or when there were enough guests to make up an eleven would play against a local team."

Eileen said she already knew that the princess was pregnant as Mike had told her in confidence. "It was only about six months since we had been to their wedding at the Abbey and as I was expecting my second baby, I was longing to know. After lunch that day Prince Philip let it slip when he interrupted an animated conversation by hauling Mike off to the cricket nets."

" 'Come on Mike,' he said. 'Let's leave these two to talk about babies.' And that evening when he was handing round pre-dinner gin and tonics, he wagged his finger at us both and said, 'It should be orange juice for you two.' "

The two remarks confirmed to Eileen that she was now permitted to openly talk to Princess Elizabeth about impending motherhood. "The princess and her husband never discussed their private lives in front of anyone," she told me, "although my husband and Prince

Philip were so close that he probably told Mike things he would not have told anyone else. Mike would sometimes pass news on to me, but I had to promise that I would never mention it to them or anyone else for that matter."

The friendship between Mike Parker and the duke would mean Eileen was often alone with the princess. At first, she was nervous because she felt Mike and Philip's intimacy obliged her to be equally friendly with Princess Elizabeth, whom she hardly knew. "Happily, she handled these situations beautifully," Eileen said. "We would chat about Scotland, which is my home country and her favorite place in the world. We would reminisce about life in the services—she had been an ATS subaltern and I had been in the WRENS. In fact, I had met both Michael and Prince Philip while I was serving in Scotland. Now thank goodness we had another topic of conversation, babies. My firstborn son was already two and a half, and now I was expecting another baby just as the queen was expecting her first. Conversation was much easier and more animated.

"The princess often spoke of her wishes for her children. She longed for them to be brought up under what she called 'normal' circumstances. 'I would like them to be able to lead ordinary lives,' she used to say, knowing that, of course, they couldn't. She would then add wistfully, 'I wish I could be more like you, Eileen.' She used to talk about her own childhood and wanted her sons and daughters to have less restricted lives than she had had. She also spoke of how her idea of happiness would be to be able to live quietly in the country with her children, dogs, and horses."

In the May of that year Princess Elizabeth and the Duke of Edinburgh made an official visit to Paris as guests of President Auriol. No one except the princess's immediate family and close friends and Mike and Eileen knew she was pregnant, but those that did considered it unwise for them to fly, so they went by train and cross-channel ferry from Dover. The visit was a huge success and the Parisians went mad in welcoming the newlyweds. But there were nasty moments. The official engagements opened with an investiture at the Elysée Palace, where Princess Elizabeth was presented with the Grand Cross of the Legion of Honor and the Duke of Edinburgh was awarded the Croix de Guerre.

"Michael told me that from the Palace they went on to a wreath-laying ceremony at the Arc de Triomphe. As they stood for the ceremony, the princess looked as if she were about to faint. Both Philip and Michael were instantly on the alert, but long years of self-discipline carried the princess through the momentary crisis. As she faltered at an emotional part of the ceremony, most of the spectators probably thought that her indisposition was due to her depth of feeling. Of course, the truth was that she was suffering from the discomforts of early pregnancy," Eileen explained.

Later in the visit they dined at the famous restaurant Tour d'Argent and Philip was "enraged' to find photographers hiding under the tablecloths of nearby tables. They ate a main course of rich duck, which was the speciality of the house. "Unfortunately, afterward the princess was violently ill. But again no one ever knew," Eileen was told by her husband.

"In those days, after the official announcement of a pregnancy it would have been unthinkable for a female member of the royal family to be publicly visible. When Prince Charles was on the way the princess was lucky if she got to the races. Indeed, I remember her at the Derby wearing a little suit with a peplum jacket that attempted to hide her bulge. And her only outings as time went on were to the private cinema at international movie mogul, who built Denham studios, Sir Alex Korda's house in Piccadilly where we would all gather to watch the latest films.

"Once having stepped out of the cars to go into the Kordas' house, the princess and I happened to be standing next to each other in the large entrance hall waiting for the King and Queen to arrive. As her father approached, he looked at us both and laughed.

" 'Who's going to be first in this race then?' the King asked with a twinkle in his eye as he surveyed our waistlines.

" 'The princess, sir,' I told him. 'I'm expecting my baby in the middle of December.'

" 'Well, if it arrives on my birthday [December 14] we'll have to have a double celebration,' he said, smiling as he led us into the foyer.

"In fact, my daughter Julie was born the month after Prince Charles, and she chose to arrive on the day that the little prince was christened in Buckingham Palace. And when the time came for her to be christened, who was one of her godfathers? Prince Philip, of course."

Philip had just become father of the future king and, surprisingly and unusually for such a macho man, was able to relate to very young children in a way that was way ahead of the established image of fatherhood in the 1940s. So, he was the perfect godfather for not only his obvious social station but his wealth of warmth and understanding to another generation.

Chapter 6

HAPPY DAYS

After the euphoria surrounding the birth of his first son, Philip's restless energy needed an outlet. The duke and Princess Elizabeth had been obliged to stay at Buckingham Palace when in London while Clarence House—which was to become their London base—was being renovated, but the confines of the palace did not suit him. Long lunches with the Thursday Club sometimes merged into dinners and occasionally into breakfasts. During this time King George VI was suffering from ill health, the severity of which was being kept from his two daughters, and the state of his condition was an increasing cause for concern. The full gravity of their father's illness was only made clear when he agreed on the advice of his doctors to postpone a planned tour of Australia and New Zealand. The King, who was difficult and bad tempered at the best of times, became irrational and would lose his temper with anyone around him. In March 1949 he underwent major lung surgery in a surgical theater constructed in the Buhl room of Buckingham Palace.

Meanwhile Philip had embarked on a course at the Royal Naval College, Greenwich, which kept him away from the palace during the week. This meant he could enjoy Windlesham at weekends, where he and Princess Elizabeth could entertain their friends rather less formally than in London. Here and later at Clarence House, Philip was the man of the house. It was he rather than the princess who reviewed the menus and decided on the meals for the day, and the staff deferred to him on domestic matters. He enjoyed the organization and liked things to run smoothly among the staff.

"I suppose I naturally filled the principal position," he told his 1970 biographer Basil Boothroyd. "People would come to me and ask me what to do."

Annoyingly for them all, the Clarence House renovations were taking far longer than expected, no doubt in part due to Philip's assiduous attention to detail. "It was a shambles," Mike Parker said. "But we got it together very quickly and they furnished it with a lot of their wedding presents."

The interior of the house made full use of those wedding presents, including white maple paneling for Philip's study, which was decorated like a ship's cabin. The house had an overall look typical of many smart postwar interiors, when it was impossible to find much variety and range of materials. Princess Elizabeth mixed the green paint for the walls of the dining room herself, and Philip scouted around to find light fittings and gadgets including one of his own inventions in his bedroom: when he pressed a button, an unseen cupboard opened. The house had a basic overall look of green wallpaper, red cushions, huge squashy sofas, and open fires. There was also a complete room furnished by donations from the people of Lancaster that served as one of the main reception rooms. There was a cinema in the basement, which was another wedding gift. To Philip's intense annoyance details of his bedroom appeared in one of the national newspapers described thus, "panelled in white Scottish sycamore with a large single bed, coverings the colour of vin rose, damask drapes and an oatmeal carpet." Whoever had been helping with the interiors had let slip the detail and no doubt he was severely reprimanded.

Unusually for the time, the staff quarters were modern and comfortable because Philip had consulted several members of staff to ask them the best way of making the workplace efficient. By far the best thing the duke installed was a "sleek white, very futuristic television set," which he put in the servants' sitting room; it had been a wedding gift from the Mountbattens.

"There was a very small household staff," Parker remembered. "The princess invited us all to lunch every day and was obviously very happy. You could hear her singing around the house. We were there long enough to see what heaven it could have been."

For the first time Philip was "king" of his own castle. Those that worked for him liked and respected him, and to his surprise they would come and ask him rather than his wife what to do. "We all thought a lot of him," former footman John Gibson confirmed. Gibson's duties were to collate the couple's many possessions, which had been in storage together with a few of their wedding presents and had not even been unpacked. There were also trunks full of clothes that had belonged to Philip's father, Prince Andrew, who had died in the Hotel Metropole Monte Carlo in 1944. His clothes had been stored in France until the end of the war, and Gibson went through them to find what could be altered and used while the remainder were stored on the top floor.

Every weekend Philip and Princess Elizabeth would go to Windlesham, where baby Charles was based, and the first thing they would do was run up to the nursery to give him his bedtime bath. "The Duke especially enjoyed these times," recalled Gibson, who was then nursery footman. In those days the aristocracy and monied classes spent very little time with their children. They were cared for by nannies, and country life was considered far healthier than the dirt and noise of a city. Certainly, for the infant Charles, Windlesham was a far preferable environment than the enormity of Buckingham Palace.

On some weekends Princess Marina, Philip's first cousin and the then Duchess of Kent, came over from Coppins, her home in Iver, Buckinghamshire. "She had a lot of show-business friends and once when I opened the door of her car, Danny Kaye stepped out. They stayed for several hours, and as they were leaving Danny Kaye turned to Princess Elizabeth and said, 'You just stand there, ma'am, I want to take a picture.' He then took a small camera out of his pocket and snapped her. Minutes later he pulled the photograph out from the back of the camera and handed it to her. The princess had never seen a Polaroid camera before and could hardly believe her eyes. Just as he was getting back into the car, Danny Kaye turned back and gave the princess a deep curtsey. She knew it was a joke and burst out laughing. 'You fool!' the prince said to Kaye as they drove off, and as he walked into the dining room and noticed there were quite a lot of drinks untouched, he suggested the staff finish them off themselves and have their own party."

"He wasn't royal to us," Gibson explained. "I always felt the old royal family just played the part, but he didn't play the part at all. He wasn't keen on luxurious things and would often ask for sausage and mash for dinner with a glass of lager, which was his favorite tipple."

On July 4, 1949—American Independence Day—Princess Elizabeth's personal standard flew from the roof of Clarence House for the first time. The house had taken nearly eighteen months to redecorate and repair, and the costs had soared to £250,000 as opposed to the original estimate of £50,000. As always there was massive criticism of the cost. It was brought to their attention that families were living in squalor with many people being out of work and unable to pay their rent. Historically this has always been the case and is not dissimilar to the uproar about the costs of renovating the Duke and Duchess of Sussex's Frogmore home in 2019. King George VI, who didn't like his daughter bearing the brunt of this criticism, eventually used his own funds to pay off the excess.

Public criticism never bothered Philip, but he liked to answer back and did so, saying estimates were exactly that—and costs nearly always exceeded them. But he knew how fortunate he was. Having celebrated his twenty-eighth birthday less than a month beforehand, he now had more than he could have ever wished for: a beautiful young wife whom he loved, a home he could call his own, a baby son and heir, and the wherewithal to make a hugely successful career in the Royal Navy. Many considered him arrogant and difficult, which he could be, but the path he had chosen was his choice, and he knew there would always be a price to be paid for marrying the heir presumptive. But at Clarence House, at least, he was free from the stuffy courtiers at Buckingham Palace and could run his life as he wished.

One idea that appealed to Philip was to run the National Playing Fields Association—it was suggested by the King and supported by Lord Mountbatten, who was its president. He took over from Mountbatten and came up with some unique fundraising ideas to finance the building of new children's playing fields and sports facilities that had been destroyed or put to other use during the war. He decided to agree to be filmed giving his appeal, and fortunately for him it was agreed the film could be shown in cinemas throughout the land. At that time, he met Frank Sinatra and his wife, actress Ava Gardner, and persuaded Sinatra to donate the royalties of two of his bestselling records to the playing fields fund. Sinatra agreed to fly back to England and give an eight-minute show at a midnight matinee at London's Empress Club. His appearance with

Ava Gardner raised £14,000 profit for the association and was the beginning of Philip's highly successful philanthropic career.

"I found him always terribly kind, most interesting and highly intelligent," Sinatra said. "He has what I consider to be the most important attribute in a man, a great sense of humor."

After the success of the Playing Fields, Philip was inundated with requests to be president or patron of this or that, make speeches and attend fundraising dinners as guest of honor. But his heart was still with the Royal Navy and he yearned to be on the move again. In October 1949, he flew out to Malta in one of the Viking planes of the King's Flight to take up his appointment of first lieutenant and second in command of HMS *Chequers*, leader of the First Destroyer Flotilla of the Mediterranean Fleet. His basic pay was one pound and six shillings a day plus allowances—making it £15 a week. The best news was that it was decided his wife would be able to join him a few weeks later, so over the next few years, her diary permitting, she could join him every time he was able to come ashore.

During the next two years, according to the princess's former governess Crawfie, she "saw and experienced for the first time the life of an ordinary girl." It was not that ordinary, however, and when Princess Elizabeth flew to Malta to join her husband on November 20, a week after Prince Charles's first birthday, she was accompanied by a lady-in-waiting, Lady Alice Egerton (the youngest daughter of the 4th Earl of Ellesmere); Mike Parker, Philip's private secretary; Bobo MacDonald, her dresser; and John Dean, the duke's valet. The corgis Susan and Crackers and one-year-old Prince Charles were left behind at Windlesham. In 1949, Malta was considered an unsuitable place for a small child, so as she herself had been left behind in 1927 when her own parents traveled, so was Charles.

Fortunately for Princess Elizabeth, Lord Mountbatten was based in Malta at the time, in his role in command of the 1st Cruiser

Squadron of the Mediterranean Fleet, and of course, he was more than happy to offer the princess any hospitality he could. So the Edinburghs, as they were known, settled in his house, Villa Guardamangia, which overlooked the harbour at Pietà. Not only did they have a staff of nineteen to look after them but Mountbatten and his wife Edwina gave up their quarters so they used his bedroom as their own. He was so delighted to have them there, he would have suffered any inconvenience, even Philip's testy behavior. He wrote to his elder daughter Patricia that at first "Philip was very busy showing his independence, sometimes rather brusquely." He later confirmed that Philip had relaxed and was "right back on 1946 terms with us and we had a heart to heart in which he admitted he was fighting shy of coming under my dominating influence and patronage!"

He later wrote to Patricia again, telling her, "Lilibet is quite enchanting and I've lost whatever of my heart is left to spare entirely to her. She dances quite divinely and always wants to Samba when we dance together and has said some very nice things about my dancing."

The princess made several trips to Malta, the longest being for eleven weeks, during which time baby Prince Charles was left behind with his grandparents, so the family was rarely in one place together. Mike Parker commuted regularly between Clarence House and Malta, keeping Philip up to date with his new interests at home, such as the National Playing Fields Association.

Philip was in his element back on board a ship. He was a strict disciplinarian and drove the crew hard in any sporting contests. In off-duty moments the Edinburghs went on boat trips with the Mountbattens, and Philip and Dickie would go waterskiing and spearfishing. Philip also took up polo, a suggestion he had initially shunned, but after lengthy persuasion from Dickie and at the suggestion of the princess he started to play what he had once called "a snob sport."

Being Philip and determined to be best at everything, under the tutelage of his uncle he excelled, and the game became one of the passions of his life. They also partied with the other servicemen and their wives, enjoying dancing together as they always had done. Lady Abel Smith, another of the princess's ladies-in-waiting, who remained with her for over forty years, recalled: "There were some very wild parties with spoons and buns being thrown, though luckily not butter. She was amazed by the spoon throwing." Apparently when the games became too boisterous, Philip would lift his wife onto the piano together with her lady-in-waiting to keep them out of the firing line.

There was only one minor blip in Philip's naval progression, when he failed a section of his command examination. "It's probably the most important exam in the navy—gunnery, torpedoes, anti-sub. I was monitoring it myself," Mike Parker explained. "Now, one of those examiners was a bloke who played polo with Prince Philip and was very jealous of him. This chap failed him on anti-sub, though Philip thought he had done a pretty good paper.

"Within a couple of hours, the local C in C, Admiral Power, sent for me. He was striding round the office with anger. 'This bloody man has failed Prince Philip,' he said. 'What's going on?' I told him I could smell a large rat. 'But is it possible for Philip to do it again, or do we just override him?' asked Power. I told him that Prince Philip had said he simply could not have special treatment, or he would have to leave the navy. Eventually I asked Philip whether he was willing to take the anti-sub exam again. 'But is that customary?' he said. I told him that in certain circumstances, it was. The next time he sailed through with flying colors."

Soon after, in July 1950, Philip was promoted to lieutenant commander and appointed to his first command, the frigate HMS *Magpie*. "Command of a ship when that comes to you, gives you a tremendous buzz," explained Admiral Robert Woodward, who commanded the Royal yacht *Britannia* from 1990 to 1995. "The C in C can be thousands of miles away and what you tell him is up to you. And you're responsible for the present and future of every man serving under you. It's exhilarating and it gives you great freedom. The command of *Magpie* had all those ingredients for Philip."

In April 1950, Princess Elizabeth's second pregnancy was announced, and on her twenty-fourth birthday she watched her husband and Dickie Mountbatten playing polo in Malta before returning to England to await the birth. On August 15, Princess Elizabeth gave birth at Clarence House to a baby girl they named Anne Elizabeth Alice Louise. Philip returned from Malta to be joined by his mother, Princess Alice, who came from Tinos in Greece for the occasion, having missed the birth of Prince Charles. The princess took time to recover from the birth and didn't return to her public duties until mid-November, by which time she was due to travel again to Malta to spend Christmas with her husband. This time both Charles and baby Anne were left in the care of their grandparents at Sandringham.

For Philip, returning to Malta and his ship meant hard work and the kind of challenge he reveled in. Second best was not good enough and HMS *Magpie* had to be the best in the fleet. He was tough, but it brought results. *Magpie* excelled at maneuvers and carried off six of ten of the first prizes in the annual regatta. *Magpie*'s tour of duty was a combination of naval exercises and ceremonial visits. In Gibraltar Philip represented the King at the opening of their legislative council; *Magpie* sailed to Jordan, Turkey, Egypt, and Iran on courtesy visits. According to Boothroyd, some said

Philip was just swanning around in what they liked to call the Duke of Edinburgh's private yacht. But he was an expert at what he did and managed to navigate out of Monte Carlo in rough conditions when other ships weren't putting to sea. He managed a nostalgic trip to his birthplace, Corfu, where he received a hero's welcome at the town hall. "Were you as hot as I was?" Mike Parker said to him as they left the building. "Was I," replied the duke. "I'm positively squelching out of this place."

When the princess arrived back in Malta to see her husband, the vessel HMS *Surprise* was put at her disposal because HMS *Magpie* did not have suitable accommodation for wives. With Philip on his own ship, there was much lighthearted fun with the exchange of signals, something the princess got the hang of pretty quickly, the best-known being:

> *Surprise* to *Magpie*: Princess full of beans
> *Magpie* to *Surprise*: Can't you give her something better for breakfast?

The royal couple paid an unofficial visit to Greece to see Philip's cousin King Paul in Athens, where they stayed in the royal palace with King Paul and Queen Frederica and enjoyed the sight of the Parthenon being floodlit in their honor. It was Princess Elizabeth's first visit to her husband's homeland, and they had a tumultuous welcome from the Greek people.

"I saw them in Athens in 1950," Sir Clifford Norton, the British ambassador, recalled. "He came into Piraeus on that funny little frigate *Magpie* of which he'd just been given command and she flew out to join him and stayed with us briefly. Both my wife and I felt that he brought her out. She was rather withdrawn, a bit of a shrinking violet in fact and he was young and vigorous and jollied her along. He didn't actually say 'Come on old girl,' but it was that sort of thing.

"She was patently in love with him and he responded. And he plainly felt great affection for her, though whether it was the same depth of love, it's impossible to say. He had a very wholesome effect on her and helped make her what she's become. She is very shrewd, but she had a protective shell around her and he brought her out of it."

The ambassador's wife, Lady Norton, gave them the key of their beach house so that they could enjoy an evening with their party after a reception on board HMS *Magpie*. The party climbed the cliffs from the beach, carrying food and the key to the house. No sooner had they rattled on the door than an upper window opened and the ambassador leaned out shouting who was making such a racket. The picnic party ignored him and carried on preparing their food. No sooner than it was ready, the ambassador appeared in his pajamas, carrying a knife and fork, and joined the party.

According to cousin Alexandra, when Philip took King Paul aboard HMS *Magpie*, he was astonished to find that Philip's quarters were full of papers on which Philip was working, including preparations for the Festival of Britain and their long overseas tour of Canada. Philip had an interest in the festival as a showpiece for the inventiveness of British scientists and for British technology. It was planned for the centenary of the Great Exhibition, in which Prince Albert had played such an important role.

Although frail, King George VI opened the festival on May 3, 1951, but he was soon struck down with an infection he could not shake off. His doctors ordered complete rest and cancelation of all public engagements. There was no choice: Elizabeth and Philip would have to take over.

*

Thus, in July 1951, Philip left Malta "on indefinite leave." It was goodbye to the Royal Navy in everything but the letter. As the crew of HMS *Magpie* lined the decks to cheer him off, he said, "I have kept my promise to make HMS *Magpie* one of the finest ships in the fleet. The past eleven months have been the happiest of my sailor life." When he arrived back at Clarence House, he looked despondently at his white naval uniforms and said to his valet John Dean, "It will be a long time before I want those again."

"His decision to retire from active naval appointments in 1951 was very carefully thought through," Parker said. "No way was he told he had to leave. He wanted to help Elizabeth and knew he couldn't do it if he stayed. There was a discussion and it became clear he could not go on. The last night before we left Malta to go home was dreadful."

Chapter 7

TWO STEPS BEHIND

King George VI's failing health meant the official east–west tour of Canada rounding off in the United States had to be adapted for the Duke and Duchess of Edinburgh, as they were then officially known. Their expected departure on RMS *Empress of Britain* was fixed for the end of September, but after the King returned from Balmoral, a bronchoscopy confirmed that he was indeed suffering from lung cancer. His doctors advised the King that he should have an operation to remove his left lung, but the true diagnosis was withheld from his family.

The operation was performed on September 23, 1951, by which time Philip had successfully hatched the plan that he and the princess should travel by air to avoid delaying the start of the tour. It was Philip's first major win over the establishment: in the early 1950s it was considered unwise and possibly dangerous for Princess Elizabeth to undertake flying the Atlantic.

Philip, of course, had been determined to get his way, and with the support of the King, their plan was that first the visit would be called off. According to Basil Boothroyd, Earl Alexander of Tunis, then the governor general, "would then lodge his horrified protests and the British government would have to respect his feelings. Then Philip would suggest the only option as being the airborne solution."

It succeeded, but it involved a great deal of diplomacy on Philip's part. He had meetings with Prime Minister Clement Attlee, whom he managed to talk round, and then Winston Churchill, the leader of the opposition at the time, who was most vigorously against the transatlantic flight.

The seventeen-hour flight to Montreal via Newfoundland on board the BOAC plane *Atalanta* was the beginning of an exhausting initiation into the intricate responsibilities of Philip being two steps behind his wife. He amused himself by spending time on the flight deck of the BOAC Stratocruiser on the way out, but he found many parts of the trip absurd and other parts deadly dull, especially being cooped up in a special train for much of the time across the vast open spaces of Canada. For an active man, being confined within a few carriages on a long train was frustrating, and he longed to get out, but being mindful of his position he knew that was an impossibility. As a precaution against the King's health taking a turn for the very worst, the princess's private secretary since 1949, Martin Charteris, kept the accession papers in a box under his bed throughout the trip.

When they landed, a nervous twenty-five-year-old Princess Elizabeth stepped out onto the aircraft gangway in Montreal on October 8, 1951, with a crowd of fifteen thousand before her on the tarmac. She was about to begin her first major royal visit where she would be the center of attention. The tour lasted thirty-three days, during which time the royal couple traveled from coast to coast and back again. It was tremendously successful, with hugely enthusiastic crowds at every stop. According to the princess, Philip was a great success, and she wrote to her mother telling her that young women screamed when he waved to them, and men shouted, "Good Old Phil!"

The Canadian authorities had taken the greatest care to ensure that everyone involved behaved impeccably, including the press, which remarked, "Philip smiled more, unbent more and was ready to smooth occasional embarrassments." To alleviate his boredom, Philip noted things along the route that caught his interest, and he devised ways in which they could be used back home. The zip fasteners worn by Canadian ratings (noncommissioned sailors) for instance could be adapted to naval uniforms, and also the Plexiglas top on the royal car, which was then made by an aircraft plant, would be perfect for back home so that the princess could be seen in all weathers.

When the royal couple made a short side trip to visit President Truman in Washington, DC, the American press were more demanding, and once back in Canada, Princess Elizabeth displayed her skill at mimicry when she mimicked the US photographers while she was doing some filming of her own. Pointing the camera at her husband, she cried out in a nasally American voice, "Hey! You there! Hey, Dook! Look this way a sec! Dat's it! Thanks a lot!"

They eventually made their way home on the liner *Empress of Scotland*, completing the last leg of the journey by train from Liverpool to Euston station in London. The King had progressed well since his operation, so much so that it seemed possible that Philip would be able to return to active service as the commander of his own destroyer. To show his gratitude, the King marked the success of the tour by making both his daughter and her husband privy councillors. Winston Churchill, who was prime minster again, welcomed the royal couple home, thanking them—in particular the princess—for the gift of her personality, which would play its part in "mellowing the human march of society the world over." Despite his oleaginous tones, he was exactly right. All seemed far better than when they had left, and Philip, inspired by his own part in the success of the tour—and encouraged by Mike Parker—devoted some time to studying Australia, where they were to visit, and went to the London Wool Exchange to learn about sheep farming.

Christmas was spent at Sandringham with the children Charles and Anne, and the King was well enough to go out shooting on several days. When they returned to London on January 29 for a consultation with the King's doctors, the following evening King George VI took his wife, his daughter Princess Margaret, Equerry Peter Townsend, and the Duke and Duchess of Edinburgh to see the hit Broadway musical *South Pacific* at the Drury Lane Theatre. The original Broadway stars, Enzo Pinza and Mary Martin, were in the starring roles, and the Drury Lane Theatre Orchestra provided the iconic score. Before the curtain call, the whole theater company lined the stage and sang the National Anthem, accompanied by a wildly cheering audience.

The following day, on January 31, the King waved goodbye to his daughter and her husband at London Airport as they set off on the first leg of the Commonwealth tour originally intended for him and his wife, Queen Elizabeth. The princess had few doubts that she would see her father again—after all, he appeared to have made a good recovery from the operation, and she wanted to believe he would get better. As a precaution, however, she was given a sealed dossier containing the draft Accession Declaration, to be opened in the event of King George VI's death. A royal standard was also tucked away in the luggage, as were black mourning clothes.

The government of Kenya had given the couple a lease on the one-story cottage Sagana Lodge as a wedding present and had been keenly asking for a visit, so the intention was that they would start their trip in Kenya before they traveled on from Mombasa on board HMS *Gothic* to Ceylon.

Lord Chandos, the colonial secretary, vividly described the scene at the airport when the couple boarded the aircraft: "The King and Queen came to see them take off and I was shocked by the King's appearance. I was familiar with his look . . . but he seemed much altered and strained. I had the feeling of doom, which grew as the minutes before the time of departure ebbed away. The King went on to the roof of the building to wave goodbye. The high wind blew his hair into disorder. I felt with foreboding that this would be the last time he was to see his daughter, and that he thought so himself."

The highlight of the first leg was to see their wedding present Sagana Lodge and then spend a night at Treetops, a renowned game-viewing lodge in the Aberdare Forest game reserve, one hundred miles from Nairobi, at Nyeri. For thirty-year-old Philip, who was well traveled, this was his first safari, and to him it was an adventure he was determined to make the most of, however brief it was.

Pamela Mountbatten, Dickie's youngest daughter, was with the royal party as a lady-in-waiting to the princess, and in her memoirs, *Daughter of Empire*, she recalled the first days, when they stayed in Government House as a guest of Governor Sir Philip Mitchell:

"After a few days in Nairobi—a whirlwind introduction to a life of cheering children, regimental inspections, lunches dinners and receptions," she said, "we travelled north on bumpy roads, engulfed by clouds of red dust to Sagana Lodge, a fishing lodge given to the Prince and Princess by the people of Kenya. Mike Parker and I were the only members of the royal household to accompany them. The Princess and I spent the first two mornings riding a couple of reliable police horses that I had managed to secure, while Prince Philip and Mike relaxed, fishing in the nearby trout stream.

"On the third evening we set off in an open jeep—the Princess and I wearing khaki shorts and slacks, drawing a few comments from Mike, who was unused to seeing us in anything other than silk or cotton dresses. We were heading for Treetops, the tree house turned miniature hotel built in the fork of a 300-year-old fig tree."

The lodge was indeed built in the branches of an enormous tree, accessible only by ladder and overlooking a lake with a salt lick, a favorite watering hole for big game. A dining area and three narrow bedrooms led on to the elevated viewing platform, where the royal party were to spend the night. Renowned British hunter and conservationist Colonel Jim Corbett was seconded to keep a discreet eye over things and not to hesitate to raise his gun should there be any danger, not only from the Mau Mau rebels, who were just beginning their campaign against British rule, but from any big game that might get dangerous.

The last quarter of a mile of the journey had to be made on foot down a track only a few feet wide, and Eric Sherbrooke Walker, the owner of the property, warned the party not to tread on twigs or speak above a whisper. As they approached, they became aware of the squealing and trumpeting of a large herd of restless elephants and a white pillowcase fluttering from the roof, which was the agreed danger signal Walker's wife, Lady Bettie, had put out as a warning. Walker asked Philip if they should abandon the idea or risk the possibility of being charged by an elephant protecting a calf. Naturally Philip, who was armed with a rifle, wanted to continue, and the group moved on as silently as they could.

There was a 50-yard (45-meter) run of comparative open ground to cross before reaching the narrow wooden struts of a ladder into the tree, but the princess did not falter and walked straight toward the ladder, ignoring the nearest elephant, which was standing 11 feet (3.3 meters) away flapping her ears menacingly. Once in the tree, the princess filmed the unfolding scene of the huge herd with her cine camera and couldn't be drawn from the array of game that gathered at the water hole.

Sherbrooke Walker takes up the story: "The Prince was greatly amused when one of the elephants carefully filled its trunk with dust. Mischievously it moved up to some doves which had settled nearby and squirted the dust at them in a powerful jet."

"Just before our arrival," Pamela Mountbatten recalled, "baboons had stolen rolls of loo paper from the minuscule loo and now the branches were festooned with large untidy swags of white paper too high for anyone to reach."

When the sunset had faded and it was no longer possible to use the cameras, the group talked in hushed voices about the game they had seen and what they might expect later. Concern was expressed for the princess's father, who had stood hatless at London airport on a bitterly cold day to wave her goodbye. Walker recalled in his book, *Treetops Hotel*: "The princess replied warmly, 'He is like that. He never thinks of himself.' She then referred to her father's long illness and the family's great pleasure when it was believed he had reached the turning point. She told us that one day he raised his walking stick to his shoulder and declared, 'I believe I could shoot now.' She was closely informed of her father's plans and was able to say he was planning to shoot on the following day. Clearly from the tone of her conversation when she said goodbye to her father, she was hoping for a complete recovery."

At sunrise, the princess—or the Queen, as she had unknowingly become during the night—was out on the balcony with her cine camera adjusting the light filter to film a rhino, silhouetted against the African dawn, at the salt lick. Philip was keeping an eye on another rhino, which arrived at the scene puffing and blowing as if a bitter battle might ensue. Mike Parker went onto the balcony and believed he was with the Queen when the new reign began, as they looked at the dawn coming up over the jungle and saw an eagle hovering over their heads.

"I never thought about it until later," he recalled, "but that was roughly the time when the King died."

After a breakfast of bacon and eggs cooked over the wood-burning stove, they all climbed down from the tree and walked back through the clearing, this time without incident. Mindful of the previous afternoon, Walker turned to the princess and said rather pompously, but still unaware of what had happened in London, "If you have the same courage, Ma'am, in facing what the future sends you as you have at facing an elephant at eight yards, we are going to be very fortunate indeed." As the princess drove away, she waved and called, "I will come again!" It was to be another twenty years before she returned.

Four hours later, the royal party were resting back at Sagana Lodge some twenty miles away when the editor of the *East African Standard* telephoned Martin Charteris, who was staying at the only local Outspan hotel. The editor anxiously enquired if the teleprinter reports coming in from London about the King's death were true. It was news to Charteris. By a twist of fate, a telegram sent to Government House in Nairobi had not been decoded because the keys to the safe holding the codebook had been misplaced. A thoroughly unnerved Charteris checked the news with Buckingham Palace, couldn't get through, and immediately contacted Sagana Lodge. He spoke to Mike Parker, who turned on a shortwave radio and heard the tolling of Big Ben and then the crackling announcement from the BBC. Mike confirmed the news with Charteris and then woke a slumbering Philip to tell him of the news. It was 2:45 p.m. local time and already 11:45 a.m. in London.

"I walked round the outside of the house, woke Prince Philip and told him. It was the toughest thing I ever did to him," Parker recalled shortly before his death in 2001. "He looked absolutely flattened as if the whole world had collapsed on him. He saw immediately that the idyll of his life and their life together had come to an end."

"He put a newspaper over his face and just remained like that for about five minutes," Pamela Mountbatten recalled. "The shock of what had happened and the enormity of the consequences, briefly disconnected Philip who knew he was going to have to break the news to his wife.

"And then he pulled himself together and said he must go and find the Princess—she was having a rest in her bedroom—and they went for a walk in the garden and you could tell, walking up and down, up and down, that he was telling her," Pamela remembered. "And then she came back to the Lodge—and one just thought, this poor girl who really adored her father, they were very close. And I think I gave her a hug and said how sorry I was. And then suddenly, I thought, my God, but she's Queen!"

The Queen has never spoken about her reaction to her father's sudden death except to say, "My father died much too young and so, it was all very sudden kind of taking on and making the best job you can." She was in shock as she had not expected it. As Princess Margaret said, "He died as he was getting better."

Three months later, there is a clue to her feelings in a touching letter to her father's assistant private secretary, Sir Eric Miéville. "It all seems so unbelievable still," she wrote, "that my father is no longer here and it is only after some time has passed one begins to realise how much he is missed." She added, "My mother and sister have been wonderful, for they have lost so much—I do have my own family to help me."

In the following hours, when preparations were made to return to England as quickly as possible, the Queen calmly and mechanically

Prince Philip's maternal grandfather, Prince Louis of Battenberg, later first Marquess of Milford Haven, in 1908 with his daughter, Princess Alice; her husband, Prince Andrew of Greece (Philip's parents); and Philip's two eldest sisters, Princess Margarita (*foreground*) and Princess Theodora. Philip's father bears a strong resemblance to Prince Charles.

Prince Philip with his English nanny, Emily Roose, and the youngest of his four sisters, Sophie, on holiday at Berck Plage in France in about 1924. Roosie was a huge influence on the young Philip.

A serious three-year-old Prince Philip posing for a formal photo session in 1924. His angelic looks belie a confident, already well-traveled little boy.

Prince Philip, by now HRH The Duke of Edinburgh, photographed for his twenty-seventh birthday in June 1948 by his good friend Baron. Philip's pose of folded arms was one he was to adopt for the rest of his life.

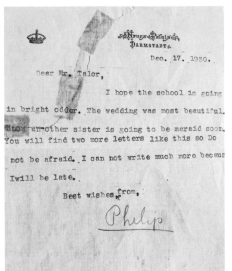

A typewritten letter full of childish spelling mistakes to the Rev. Harold Taylor, Philip's headmaster at Cheam School, just before Christmas 1930. Philip writes about his youngest sister Sophie's wedding to Prince Christoph of Hesse in 1930. The next wedding he mentions was probably that of his sister Cecile, who married the following February.

Philip's mother pictured with her four eldest children in 1916. (*From left*) Margarita, Sophie, Theodora, and finally Cecile. Their mother wears the Meander tiara, most recently worn by Zara Phillips on her wedding day.

Enjoying an archery class at The Elms school in Paris, 1931. (*From left*) Jacques de Bourbon, Prince Philip, Alan Reeves, Martha Robinson, and Princess Anne of Bourbon-Parma (later the wife of King Michael of Romania).

The wedding of Philip's sister Cecile to Hereditary Grand Duke Donatus of Hesse-Darmstadt on February 2, 1931. (*From left*) The Marchioness of Milford Haven, Philip's maternal grandmother; Philip's sister Margarita; Prince Gottfried of Hohenlohe (*partly obscured*); Grand Duke Ernst Ludwig; Philip, at the front, in his starched "Eton collar"; Prince Ernst of Hohenlohe-Langenburg.

Prince Philip in 1936 at Lynden Manor, the home of his maternal uncle George and his wife, Nada, the Marquess and Marchioness of Milford Haven. With him are his cousins Lady Tatiana Mountbatten and David, Earl of Medina, Philip's great friend and best man at his wedding.

Prince Philip and his uncle Dickie Mountbatten, who was said to be the marriage broker and greatest influence on Philip's life, at a dinner in 1948, the year after Philip married Princess Elizabeth.

Prince Philip and another important mentor, the redoubtable Kurt Hahn, founder of Gordonstoun School, Schloss Salem in Germany, and in 1956 the Duke of Edinburgh's Awards scheme. Here, in June 1964, the two men attend a dinner given in seventy-seven-year-old Kurt Hahn's honor by the Friends of Gordonstoun.

Marriage to Princess Elizabeth on November 20, 1947. "Lilibet is the only thing in this world which is absolutely real to me and my ambition is to weld the two of us into a new combined existence," Philip wrote to his mother-in-law two weeks later. It was to be the blueprint for their life together.

Princess Elizabeth and Prince Philip during her 1950 visit to Malta, where the duke was stationed as a naval officer before her accession as Queen two years later. The princess was pregnant with their daughter, Anne, at the time.

In the quadrangle of Windsor Castle to celebrate Prince Philip's ninety-ninth birthday on June 10, 2020. While self-isolating during the coronavirus pandemic, the Queen and Philip posed briefly for an official portrait, the first since their seventieth wedding anniversary in November 2017.

wrote letters and telegrams while Philip sat beside her. "She was sitting erect fully accepting her destiny," Martin Charteris recalled.

"I asked her what name she would take and she said, 'My own of course.'"

"Poor guy," Parker recalled, talking in 1999 about Philip. "He needed something to do. But he was there with the Queen; that was the thing; he was like a bloody great pillar." Back in London, the news had been relayed to Prime Minister Winston Churchill four hours previously. Operation Hyde Park Corner, with coded plans for the death of the King, was already in full swing. Churchill's private secretary, Jock Colville, recalled that when he went to Churchill's bedroom, he was sitting alone with tears in his eyes staring into space. "I had not realised how much the King meant to him," he said. "I tried to cheer him up by saying how well he would get on with the new Queen, but all he could say was that he did not know her and that she was only a child."

A child she was not. The mourning clothes that had been packed so carefully had gone on ahead with the official luggage to Mombasa, and the new Queen was forced to wear a floral frock and white sandals instead of her black dress, which she was not happy about, as she wanted to show proper respect for her father. She requested no photographs be taken as she left the lodge for London, but there were a couple of photographers already gathered outside.

"We stood silently outside the lodge," one recalled, "as the cars drove away in a cloud of dust, not one of us taking a shot at that historic moment. Seeing the young girl as Queen of Great Britain as she drove away, I felt her sadness, as she just raised her hand to us as we stood there silent, our cameras on the ground."

When the Queen and the duke arrived back in London on February 7—the new Queen changed into black mourning clothes that had to be taken on board as soon as they arrived—they found a nation in mourning. Flags were at half-mast, cinemas and theaters were closed, and sports fixtures canceled. The diplomat Sir Evelyn Shuckburgh described the poignant scene as they walked down the steps of the aircraft. "There was a touching picture of [the Queen] walking down the steps from the aircraft with the Privy Council lined up to greet her. One could just see the backs of their poor old heads: Winston, Attlee, AE [Eden], Woolton and so on. The twentieth-century version of Melbourne galloping to Kensington Palace, falling on his knees before Victoria in her nightdress."

Philip had waited his turn to exit the plane. He knew that his role as head of the household had changed forever. Furthermore, his hopes for a continuing career in the Royal Navy were dashed.

Although the death of the King at such an early age could not have been foreseen, the Queen's whole life had prepared her for the change of circumstances. Not so Philip, who described his feelings years later: "Within the house, whatever we did, it was together. I suppose I naturally filled that position. People used to come to me and ask me what to do. In 1952 the whole thing changed, very, very considerably."

He was on his own. But assertive personalities like Philip do their best when the odds are against them. In that brief moment in the Kenyan bush, he had lost his career, his home, his wife, and life as he knew it. A lesser man might have crumbled, but after a moment drowning, Philip came up for air and was determined to stay on top. He knew even then it was going to be a fight. And it was.

Chapter 8

CHANGE FOR THE WORST

Philip spent the first few months of the new Queen's reign in a low mood, experiencing what is called in psychological terms delayed emotional shock. He tried to work out the best method of supporting his wife without "getting in the way," but he was deeply despondent about having to move out of the first home he had ever been able to call his own, Clarence House.

Princess Alice, who had been in America at the time of the King's death, wrote to her son telling him she understood how difficult his new responsibilities would be and how she envisaged they would involve him in a great deal more personal self-sacrifice than he had been expected to give beforehand. She also told him that his late father, who had died in 1944, would be with him in "spirit" to help him along. In spite of her fragile mental health, Princess Alice understood her son and was always there for him, which he seldom spoke of. The Queen appreciated Alice's concern and was happy when the elderly lady moved into Buckingham Palace in 1967 for the last two years of her life.

Winston Churchill's insistence on the royal couple moving as soon as possible provoked lots of below-stairs rumors among the staff at Buckingham Palace about how differently things were done "across the road," as they called Clarence House. Naturally, they were anxious about their jobs, especially when "PP," as he became known, began a departmental tour of inspection within a couple of days of their arrival at the palace in early 1953. For the first few months at the palace, the Queen and the duke used the Belgian Suite on the ground floor, at the back northwest corner of the building, eating in the Carnarvon Room, where the late King used to lunch with his prime minister every Tuesday during the war. Later on, the Queen and the duke moved to their rooms on the first floor, formerly occupied by King George VI and his father and grandfather before him.

The work of organizing the late King's wardrobe and uniforms was so difficult that his valet, Mr. Tom Jerram, was still working on it two years after his death. The late King's clothes remained on the top floor of Clarence House until the Queen Mother's death in 2002, when they were moved back to Buckingham Palace.

Once inside Buckingham Palace, Philip needed a project, so together with Mike Parker, they duly went into every one of the four hundred rooms and asked every available member of staff exactly what he or she did and why. Philip's naval training meant he was a stickler for timekeeping and efficiency, and he could not understand the ineffective system of staggered meals in the servants' hall, so he suggested introducing a cafeteria. The archaic mechanics of the palace both fascinated and irritated him. When he discovered that to transmit a simple order from the Queen or himself it took several footmen to pass it on to the correct recipient, he likened it to A. A. Milne's poem "The King's Breakfast." Instead he decided he would simply send down a personal note written in pencil requesting his requirements. Sometimes he would call the Royal Mews or chef's office and the surprised chauffeur or cook would recognize the duke's voice and he would give his orders personally. To him it seemed a perfectly natural thing to do.

Of course, the old-school staff were not used to this and used to joke it was like being on board a huge ship with Philip at the helm, as he used to be on board HMS *Magpie*. They weren't far wrong. Philip was impatient, but he was also perceptive and missed nothing. He was determined the palace machinery would run efficiently under his command, and it was an outlet for his energies to get it to do so.

Because of his culinary awareness, his greatest interest and biggest challenge was the old-fashioned palace kitchens on the ground floor on the south side of the building. He'd suddenly appear and ask anyone who happened to be on duty what the various fittings and equipment were for. It drove him mad that the dining room seemed to be miles away from the kitchens and all the food had to be carried from oven to table. He longed to rebuild the kitchens, but the cost was prohibitive, so he decided to temporarily abandon his scheme to move them but did not give in. Eventually, the main kitchens were left in place, and the duke's idea of a completely modern kitchen fitted with the very latest equipment was installed by the royal dining room for preparing family meals.

According to Frederick Corbitt, who worked as deputy controller of supplies for twenty years, until the early 1950s, small things as well as big attracted the duke's notice. Even the blocks of ice that used to be stacked outside the kitchen larder at Sandringham came to his notice, and he insisted that a bench be made to accommodate them.

"What difference it made, none of us could discover," he recalled. "But the duke was satisfied. The Queen, when she could spare the time, went into details of everything with her husband, but in general she left it to his judgment and generally backed up any of his ideas." These also included putting his decorating skills to work modifying and redecorating the private apartments overlooking Constitution Hill and appointing a new office for himself with Mike Parker as his official private secretary.

In spite of his newly found responsibilities, Philip still felt rudderless. Small things irritated him: he could not bear the piper that played every morning beneath the Queen's window, for instance, and hated that no one could make an appointment with him except through his page. Having started to tackle the inefficiency of how the palace was run, he then came down with a second attack of jaundice in late 1952 and was forced into bed. (He'd had a previous attack earlier in June, and at the time his immediate engagements had to be canceled.)

As the new monarch, the Queen now had many duties from which Philip was excluded. She had her weekly meetings with the prime minister, and every day she received red boxes full of state papers—Cabinet minutes, Foreign Office telegrams, documents, briefs, and drafts—none of which were shown to Philip, as he simply didn't want to get officially involved. "It was bloody difficult for him," said Mike Parker. "In the navy, he was in command of his own ship—literally. At Clarence House, it was very much his show. When we got to Buckingham Palace, all that changed."

In his new role as consort, Philip sought the guidance of Prince Bernhard of the Netherlands, who as the husband of Queen Juliana had fifteen years' experience as consort, four of them since she took the throne. Bernhard was one of the founders of the World Wildlife Fund and its president before Philip took on that role. Bernhard gave him the benefit of his advice: "You are new at this thing and you probably don't realise what you are up against. Practically everything you do will be a subject of criticism. You can't ignore it because some of it may be justified. And even if it isn't it may be politic to heed it. But don't let it get you down. In this job, you need a skin like an elephant."

Another irritant was that the palace was staffed with courtiers who answered only to the monarch. "Philip was constantly being squashed, snubbed, ticked off, rapped over the knuckles," said Mike Parker. "It was intolerable. The problem was simply that Philip had energy, ideas, get-up-and-go, and that didn't suit the Establishment, not one bit." The same thing went for Windsor Castle, which became their weekend retreat instead of Windlesham. Another major blow to Philip that year came when it was decided that their children and their children's children should bear the name Windsor, after the Queen's family, not his name, Mountbatten. Philip was furious and deeply wounded. It was emasculating. It was cruel. "I am the only man in the country not allowed to give his name to his children," he protested.

"It hurt him, it really hurt him," Countess Mountbatten recalled. "He had given up everything—and now this, the final insult. It was a terrible blow. It upset him very deeply and left him feeling unsettled and unhappy for a long while. Of course, I don't blame the Queen."

It was the elder statesman Churchill—encouraged by Sir Alan "Tommy" Lascelles, who was forty years older than the Queen and her private secretary—who had decided on this, and together they forced the Queen's unsophisticated hand. She was too young and inexperienced to stand up for what she wanted for her husband, which was the name Mountbatten-Windsor.

Frustration, irritation, and disappointment were daily occurrences for Philip, but outside the palace, he soon found roles to which he could apply his extensive energies. The Queen made him ranger of Windsor Great Park, in effect estate manager. He subsequently took an overseeing role at all the royal estates and greatly improved their efficiency. He was also made chairman of the Coronation Commission, which included the Duke of Norfolk, Winston Churchill, Clement Attlee, and the Archbishop of Canterbury. The commission would consider every aspect of the coronation, including the question of whether to permit the ceremony to be televised. Meanwhile, the Royal Mint had to issue new coins bearing the Queen's head, and Philip was made president of the committee to advise on the design of new coins and medals.

The first meeting of the Coronation Commission took place on May 5, 1952, more than a year before the actual event. The Duke of Edinburgh was in the chair and gave a typically brief speech to get things going: "First as Chairman, welcome to the first meeting of the coronation commission. There is a tremendous amount of work to be done, so the sooner we get on with it the better." There is little doubt that his efficiency and refusal to dwell too long on any unnecessary subjects contributed to the success of the organization.

To this end, the ballroom at Buckingham Palace was marked with tape to indicate an approximate shape of Westminster Abbey, and the Queen with a sheet pinned to her shoulders to represent her coronation cloak went through the rehearsals in minute detail. For Philip and Mike Parker, who was always at his side, the rehearsals, although necessary, became another source of frustration as they went about their business in an increasingly crowded calendar. Philip particularly disliked the number of official photographs on the agenda, each requiring a change of uniform. They were, he thought, an imposition and a waste of time. Then, on March 24, eighty-five-year-old Queen Mary, who lived at Marlborough House, died in her sleep. As per her wishes her granddaughter's coronation was to go ahead, despite the official period of mourning, on Tuesday, June 2, 1953 as planned.

Just before dawn on the morning of the coronation, word reached

Buckingham Palace that Everest had been conquered. Two members of the 1953 British Mount Everest expedition, led by Brigadier John Hunt, had planted a Union Jack on the mountain's summit at 29,002 feet (8,840 meters). The Duke of Edinburgh, who was patron of the expedition, was overjoyed at the news that New Zealander Edmund Hillary and his Nepalese guide Tenzing Norgay had reached the summit on Friday, May 29. The climbers had brought out the rum and toasted their patron, "who had followed their progress with keen interest."

The conquest of Everest was probably the last major news item to be delivered to the world by runner, and the encoded message to *The Times* was received and understood in London in time for the news to be released on the morning of the coronation. "The Queen and the Duke of Edinburgh and other members of the royal family were delighted," the *Daily Mail* wrote. "She sent her congratulations to the expedition." Eileen Parker recalled pithily, "My husband and Prince Philip were more interested in watching that than going to the ceremony." Indeed, they probably were, and when the leader of the expedition returned and was knighted, Sir John Hunt became the first director of the Duke of Edinburgh's Award.

There had been some debate about whether Philip should ride in the gold state coach with the Queen, go on horseback, or travel in a separate coach, as there was no precedent for a reigning Queen going to her coronation together with her consort. In the end, Philip pointed out the only sensible thing to do was to travel with the Queen, where he would be equipped with a radio-telephone on the seat beside him so he could keep in touch with everything else going on.

Philip's role in the coronation was to kneel before his wife, taking the ancient oath of fealty: "I Philip, Duke of Edinburgh, do become your liege man of life and limb and of earthly worship; and faith and truth will I bear unto you, to live and die, against all manner of folks. So help me God." He then had to stand and kiss her cheek and back away. At the rehearsal, he did not play his part with any conviction. In fact, he mumbled the words at high speed, missed the Queen's cheek, and retired backward fast. The Queen told him off: "Don't be silly, Philip. Come back here and do it properly."

Of course, he performed seriously on the day, but his touch on the crown was a little heavy-handed, and the Queen had to fleetingly adjust it.

Cecil Beaton, who had been commissioned to take the official photographs, gave one of the most vivid descriptions of the day, on entering the abbey:

"Gold sticks [gentlemen-at-arms of the Queen's bodyguard] stationed around the cloisters showed us on our way. They were already frozen blue. One of them asked me if I had heard the good news that Hunt had climbed Everest.

"The guests, the peeresses en bloc—in their dark red velvet and foam white, dew spangled with diamonds. The minor royalties and the foreign royalties and representatives of states. The mother of the Duke of Edinburgh, a contrast to the grandeur, in the ash grey draperies of a nun. . . . That great old relic, Winston Churchill, lurches forward on unsteady feet, a fluttering mass of white ribbons at his shoulder and white feathers in the hat in his hand. Then the most dramatic and spectacular, at the head of her retinue of white, lily-like ladies, the Queen."

Rain had fallen solidly throughout most of the ceremony, soaking everyone outside, especially those in uniform who were unable to take any shelter. There was profound relief when the great ceremony was over and had gone without a noticeable hitch.

Then as now, both the Queen and Philip enjoy it when things go slightly wrong, because their lives are so regimented. They were treated to one such moment in the procession back from the abbey when one of the attendants walking beside the gold state coach started to head off in the wrong direction, toward Hyde Park. John Taylor, the footman walking next to him, noticed straightaway and signaled to the Queen, who told the duke, who yelled out of the window at Taylor, "Where does that man think he is going? Get him back!"

Nothing had been left to chance, so the duke, with his walkie-talkie next to him on the upholstered seat of the coach, tried to coordinate the footman, but even he couldn't get to him, so a lot of discreet signaling went on.

Back at the palace, Cecil Beaton had to get the official pictures done as soon as possible for the thousands of publications waiting for them. Philip was at his most officious and tried to take control, which was very much unappreciated. "I could see that Cecil Beaton was getting very, very irritated because he is a professional photographer and the Duke of Edinburgh was telling him what to do," Lady Anne Glenconner, one of the maids of honor recalled.

Despite the tensions, Beaton still had time to note what was going on when he was not in front of his camera, and he later made some acerbic observations: "The Queen looked extremely minute under her robes and crown, her nose and hands chilled and her eyes tired. The Duke of Edinburgh stood by making wry jokes, his lips pursed in a smile that put the fear of God into me. I believe he doesn't like or approve of me. . . . Perhaps he was disappointed that his friend Baron was not doing the job today: whatever the reason he was adopting a rather ragging attitude to the proceedings."

As the rain continued to pour down, the crowds called the Queen and Philip back onto the balcony at least half a dozen times. After their final appearance, at midnight, the crowd, which was by then a solid mass all the way to Trafalgar Square, started singing "Auld Lang Syne." "The Queen led us out and we gazed at this extraordinary throng of people stretching for miles down the Mall," Lady

Anne Glenconner recalled. "You couldn't put a pin between the people. It was just a sort of roar of love for her."

Earlier that evening, the Queen had given her historic coronation broadcast to the world. It was broadcast from the Home Service and during the program she set the tone for her reign and the Duke of Edinburgh's important part in it: "Throughout my life and with all my heart I shall strive to be worthy of your trust. . . . In this resolve I have my husband to support me. He shares all my ideals and all my affection for you. Then, although my experience is so short and my task so new, I have in my parents and grandparents an example which I can follow with certainty and with confidence."

Eight days later, it was Philip's birthday, and Mike and Eileen Parker threw a cocktail party at their home in Launceston Place in his honor. Philip's sisters, who had all been invited to the coronation, were also there. Margarita and Theodora were heavily built while Sophie, the youngest, was tall and slender. She had been married twice and her second husband was Prince George of Hanover. They all loved being with their younger brother in informal surroundings and chatted all evening, sharing private jokes in German. Philip spent much of the evening explaining to Prince Alfonso of Hohenlohe-Langenburg how the glassblower had managed to trap a bubble of air in the stem of his champagne glass. Philip was always completely at ease with the international set of glamorous rich playboys, many of whom he had known since childhood, and Alfonso, who later married the fifteen-year-old Fiat heiress Ira von Furstenberg, was one of those whose company he enjoyed.

While the coronation ceremony itself had gone smoothly, the event created a new concern for Philip and the Queen. During the coronation, Princess Margaret made an innocent gesture of brushing an imaginary piece of fluff from the lapel of Group Captain Peter

Townsend's uniform, which was reported by the press as being done "with a tender hand." The resulting furor threatened to propel the Queen into a constitutional crisis as the press on both sides of the Atlantic endlessly discussed what Margaret had been up to with the handsome Townsend.

The Queen and Philip were aware of the intensity of their relationship: a few weeks before the coronation Princess Margaret had informed them over lunch that she wanted to marry Peter, whom she had known since she was fourteen. He was sixteen years older than her, but more pointedly at the time when divorce was taboo, especially for a member of the royal family, he had just obtained a divorce from his wife, Rosemary.

Philip's main concern was for his own wife and how the potential crisis would affect her, especially when she was still trying to grasp so many other affairs of state. He was annoyed at the amount of publicity the tiny gesture had caused but tried to keep out of it, only listening to what he was told and then making light of it. However, he was quite aware of the threat the problem could cause and was annoyed at the apparent selfishness of both Margaret and Townsend for placing the Queen in such a delicate situation so soon after the beginning of her reign.

Philip had nothing against Townsend, whom he had first met at Balmoral when, as the King's equerry, he was a member of the shooting party. Once Princess Elizabeth's engagement had been announced, it was not in Townsend's character to pass judgment on Philip one way or another, and he never did. "I was prepared to like Philip," Townsend said many years later. "I knew him first through my brother Michael, who was a captain of a destroyer in the war. Philip sailed under him later and when Philip became a pilot, my admiration for him increased because of my own love of flying.

"The one thing we did do was fight battles against each other on the courts. Badminton and squash. Philip would fight me to a standstill. He wanted to win every time. One time he was so intent on the game that he nearly broke my wrist. And when I went into exile in 1953, he did not exactly walk me to the door and say good-bye, although we had known each other for many years and had dined together with the Queen and Margaret.

"During those times that we were together he was always polite and friendly. Never imperious. He is a German but he does not look very German. He is certainly trenchant and his views are trenchant. I would say he was intelligent without being an intellectual. When I was there, he could be abrupt and he had this staccato way of talking, although he would often end things up with a joke or a quip."

There is no evidence that Philip disliked Townsend, as has been widely reported, or vice versa. But it would be strange if Townsend hadn't been slightly wary of Philip, as so many of the courtiers were. In an interview with *Daily Express* columnist the late Jean Rook, Townsend said it was a "great myth" that Philip was out to get him. "But if he was or did when I wasn't around, I wasn't aware of it. He's a hard-hitting extrovert, not my sort of man, but I liked him."

Philip had known Princess Margaret, or Margo as he called her, from the time she was an attention-grabbing little sister to when she blossomed into a society beauty, but they were never the closest friends. He found her entertaining but selfish and demanding; and when Margaret was younger, she said she found Philip "cold" and disliked being subjected to his constant sarcastic teasing. Once she became used to it, her subtler wit triumphed over his and they became sparring equals. The only comment she ever made about him was that she liked him.

It was probably the combination of the two sisters and their mother that Philip found most trying. When they were together, they formed a powerful trio. They frequently lunched together and conversed in French using a subtle code to illustrate what they meant. If, for instance, the Queen Mother thought anyone in the family was shirking, she would tell her daughter to remind them of their duty, or *devoir* as she called it in French. Sometimes in a loud stage whisper she would simply say the word "*devoir*," and the Queen and Margaret knew exactly what she meant.

Philip kept well out of the way on these occasions. He knew exactly what they were gossiping about but preferred not to get involved and to leave them to it. He knew better than anyone how close the Queen was to her sister and how she longed for Margo to find happiness with the man she loved as she had done herself. It came as a shock, however, when Princess Margaret announced over lunch with him and the Queen that she and Townsend were in love and hoped they might get married. At this stage the Queen Mother knew nothing about it, but Townsend then told the Queen's private secretary, Tommy Lascelles.

"My only comment at the time," Lascelles later recalled, "was that, as Townsend must realise that there were obviously several formidable obstacles to be overcome." This differs from Townsend's account in his memoirs written in 1978, in which he said that Tommy was "visibly shaken" and could say nothing except, "You must be either mad or bad."

Whatever was said, it appears Lascelles was not quite as unfeeling as history relates. The very next day, he spoke to the Queen, reminding her about the royal marriages act of 1772 in which the Queen as titular head of the Church of England could not give her formal consent to the marriage of her sister to a divorced man without the agreement of her prime minister, who at that time was Sir Winston Churchill. Lascelles confirms that when he discussed the matter with the Queen, the Duke of Edinburgh, and Princess Margaret in January 1953 "no conclusion was reached."

Once the coronation was over and the press took up the story,

Lascelles went to see Churchill at Chartwell and found him more concerned about the aspect of the Commonwealth and their possible reaction to the marriage and its consequences if the Queen were to die and any child of the union would then be in line to the throne.

According to Lascelles, Churchill "made it perfectly clear that if Princess Margaret should decide to marry Townsend, she should renounce her rights to the throne." Churchill also said that Townsend should be offered "employment abroad" and wait until Princess Margaret was twenty-five before revisiting the situation. Eventually the Queen agreed, as it was the line of least resistance, but in retrospect it meant the lovers still retained hope that they would eventually be together. Far from preventing the love affair, of course, it made it all the more poignant, and when Townsend was sent to Brussels on a convenience posting and Margaret joined her mother on an official visit to Africa, they wrote to each other every day.

Years later, Prince Philip pointed out it was a disastrous decision and thought it would have been so much better to say no straightaway. There was however one advantage for Philip out of the whole unhappy business, which was prompted by Lascelles when he asked Churchill to remind the Queen that if anything should happen to her, Princess Margaret would become regent. Churchill proposed a new regency act of 1953, and for this the Queen requested that "in the event of a Regent becoming necessary in my lifetime, my husband should be Regent and should be charged with the guardianship of the Sovereign."

This meant the removal of Margaret's potentially most powerful constitutional role, which did not please her. But worse was to come when the new prime minister, Sir Anthony Eden, although sympathetic to her plight, traveled to Balmoral and had to warn Princess Margaret that she would have to renounce her royal rights, functions, and income should the union go ahead.

In his autobiography *Time and Chance*, published in 1978,

twenty-three years after the event, Townsend described the tensions and dramas that led to the end of the affair, which came to a head in October 1955, saying, "We felt mute and numbed at the centre of this maelstrom."

Numbed as she was, Princess Margaret knew she owed it to her mother and sister to talk things over with them once again and left for Windsor Castle, where together with Philip they spent a difficult weekend, leaving Townsend at the mercy of the frenetic press. What happened or what was said has never been disclosed, but finally they faced up to the gravity of the situation together.

When the Queen Mother, who disliked any kind of moral confrontation, blandly said her daughter "hadn't even thought where they were going to live," Prince Philip was incensed by the triviality of the statement. He replied with heavy sarcasm, "It is still possible, even nowadays, to buy a house." The Queen Mother was so annoyed by him, she left the room angrily, slamming the door. Later that day, Margaret rang Townsend "in great distress." She did not say what had passed between her sister and brother-in-law, but according to the helpless Townsend, doubtless "the truth was dawning on her."

On Monday October 31, 1955, Margaret and Townsend met for the last time, at Clarence House. Their love story ended with the words that Townsend had written for her to say if she wished to, which was to end what he described as "a miserable trial by ordeal, held in public."

After they met, his words became part of the statement that was broadcast to the world at 7 p.m. that same evening. "I have decided not to marry Group Captain Peter Townsend. I have been aware that, subject to my renouncing my rights of succession, it might have been possible for me to contract a civil marriage. But, mindful of the Church's teaching that Christian marriage is indissoluble and conscious of my duty to the Commonwealth, I have resolved

to put these considerations before others. I have reached this decision entirely alone and in doing so I have been strengthened by the
unfailing support and devotion of Group Captain Townsend. I am
deeply grateful for the concern of all of those who have constantly
prayed for my happiness."

By this time, Philip had other things on his mind, and as far as he
was concerned the matter was closed. What really interested him
was an invitation he had received to open the 1956 Olympic Games
in Melbourne, Australia. With the Queen's support, he decided to
embark on a forty-thousand-mile world tour on board the recently
commissioned HMY *Britannia*, which he would join in Melbourne
and use as his floating home so he could visit some of the far-flung
outposts of the Commonwealth on what he called his "personal
contribution to the Commonwealth Ideal."

The extended tour, which included New Zealand, Ceylon, the
Gambia, the Antarctic, the Galápagos Islands, and the Falkland
Islands, meant Philip being away from home from mid-October
1956 to mid-February 1957. The Queen may not have been completely happy about the idea, but it was her way of acknowledging
her husband's huge personal sacrifice in giving up his naval career
to support her. She understood his frustrations, his moods, and his
boundless energy, all of which needed an outlet, and it was an opportunity for him to do what he loved best—being at sea and being
in control of his own life.

The charming, urbane Mike Parker accompanied him throughout the voyage under the command of Rear Admiral Sir Conolly
Abel Smith. It also included a crew of 277 officers and ratings, an
office with two lady clerks, and various others, including artist Edward Seago and Viscount Cilcennin, who had recently resigned as
First Lord of the Admiralty. Philip invited the latter not only as a

friend, but as a man of great experience in the political world who could give invaluable assistance should it be needed. Cilcennin was not a well man, and Philip knew the voyage would help him as he would be able to have daily treatment for his arthritis in the sick bay on board the royal yacht.

As the Queen waved goodbye to her husband as he boarded the VC-10 aircraft bound for Australia, neither of them had any inkling of the personal problems that lay ahead. The Queen had enough to worry her with the Suez crisis, and Philip had to cancel a planned stop in Singapore because of anti-British riots. But it was the length of the trip and then the abrupt resignation of Philip's closest friend and equerry, which followed news of Parker's impending separation, that caught the headlines. Parker had been spending an inordinate amount of time away from his wife, Eileen, and eventually began an affair, which she discovered. They agreed no mention of the situation should be made public, and Parker embarked on his trip on board HMY *Britannia* confident that was the case. Unfortunately, Eileen Parker's lawyer chose to make the announcement of the separation as HMY *Britannia* arrived in Gibraltar, and to make matters worse, instead of releasing it through Reuters he gave the "scoop" to journalist Rex North of the *Sunday Pictorial*.

It was only two years since the Townsend affair had rocked the monarchy, and the press was determined to make as much fuss of the situation as they could, as it had been proven that anything to do with royalty and divorce sold newspapers. The American press took full advantage of the situation. The *Baltimore Sun* revealed that London was awash with rumor that the Duke of Edinburgh too was involved with an unnamed woman, whom he was meeting regularly at the apartment of a court photographer. Parker duly resigned despite both Philip's and the Queen's efforts to persuade him to stay. Parker's story might have died, but Philip's did not, and when the Queen's press secretary Commander Richard Colville denied the news of a "royal rift," it only served to encourage the British newspapers, which now had the excuse they needed to go into print.

In a letter from February 1958, Princess Margaret touched on the controversy when writing to her friend Sharman Douglas, whose father had been the US ambassador in London in the late 1940s. "I see the fine old press in your country tried to make out the Queen wasn't getting on with my b-in-l [brother-in-law]. So of course, the stinking press here repeated it all the sheep like, like the nasty cowards they are. However, all is well and he's terribly well and full of fascinating stories of his journeys and it's very nice indeed to have him home again. The children are thrilled."

At the end of the tour, the Queen flew out to Lisbon to join Philip on a state visit to Portugal as planned. During the long voyage, Philip had grown a full naval beard, which he shaved off before boarding the Queen's plane. He found the entire party on the plane, including the Queen, wearing false ginger whiskers. When the royal couple emerged to meet the reporters on the tarmac, they were smiling happily. *Time* magazine reported that this was "an all's well signal that spread to the four corners of the earth."

Later Mike Parker admitted the duke had been "incandescent" about the rumors and publicity. "He was very, very angry. And deeply hurt." It was not the first time Philip would feel this way and it was not to be the last. But it was the last time he would have Parker at his side. Such was their friendship he was not banished from royal company, as is so often the case when royal members of the household attract an unwanted scandal. Instead, the Queen invested him with the Royal Victorian Order in recognition of his services and Parker continued to see Philip as a friend, if not as an employer.

Chapter 9

CHARLES AND ANNE

Philip enjoyed fatherhood. He loved babies and was delighted when Princess Elizabeth became pregnant soon after their marriage. They had both hoped for a son to secure the succession, and as soon as he arrived their happiness appeared complete. When Anne was born two years later, she proved to be everything her sensitive brother was not. Baby Charles grew into a sweet-natured but painfully shy, timorous little boy and would have an increasingly difficult relationship with his father, who would have much more fun with his boisterous daughter, Anne.

Prince Charles celebrated his fourth birthday in the white-and-gold music room at Buckingham Palace. Fourteen children were invited, and the corridor outside was cleared of its impedimenta of chairs and tables and ornaments so that the prince and his guests could run up and down. In the forecourt below, the band of the Grenadier Guards entertained the youthful revelers with a selection of nursery rhymes and then, as a special treat, with a rendition of Charles's favorite song, "The Teddy Bear's Picnic."

It was as one observer surmised, "probably the lightest-hearted party given at Buckingham Palace since the period of the Crimean War when Queen Victoria still had children young enough to romp in the same spirit." It was also notable for something more contemporaneous: this was the first time Philip had been present at one of his son's birthday parties.

Prince Charles was born on November 14, 1948. The birth that foggy night had not been an easy one. The official bulletin pinned to the gates of Buckingham Palace announced that "Her Royal Highness and her son are doing well." It was later revealed that she had been given a pain-killing anesthetic. It is commonly supposed that forceps were used to deliver the 7-pound 6-ounce (3.34 kilogram) boy. In fact, he was born by cesarean section, but such was the prudishness of the age that this was never officially disclosed. Even the princess's friends were not informed. "Breast feeding," as one of her confidantes remembered, "was never spoken of." Pregnancy, and especially a royal pregnancy, was a condition that polite society feigned to ignore.

In another indication of the contemporary attitudes, Philip did not attend his wife during her confinement. Nor, for the first time in more than a century, did the home secretary. A few weeks before the birth, the King had issued the formal announcement that the archaic custom, dating from the reign of James II when his wife, Mary of Modena, had been accused of deceptively producing a changeling son to ensure the succession, was to be discontinued.

When the princess's labor started, Mike Parker remembers the royal family gathered in the equerry's room to await news of the birth. The King was stretched out by the fire and Philip was pacing the floor. Eventually Parker took him off for a game of squash.

"Well, time stretched a bit and he was getting restless," Parker said by way of explanation. When the King's private secretary, Tommy Lascelles, brought the good news that the princess had given birth, Philip bounded into the Buhl room, once a part of the children's quarters and later converted into a surgical theater for an operation on the arteries on the King's legs. Still wearing his sporting flannels and open-necked shirt and sweating with exertion, according to the official statement he "went into the Princess's room to see her" and then "went to see his son who had been taken to the nursery." His wife was still drugged and did not come to for some minutes more. The princess would later say that her husband's face was the last she saw before she slipped under the anesthetic and the first she saw when she came around again.

Philip sent a telegraph with the news to his mother, Princess Alice, who was living on the Greek island of Tinos, in a house without a telephone. She wrote to him at once saying: "I think of you so much with a sweet baby of your own, of your joy and the interest you will take in all his little doings. How fascinating nature is, but how one has to pay for it in the anxious trying hours of the confinement."

Princess Elizabeth had seen little of her husband during the early months of her pregnancy: Philip, still a serving naval officer and frequently away, also contracted German measles and had to be kept apart from his expectant wife. The princess, who had taken a matter-of-fact approach to her pregnancy, was beguiled by what she had produced.

"I still find it difficult to believe I have a baby of my own," she remarked. In the long human tradition, she set about searching for family resemblances in his features. His hands attracted her attention. They were, she said, rather large "but fine with long fingers." Philip, always matter-of-fact to the point of indifference, declared that he looked like "a plum pudding."

The infant was cared for by a pampering retinue of nannies and under-nannies and nursery maids, and he had a grandmother who doted on him. The love of his mother and father, however, like his food and clothing in those austere postwar years, was severely rationed. It had to be fitted in between their official duties. Even when time and duty permitted, the emotional needs of the little prince were not always paramount on their agenda.

A month after his birth, the infant was christened Charles Philip Arthur George in the music room at Buckingham Palace, as the private chapel had been destroyed by a bomb during the Second World War. His godparents—or sponsors, as royal godparents are called—were King George VI, his great-grandmother Queen Mary, his aunt Princess Margaret, his paternal great-grandmother Victoria Marchioness of Milford Haven, his great-uncle David Bowes Lyon, Earl Mountbatten's daughter and his cousin Lady Brabourne, and his great-uncles Prince George of Greece and King Haakon of Norway. Princess Alice did not attend but received all the news of her new grandson's progress from her younger sister, Louise. She said the baby was like Philip, but the Duchess of Kent thought he was more like Lilibet.

"I am so happy for Philip," she wrote, "for he adores children and also small babies. He carries it [the baby] about himself quite professionally much to the nurses' amusement."

Many years later, the Queen's cousin Margaret Rhodes told me that he liked nothing more than dandling little children on his knee and making them gurgle with laughter. It was when they grew and developed their own personalities that Philip seemed to lose interest.

In the event, it was nanny Helen Lightbody who assumed the major role in Charles's formative early years. She arrived at Buckingham Palace two days before Charles's first Christmas and stayed with him until he went off to school eight years later. She would have stayed longer had she not fallen foul of the Duke of Edinburgh. "Charles absolutely adored her," recalled Eileen Parker. It was nanny Lightbody who got him up in the morning and gave him his last goodnight kiss. He then played in his nursery until he was taken downstairs to spend half an hour with his mother and also his father on the rare occasions he should happen to be around.

Despite his frequent absences, Philip always had the say in the upbringing of the children. He was only twenty-six when Charles was born and harbored a young man's ideal that he would like his firstborn to be in his own image. As Charles grew into a shy, diffident child, Philip was determined to make a man of his son and with this in mind organized for him to be driven three times a week to a private gym in Pavilion Road, Chelsea, where a small class of young boys were instructed in physical training and also boxing.

"I think Philip tolerated Charles but he wasn't a loving father," Eileen Parker said when I interviewed her many years ago. "I think Charles was frightened of him. I never saw him spank his children, but he had a rough manner and could be incredibly cutting." Charles was always in need of reassurance and did not respond well to his father's truculence. "He became very quiet when Philip was around; he was not confident with him," Mrs. Parker observed.

Tough and determinedly independent, Philip had been brought up to fend for himself in a way that left little room for other people, even his own children. "When I was only a year old, I had to leave my family home and, since I was eight years old, I've always been at school," he explained shortly before his judicious marriage to the heir to the throne. "First Paris, then Baden, then Gordonstoun, then the Navy since I was seventeen."

Self-reliant by nature and necessity, he had little intuitive sympathy for anyone less capable than himself. Though often fair-minded, he was more frequently rude and intolerant. Denied the emotional continuity of a settled family life, he had constructed a protective persona of vigorous independence that took slight account of others, his own son included.

"He was very tough with Charles," Eileen Parker said. "There was always the Gordonstoun thing." It was, she said, his guiding precept. There were aspects of Hahn's teachings that Charles would eventually embrace. His father's muscular interpretation of the doctrine cast a fearful shadow over his early life, however. Like his grandfather, George VI, and his great-grandfather, George V, he suffered from knock knees and had to wear orthopedic shoes to correct his flat feet. He was "chesty" like his mother and suffered unduly from colds. His hearty father made no concessions to his son's infirmity.

The Parkers' daughter, Julie, born a month after the prince, would often come from playing with Charles and ask her parents, "Why is Prince Philip cross with Charles? Why isn't he nice to him?"

Philip's method of teaching his son to swim, for instance, was simple and to the point. Over his objections, Charles would be dragged into the Buckingham Palace swimming pool. Sometimes he would be thrown in. On one occasion, his nanny Lightbody objected to the treatment being meted out to her three-year-old charge on the diplomatic grounds that he was "chesty." Philip replied: "It's ridiculous to make such a fuss of him. There's nothing wrong with him!" In the protesting boy went.

As the nanny had worried, Charles duly came down with a cold. She was furious, but even that determined Scotswoman shied away from a direct confrontation with the irascible Philip. "The trouble is, I can only say so much," she angrily complained. It was with an understandable sense of trepidation, therefore, that Charles would await his father's barked command ordering him into his presence. But if it reverberated loudly in his imagination, it featured less resoundingly in reality. Right from the beginning of his marriage, Philip established what became a lifetime's habit of being absent from his home for long periods, and Charles saw very little of his father from one year to the next. He was rarely around, even at

Christmas, which was why the first of his son's birthday parties he attended was his fourth.

As we have seen, originally Philip had no intention of settling into the cozy, claustrophobic domesticity of royal life. He insisted on pursuing his naval career and detested what he called "loose ends." He remarked, "Either I stay in the navy and work, or I retire on half-pay and give my full time to the other things I now have to do." He chose to stay in. He was based at the Admiralty when Charles was born. He then attended a staff course at the Royal Naval College, Greenwich. Within a year, he was back in the Mediterranean as second in command of the destroyer HMS *Chequers*. So began the series of separations from his parents that were to blight Charles's young life. It established a pattern that has carried through into his own adulthood—with all its dire consequences.

It was not, of course, unusual for children of aristocratic families to be placed in the care of nannies. Indeed, at the turn of the twentieth century, one child in ten was brought up by someone other than the child's own mother or father. But even when judged by the standards of the time, Philip and Elizabeth saw remarkably little of their offspring.

The declining health of King George VI compelled the princess to assume more of the royal workload. Her accession to the throne upon his death from cancer in 1952, which moved her family out of Clarence House and into the impersonal vastness of Buckingham Palace, resulted in her seeing even less of her children.

"From the moment the King died the Queen didn't have a minute to spare," observed the court correspondent of the time, Godfrey Talbot. "She immediately had to take over the responsibilities of State. She had been trained since the cradle by her father that duty came before everything, including family. She reluctantly had to abandon her children and they virtually didn't see their parents for months on end." Talbot had a slightly one-sided view of Philip's parenting. Although the duke was impatient, it worried him that in the early days of his marriage, when he was still a serving officer and frequently away, that his son was completely surrounded by women—his mother; his nanny; his governess; and his grandmother, the Queen Mother. Like many fathers of that era, Philip didn't want his son to be mollycoddled.

Eventually, it was to the overall care of the new Queen Mother that Charles was entrusted for several months of each year. She was, said Talbot, a tender shoulder to cry on. "During the first years of the Queen's reign the Queen Mother was both mother and father," he observed.

But if the distancing from his mother was the consequence of her royal duty, the new Queen was not always as reluctant to be parted from her son as the old court correspondent suggested. But she spent her twenty-fourth birthday in Malta watching her husband and uncle playing polo before returning to England to wait for the birth of her second child. On August 15, 1950, the princess gave birth to a baby daughter in their newly refurbished marital home, Clarence House. Two years earlier, King George VI, on the advice of his private secretary, had swiftly issued Letters Patent to say any child born to his eldest daughter would be known as Prince or Princess. As special decree published in the London gazette in November 1948 stated: "The children of Princess Elizabeth and the Duke of Edinburgh are to enjoy the style and titular dignity of Prince or Princess before their Christian names." Had this not been issued, the infant would have been known simply as Lady Anne Mountbatten and would not have been a princess until her mother acceded to the throne.

Philip adored his baby daughter. "It's the sweetest girl," he said ("with quite a definite nose for one so young," photographer Cecil

Beaton remarked cattily). She was twenty-one months younger than her brother, but later what she gave away in age she soon made up for in temper and physical determination.

Philip's eldest sister, Princess Margarita of Hohenlohe-Langenburg, was chosen as a godparent, as was his mother, Princess Alice, and his uncle, Dickie Mountbatten. From Princess Elizabeth's side her mother and the Rev. Andrew Elphinstone were chosen. For the first and last time, Philip's side outnumbered his wife's by three to two, indicating his status as the head of the family. The ceremony took place in the music room at Buckingham Palace on October 21, 1950—appropriately for Philip it was on the anniversary of the Battle of Trafalgar, one of the greatest naval victories in maritime history.

Philip had been promoted to the rank of lieutenant commander in the Royal Navy on the day Anne was born and given command of his own ship, the frigate HMS *Magpie*, so it was an auspicious day for him. He also helped choose the names Anne Elizabeth Alice Louise—and had registered her with the Westminster food office to get her the ration book that was still required in those austere postwar years.

Princess Elizabeth took some time to recover from the birth and spent the late summer at Balmoral before joining Philip in Malta for a holiday, leaving her baby daughter and her son to spend Christmas without them at Sandringham in the company of the ailing King, his Queen, and of course, the nannies. She also wanted to see the husband she saw so little of. The habit of separation was being established early—even before she ascended the throne.

His parents' long absences did at least give Charles the chance to get to know his only surviving grandfather, if only just: his one recollection of the last British emperor of India is of someone much bigger than himself sitting beside him on a sofa while his third birthday photograph was being taken. Even the ramrod-backed Queen

Mary unbent a little when he was with her. He had to bow to her when he was first ushered into Marlborough House, where she had resided since the death of George V. Although "Gan-Gan"—as he called her—was an intimidating presence, she let her great-grandson play with her collection of jade, a treat she had denied her children and granddaughters.

Philip took a more detached view of his son than of his daughter. He did not attend six of Charles's first eight birthdays. Nor was he welcome when he did make one of his rare ventures into the nursery. The staff there, led by nanny Lightbody, had taken against their mistress's consort. They disliked his dictatorial manner and what they saw as his bullying methods of child-rearing. They "ganged up on him" and went out of their way to protect their charges—Charles in particular—from their father.

"Nanny Lightbody saw through him," one member of the palace household recalled. She tried to avoid a direct confrontation with her employer but was never in any great hurry to carry out all of his instructions. Philip, for instance, wanted his son playing out of doors, regardless of the weather. Nanny, wary of Charles's chesty condition, would declare to her assistant, Miss Anderson, and the governess, Miss Peebles: "I'm not going to let him do that. I'm not going to have the responsibility. His father wants him to do it but I'm not allowing it: The Queen wouldn't like it."

For all the pomp and palaces, it was not an ideal environment for a little boy whose most noticeable characteristic, as everyone remarked, was his "sensitivity." He needed encouraging. "He was very responsive to kindness but if you shouted at him, he would draw back into his shell and you would be able to do nothing with him," Miss Peebles observed. He was always very subdued in the presence of his father, whose demands he found so hard to live up to and whose caustic dismissal of his childish qualms only served to further undermine his already delicate sense of self-worth.

Those long separations from his mother also had a noticeable effect on him. He found them, Talbot noted, "very upsetting and bewildering."

His more robust sister, on the other hand, quickly learned to take them in her independent stride, but then everything Anne did was marked by a self-reliance Charles could never match. His reticence irritated Philip, and father and son had a fractured relationship for the remainder of his formative years.

"A resilient character such as Philip, toughened by the slings and arrows of life, who sees being tough as a necessity for survival, wants to toughen up his son—and his son is very sensitive," Countess Mountbatten observed. "It hasn't been easy for either of them."

"He just can't resist coming out with these personal remarks," said Lady Kennard, a childhood friend of both Princess Elizabeth and Philip. "He's at his worst with Charles, but he could be quite sarcastic with Anne too."

Neither the absences nor his lack of sensitivity prevented Philip from being a decent father when he wanted to be. He taught his children to ride and rode along beside them when they learned to canter and encouraged them to learn to jump their ponies. When he saw how adept Anne was and how much better than her brother, he contacted Sir John Miller, Crown equerry and head of the Royal Mews at Buckingham Palace, and told him "to get on with it." Charles was still at the end of a leading rein when Anne was off galloping before she had even learned how to trot. Philip had no reservations about letting his daughter expose herself to the dangers inherent in equestrian sport. "It was almost as if he treated her as a son," one observer recalled. He also taught Charles to shoot and played bicycle polo with him.

When they were at Balmoral, he would take both Charles and Anne out in his Land Rover with sleeping bags and cooking equipment and spend the night in one of the many cabins on the estate. They would cook sausages over a fire and spend the night in their sleeping bags in a bothy built in Queen Victoria's day as a picnic hut. He also taught them to sail, which Anne loved, but Charles, who was often seasick, did not respond so well. Charles later recalled: "I remember one disastrous day when we went out racing and my father was, as usual, shouting. We wound the winch harder and the sail split in half with a sickening crack. Father was not pleased."

In 1956, Philip first made his views on the education of the heir to the throne public. "The Queen and I want Charles to go to school with other boys of his generation and learn to live with other children, and to absorb from childhood the discipline imposed by education and others," he said.

The fact that Charles turned out to be only an average scholar did not worry him as much as his son's lack of athletic ability. His daughter was better at everything and became a first-class tennis and lacrosse player and, most notably, an Olympic three-day event rider. He said that he would prefer his children weren't at the bottom of the class all the time, but somewhere around the middle would suit fine. In spite of the evidence to the contrary, Philip never accepted that he was a forceful father, telling his biographer Basil Boothroyd that the children were all encouraged to do their own thing as long as they stuck to it.

"From the beginning," he said. "I was careful not to make a rigid plan—I haven't for any of them—until some sort of foreseeable situation."

Prince Charles was a slow developer, and Philip was insistent that after his early education with a governess at home, he would be sent away to school. He concluded that the competition with other children his age would spur him on to do better, but the Queen thought Charles was better off being taught on his own. At the time, sending Charles away was considered a daring break from royal tradition, and it did not meet the approval of the palace old guard, most of whom had come to dislike Philip's decisions on a point of principle.

The first stage of what the Queen and Philip called the experiment went reasonably well though. On November 7, 1956, Prince Charles became the first heir to the British throne to go to school and was delivered to Hill House, the pre-preparatory school in Hans Crescent in Knightsbridge, run by Colonel Henry Townsend. Charles seems to have been reasonably happy there but preferred the comfort and safety of the palace he was driven home to every afternoon. Then even that lifeline of security was broken when Philip decided it was time he was sent away to boarding school, as he explained:

"When Charles first went to school one of the problems we were confronted with was, 'How do you select a prep school?' In the end, he went to Cheam where I had been. But this is something better understood in this country than almost anything else—that people very frequently do what their fathers have done. People say, 'Oh, he has gone because his father went.' "

Philip had also pointed out in an unguarded moment that Charles and his sister would always be different. "There's always this idea about treating them exactly like other children," he said. "It's all very well to say they're treated the same as everybody else, but it's impossible."

No matter how hard he tried to mingle, Charles always stood out. He had never learned to fend for himself, despite his father doing his best to teach him, and he had never had the opportunity to make friends. He would inevitably be singled out by the teachers, but also, more disconcertingly, by his contemporaries, who would all be told to treat the newcomer like everyone else, thus ensuring that they did not.

Charles hated Cheam. The Queen remembered him literally shuddering with apprehension on the journey there. He was only eight years old. "He felt the family separation very deeply," said nanny Mabel Anderson, who also remarked, "he dreaded going away to school." He was used to the coddled security of the matriarchal palace society of nannies and nursemaids and nursery footmen, and suddenly he was on his own, one of twelve lowly new boys in a school of more than a hundred pupils. It was for that exact reason that Philip had insisted he go away to school and face up to the burden of his position. On July 26, 1958, as his first full year approached, the Queen broadcast a message at the Commonwealth Games in Cardiff. She would have delivered the speech in person but for a bout of sinus trouble, and Prince Philip presided in her stead, so it was her prerecorded voice that Charles and some of the other boys were invited into the headmaster's study to hear.

The Queen's voice declared: "The British Empire and Commonwealth Games in the capital, together with all the activities of the Festival of Wales, have made this a memorable year for the Principality. I have therefore decided to mark it further by an act, which will, I hope, give as much pleasure to all Welshmen as it does to me. I intend to create my son, Charles, Prince of Wales today. When he is grown up, I will present him to you at Caernarvon."

With that title came a host of others. He was nine years and eight months, and according to Charles the whole thing produced a great sense of embarrassment at the grandiosity of his destiny. Philip would have none of that. He considered his son fortunate to have a path clearly mapped out for him, unlike when he was a child and had to struggle for everything while his family lived in exile in France.

*

Philip had already planned the next step in his son's education and claimed he discussed the pros and cons of a Gordonstoun versus an Eton education. Not unnaturally Charles, who was always anxious to please his father, agreed to the former although he expressed a preference for Charterhouse, where some of the friends he had finally made at Cheam were going. Philip, who had a dislike bordering on contempt for the British establishment and many of its elitist institutions, was not to be swayed. He felt that Gordonstoun's fresher and ostensibly more rounded approach to education was more suited to the latter part of the twentieth century than that offered by any of the longer-established schools. He was aware of his son's shyness and tendency toward self-effacement and was of the opinion that his alma mater, with its emphasis on self-reliance, would help mold Charles into being a more confident and self-assertive young man.

There was also the security advantage. If he went to Eton, Philip explained, "every time you hiccup, you'll have the whole of the national press on your shoulders. If you go to the north of Scotland you'll be out of sight." Discussions that included the Queen Mother, the Dean of Windsor, and Earl Mountbatten were, Philip considered, a waste of time. He brought them to an end by ruling that what was good enough for him was good enough for his son. Thus, the next educational wheels of the heir to the throne were set in motion.

In the cases of his other children's education Philip got it more or less right. His firstborn, on the other hand, had ample cause to lament his father's choice of school. As biographer of Charles's early life Dermot Morrah noted, "In effect the decision meant an attempt to mould him in his father's image to which . . . he did not naturally approximate."

Prince Charles loathed Gordonstoun. He found it hard to adapt to its austere environment, to rise to its athletic demands, and to make friends. Toughest of all for the young prince to bear was the attitude of the other boys. He was immediately picked upon "maliciously, cruelly and without respite," one fellow newcomer recalled.

For Charles's protection, cobwebbed rules started to be enforced and new ones were introduced, much to the chagrin of the four hundred boys already at the school. Smoking, in a school where corporal punishment had always been disavowed, became a caning offense. Drinking, while never previously condoned, now carried the threat of expulsion with it. Just as Britain was about to embark on the social revolution of the Swinging Sixties, Gordonstoun was making a determined effort to stop the clock.

These changes were enacted by the headmaster, Robert Chew, who had a glass eye that wandered off in disconcerting directions and who had been at the school since its inception. He took great pride in the honor of having the heir to the throne under his wing. The changes had nothing directly to do with Charles, but Charles was blamed and he was made to pay a cruel price. It's doubtful that Philip had any idea of what was going on, because Charles never confided the extent of his unhappiness to his abrasive father. Philip dutifully wrote to him encouraging him to "man up" and learn to be strong and resourceful, rather than sympathizing with his subdued state of mind.

It was impossible for Charles. One night one of the senior boys had the bright idea of making a tape recording of Prince Charles snoring. Having waited until he was asleep, several boys crept up to the open window of Charles's dormitory and lowered a microphone by an extension cable to just above his head. It was easy enough to do because Charles's bed was right next to one of the windows that by Gordonstoun regulations were always kept open.

The plan worked like a charm, and a little later that night the excited plotters listened gleefully to the loud snores of the future king on their tape recorders. Luckily for Charles, his housemaster heard about the escapade and confiscated the tape. But one boy swears he made a second tape recording taken from the original on his own machine. So somewhere in Britain, in the privacy of a drawer, lies a historic tape of Prince Charles snoring.

One of the old school retainers remembered Prince Philip's time there and said: "He is not at all like his father when he was here. Prince Philip was one of the wild boys. He got up to one or two tricks, I can tell you that."

Certainly, Prince Philip was remembered at Gordonstoun, not because he was a prince, but because he was a character in his own right. Without a doubt he had been "one of the lads"—the expression at the school to express the ultimate admiration. The duke was often referred to as a "good man" or a good "shade"—praiseworthy categories that sorted the wheat from the chaff in Gordonstoun terminology. Charles, of course, was told about his father's exploits at the school, and it seemed as though he was always trying to live up to the duke's great reputation, not by misbehaving and having adventures, but by striving to excel at everything he did.

Normally Charles had middle-of-the-road views and was never extreme about anything. He prepared his speeches diligently, but there were none of the quick flashes of inspired thought or sudden witty comments for which his father is famous. One of the rare occasions when Charles blossomed out occurred during the mock elections held at the school. Charles became a vociferous supporter of the Scottish Nationalists, and wearing his Stewart kilt, he marched up and down the grounds during the "campaign," shouting "Scotland forever," "Freedom for the Scots," and "Down with the rule from Whitehall." Together with his other political supporters, he held aloft a large banner saying, "Vote for the Scottish Nationalists."

During his time at Gordonstoun, Prince Charles took two terms off to attend Timbertop School in the outback of Australia. Afterward he told his pen friend Rosaleen Bagge he was very happy in Australia, perhaps happier there than he had ever been in his life. Finally, Prince Philip had done the right thing by his son, as it was his idea that Charles should go to Australia, and he assigned his equerry, Sir David Checketts, to stay nearby with his wife and family, to be available to smooth out any problems if they arose. Charles had accepted the idea with alacrity, even though the school was in the wilds of Victoria and had the reputation of being pretty tough. The view of everyone at Gordonstoun was that Charles was not happy with the type of education being meted out to him there and was looking forward to a change. Gordonstoun had very little to offer a boy of Charles's temperament and personality, and with his inward-looking and artistic nature and lack of interest in sport, maybe Charles would not have been happy at any boarding school.

At least at Gordonstoun he had his grandmother relatively nearby at Birkhall, and she was delighted to have her grandson join her there for weekends when she came north. What she wouldn't do, however, was intervene on his behalf, which he pleaded with her to do, to try to persuade his father to take him away from Gordonstoun. He was there, and there he was going to stay. "At least he hasn't run away yet," Philip replied when he was asked how he was getting on there. That kind of escape was never an option, as much as Charles dreamed of doing it. He was trapped; he had no choice except to get on with it and make of the situation what he could.

When he returned from Australia, he was made head of house and a term later Gordonstoun's equivalent of head boy: guardian. The radical experiment in the prince's education, as planned by his father, had come to its conclusion with the subject sitting high on top of the pile.

But what had been achieved and at what cost? He had learned how to keep his emotions in check, how always to present a brave face. But the little boy who cowered when his father raised his voice still lurked under the surface. He still talks about the humiliating day his parents came to Gordonstoun to see him perform extremely credibly in the role of Macbeth.

"I had to lie on a huge fur rug and have a nightmare," Prince Charles remembers. "I lay there and thrashed about and all I could hear was my father and ha ha ha. I went to him afterward and said, 'Why did you laugh?' and he said, 'It sounds like the Goons.'"

There was no way his father could turn Charles into the man he wanted him to be, in spite of putting him through the refined hardship of Gordonstoun and Timbertop. There was no way either Philip was going to admit that his insistence on sending him to Gordonstoun was a mistake or that Charles was going to step down from his stance that he had been "emotionally estranged" from his parents, who had been "unable or unwilling" to offer the kind of affection he craved.

As we have seen, it quickly became apparent that Princess Anne was a very different character to her brother. She was and still is her father's favorite, and as much as he bullied and belittled Charles and frequently reduced him to tears with his banter, his dominant sister took it all in her stride and, according to Charles's biographer Jonathan Dimbleby, Philip openly indulged her often brash and obstreperous behavior. The Queen, friends observed, was not so much indifferent as detached, deciding that in domestic matters she would submit entirely to her husband's will.

"He always had more fun with Anne," Eileen Parker observed. "Charles is more like the Queen, while Anne is very like Prince Philip." As Philip himself would later admit, "Perhaps I did spoil her at times."

"Anne would boss Charles; she would take command of things," recalled Mrs. Parker. "If she saw a toy she wanted, she would grab it. She also grabbed everything that Charles wanted—and everything he had she wanted, including attention from their father."

Philip paid more attention to his daughter than he did to his son because she was more responsive. He laughed with Anne in a way he never did with Charles. He made acerbic remarks to tease her, but she could deal with them, cheerfully braving his ridicule, saying anything she wanted, laughing back at him and with him, as she did when they were playing a game involving car number plates.

To keep the children amused on long car journeys, Philip would call out the registrations of passing vehicles and ask them to make a sentence out of the letters. One car had the number plate PMD.

"That's easy," said Anne. "Philip's my dad!"

He provided them with two pairs of boxing gloves and showed them the basic points of self-defense, which Charles had already learned from his time in the junior Pimlico gym. "They tore into each other and nearly killed each other," Philip explained afterward. There was no place for boxing gloves in the royal nursery after all, he decided.

Unlike Charles, Anne remembers her childhood as halcyon days of picnics, animals, and outdoor life in which they thrived on the relative freedom they had. She maintains her parents were supportive of most of the ideas they had and never really "quibbled" about whatever they wanted to do. Afterward they might suggest with a faint touch of sarcasm if things had gone wrong, that perhaps it wasn't really such a good idea.

Anne is as like her father as Charles is unlike. They are energetic, brisk, and efficient, and both like to fit in as much in a day as they possibly can. Anything else is a waste of time. Like her father, Anne gained a reputation as something of a flirt, and as a teenager former head coachman Steve Matthews remembers her being in one of the stables at the Mews in Windsor sharing a passionate kiss with a young groom. They were rolling about in the hay when her father appeared. Panic stricken, she signaled the groom to hide her, which he did by standing in front of the stable door so no one could enter or see inside. Luckily for them all, the duke moved on.

Philip was instrumental in steering the path of his daughter's education, but this time the Queen was more involved. Anne had started her education at Buckingham Palace with governess Miss Peebles along with two other girls to make up the numbers. Being such a self-assured child, Anne would have enjoyed a London day school, but both Philip and the Queen thought, quite correctly in retrospect, she would be better educated and get into less trouble at home. But by the age of twelve she had outgrown the schoolroom, and Philip gave her the opportunity of deciding if she would like to go to boarding school like her cousin Princess Alexandra, who had gone to Heathfield. She readily agreed, although she later admitted it would not have made any difference if she had said no.

After much discussion, Benenden School in Kent was deemed the most suitable place to send Anne. Friends had recommended the school, and it was close to Lord and Lady Rupert Nevill's Sussex home, Horsted Place. Rupert Nevill was a good friend of both Philip and the Queen and later became Prince Philip's treasurer and then private secretary until he died prematurely in 1982. They were very close friends, and if she needed to, Anne could make weekend visits, which she did in the beginning. Before a final decision was made, Philip, who knew little about girls' education, insisted on meeting the headmistress, Miss Elizabeth Clarke, and she was invited to lunch at Windsor Castle.

"I received an invitation to lunch and, realising it was not because of my scintillating conversation and sparkling personality, I guessed it might have something to do with education," she recalled when speaking to Anne's biographer Brian Hoey. "When I arrived at the castle there was just the family, the Queen, the Duke of Edinburgh,

Princess Anne and myself. But far from being a formal, uncomfortable occasion it turned out to be a pleasant easy meal of the sort that one might have enjoyed with the parents of any girl who was being thought of as a prospective parent."

Anne remembers the occasion. "When I met the headmistress for the first time she said, 'We do not encourage hippomania [a passion for horses].' My father turned to me and said, 'That does not mean you're mad on hippos.'"

A few days later Miss Clarke received a telephone call from the Queen informing her that it had been decided to send Princess Anne to Benenden, if she was acceptable. Anne was excused the formality of an entrance exam after Miss Clarke had spoken to the princess's tutors at Buckingham Palace and they assured her the princess was up to the academic standard.

In September 1963, the Queen traveled with Anne on the royal train from Balmoral and then drove to Kent from London. The car was late arriving, which was embarrassing for Anne as the three hundred pupils and forty staff lined the drive to welcome their new colleague. Apparently Princess Anne was so nervous at the prospect of her new school, she had been physically sick on the way, which explained the delay. Nothing was known about this until later, when Miss Clarke found out about it by accident and cited it as an example of the extraordinary discipline the princess had learned even at the age of thirteen.

Anne was as much her father's daughter as Charles was the polar opposite. She admits she didn't fit the image of a princess and could be as rude and abrasive as her father. "It's difficult to take an intelligent interest in something and wear a grin," she has said by way of excuse for her glum expressions. She also has his excess of energy and hatred of sitting around doing nothing.

When she left school after five years, she had a difficult time. She had few friends, no boyfriends, and was not sure what she wanted to do. Philip realized the problem with his surly teenage daughter and spoke to some of his polo-playing friends who had children of a similar age. The invitations to parties flooded in and Anne began to enjoy a normal teenage life. She has Philip's dedication to do a job well and see it through. She is a very hard worker, incredibly brave, and not particularly imaginative, just like her father. She has his good qualities as well as his bad and throughout the next stages of her life maintained her close bond with him.

Looking back at the lives of his elder two children, Prince Philip did his best as a parent. He had been raised within a close family himself, but they provided little stability. His father did not have a job or provide a home, and the family quickly dispersed.

I remember talking to Diana, the late Princess of Wales, about what she called Charles's "emotional retentiveness," which she put down to his childhood. Diana reckoned that if Charles had been brought up in the normal fashion, he would have been better able to handle his and her emotions. Instead, she said, his feelings seemed to have been suffocated at birth. According to her, he never had any hands-on love from his parents. Only his nannies showed him affection, but that, as Diana explained, was not the same as being kissed and cuddled by your parents, which Charles never was. When he met his parents, they didn't embrace: they shook hands. Because of his upbringing he couldn't be tactile with his own wife. She said, "The only thing he learned about love was shaking hands."

The Windsor men are notorious for their short fuses and Charles was no exception. When he was angry with Diana, he would shout at her, scream and throw things, and didn't seem to be able to control himself. He would always apologize afterward, and Diana put it down to the way he had been so thoroughly spoiled as a little boy. So according to Diana, Philip was not a particularly good parent. At that time the Queen was so busy with affairs of state she had to leave much of the upbringing of their eldest to Philip, and he left it to the nannies.

Being far tougher and of a completely different disposition, Princess Anne failed to notice the lack of tactile love. She had all the affection she wanted from her father and couldn't understand Charles whinging about his childhood, which she considered very happy. But her first husband, Captain Mark Phillips, suffered because of Anne's emotional coldness and told Diana he never knew what was going to happen. During their divorce he said it was particularly difficult because Anne never bothered to tell him anything at all.

Chapter 10

THE MIDDLE YEARS

When Mike Parker resigned in 1957 after ten years as Philip's closest friend and confidant, it was the end of an era. He was, of course, replaced as equerry and private secretary, but no one outside the royal family ever became so close to Philip. On February 22, Prime Minister Harold Macmillan told the cabinet that he had proposed to the Queen that her husband should be given "the style and dignity of a Prince of the United Kingdom" and she had accepted.

The palace issued an announcement in which the Queen stated she was "pleased to declare her will and pleasure" in announcing that "His Royal Highness the Duke of Edinburgh shall henceforth be known as His Royal Highness the Prince Philip, Duke of Edinburgh." The new title, the announcement continued, was "in recognition of the affection in which the people held him and of his services to the nation and the Commonwealth."

The sniping at Philip stopped. Instead of being regarded as an irksome responsibility, he began to be seen as what he always was—an invaluable asset to the monarchy, helping to support the Queen as she shaped her role in a less reverential age. Although Philip's popularity was on the up, the institution of the monarchy would come in for an enormous amount of press criticism during the 1960s and '70s, especially about the cost of keeping a family who appeared to do very little.

During the ensuing twenty years, Philip's impatience and enjoyment of attractive female company did not prevent the marriage from evolving into a solid and understanding one. They had their difficulties, but whatever was lacking in their marriage, respect for each other was not. They appeared to enjoy being together as much as they were content to often travel and live apart. The Queen knew that in order to keep Philip happy, she had to give him as much freedom as she could. She came from the old school of marriage, which believed that, unlike today, a husband has the right to his own personal freedom and there is no point in trying to control him more than necessary. As with so many marriages, theirs was held together through its awkward moments by his wife's patience, tolerance, and ability to deal with a difficult man. It was fortunate for her husband that Elizabeth believed that a man should be master in his own home and to recall that in their wedding vows ten years before she had promised to love *and* obey.

In private, the Queen has always deferred to her husband. At formal meals, protocol demanded that she presided over the royal table. In private, she gave up her place to her husband. On family decisions, she gave way to him—sometimes against her better judgment. But within the family circle Philip was boss. "I'll see what Philip thinks," she told friends before deciding to do anything concerning their personal life. They had what many would consider a very old-fashioned marriage.

"It's a waste of time trying to change a man's character," she once told a friend. "You have to accept him as he is." And she did.

When the Queen was in her early thirties. she said, "There is nothing worse than trying to fence a man in and stop him from doing what he wants." But she had her own wifely wiles. When Queen Juliana of the Netherlands asked her, "What do you do when Philip wants something and you don't want him to have it?"

"Oh, I just tell him he will have it and see that he doesn't," she replied.

After ten years of marriage, she had the measure of her husband far more than he would have cared to acknowledge. Their private message to each other when events separated them was this simple verse from the Old Testament: "The Lord watch between thee and me when we are absent from one another."

Among the numerous royal tours undertaken by the couple was an important North American trip in October 1957, where the impact of the duke and the Queen as a young and energetic royal couple was an instant success. The trip was significant coming in the aftermath of the Suez crisis and an unprovoked attack on the Queen by Lord Altrincham, in which he undermined the very Britishness of the monarch and her upper-class way of speaking. After taking part in Virginia's 350th anniversary celebrations, they arrived in New York City, where, according to the *Daily Mirror*, "more than 600,000 wildly cheering Americans hailed the Queen as the 'Belle of New York' as they drove through a storm of ticker tape in a brilliant climax to the American tour." They were both taken aback by what they saw as the American insecurity and need to be liked and the enormous weight of the responsibilities of the president of the United States, a feeling which remained with them throughout the ensuing years of eleven presidents.

Philip took on more and more worthy causes and military positions, which together ran into hundreds, while he helped his wife come to terms with the modern age of television, in particular her early

Christmas broadcasts. The words were supposed to be her own, and eventually they were, but in the very beginning suggestions were made to her, with the final draft being Philip's.

"The most difficult thing in the world," a BBC official said, "is to give a personal message, that is in fact not personal." But it worked as Philip, knowing her better than anyone else, knew exactly how to phrase the words of her speech. His ability to make his wife laugh before she went on air was again invaluable, as it improved her performance and made her more relaxed with all the technicians and production staff involved. The rehearsals for the 1957 broadcast, the first to be televised, began in early October, when legendary producer Antony Craxton and his team arrived at the state dining room in Buckingham Palace to begin work on the presentation. The Queen walked in at three o'clock as planned and promptly froze. Peter Dimmock, the head of the BBC's outside broadcasting, recalled how the Queen kept on telling him, "I am not an actress." He added: "She was not and the first two takes were less than encouraging. Prince Philip came in and suggested a few alterations to the script. It helped—but not much, and every time the Queen started to speak nerves pushed her voice up a couple of octaves."

Eventually, it was Prince Philip who saved the day. When the Queen entered the library at Sandringham, where the live broadcast was to take place, he remained in the room throughout, watching on a spare camera on the reserve circuit. He told a silly joke, and the Queen at last relaxed and managed to do what Dimmock had been trying to get her to do for weeks—smile naturally for the cameras.

The message was a resounding success when it was broadcast at 3 p.m. Instead of the gushing sycophancy often attached to the royal family, it was a positive story. The *New York Times* and the *New York Herald* published the text of the broadcast in full, and London's *Daily Mirror* reported the Queen spoke with "easy friendliness," which showed the monarchy still had an important part to play in the fast-changing world. Prince Philip took no credit. He considered that helping his wife over the hurdle of doing a live television broadcast for the first time was part of the role he had chosen to play when he married her. Whatever other husbandly attributes he might have lacked, loyalty was not one of them.

Early in 1959, the Queen became pregnant for the third time, but it was decided to delay the announcement until after their planned six-week tour of Canada. When it came, it took the world by surprise as Prince Charles was eleven and Princess Anne nearly ten, and it became a talking point as to why they would choose to increase their family after such a long gap. The Queen confided to friends that she was delighted and had wanted this pregnancy very much as she and Philip had been trying for another baby for quite some time.

Shortly after the baby boy was born on February 19, 1960, Philip's mother arrived in England and was able to visit the infant at Buckingham Palace. She was thrilled he was to be called Andrew. When she was back in Greece, she wrote to her son saying: "I am so happy about papa's name being given to the baby. The people's delight here about this is really touching." She wrote of unknown people waving to her in the streets, calling out her husband's name. She continued, "He is not forgotten and still much loved."

The pregnancy once again raised the thorny issue of the family name that had so upset Philip in 1952. The Queen had "absolutely set her heart on a change" and wanted to get it sorted for once and all to appease her husband and his uncle Lord Mountbatten. A double-barreled name, including his, for the future generations was therefore proposed. The matter was discussed in the cabinet and it was revealed that "those members of the royal family who would have to use a surname because they were no longer entitled to be called a prince or princess should use the name Mountbatten-Windsor."

On February 8, 1960, eight years after her Accession Council, the

Queen finally issued a new declaration of her "will and pleasure." "While I and my children will continue to be styled and known as the House and Family of Windsor my descendants, other than descendants enjoying the style, title or attributes of Royal Highness and the titular dignity of Prince and Princess, and other female descendants who marry and their descendants, shall bear the name Mountbatten-Windsor."

Just before the birth of Prince Andrew, Buckingham Palace announced that Princess Margaret was to marry a commoner, the photographer Antony Armstrong-Jones. There was much tutting among the royal court about his suitability for the princess, but Philip was not part of the spiteful backchat and preferred to keep an open mind. Although Antony Armstrong-Jones and Philip were completely different characters, Philip always welcomed newcomers into the family, remembering his own early difficulties. As a young man and budding photographer, Tony had briefly worked in Philip's friend photographer Baron Nahum's studio as a jobbing assistant. By 1956, his talent proven, he had photographed the Queen and Philip with Prince Charles and Princess Anne in the gardens of Buckingham Palace.

Although he irritated Philip, who used to swear and shout at him when he was late for a shooting party—which he invariably was—he liked him well enough. Tony was amusing and took care to familiarize himself with the complicated royal etiquette as a matter of politeness. In one of his early letters to Armstrong-Jones, Philip had an arrow pointing at the signature "Philip" with the words "try and bring yourself to call me this!"

Princess Margaret could also infuriate Philip, who found her behavior exasperating. However, mindful of his wife's love for her younger sister, he put up with Margaret's various exploits, taking neither one side nor another, again preferring to keep out of any controversy. If proof of his loyalty to his sister-in-law were needed, Philip accompanied Princess Margaret down the aisle on her wedding day on Friday May 6, 1960. It was the first royal wedding to be broadcast on television and was later estimated to have had 300 million viewers tuning in around the world.

Philip rode with the princess from Clarence House to Westminster Abbey in the glass coach, taking care not to crush her silk organza dress, with more than 30 yards (30 meters) of fabric in the full skirt alone, designed by favorite royal couturier Norman Hartnell. Before they left, he paced up and down along the wide corridor of Clarence House, chivvying Margaret to hurry up as, being a naval man, he hated the thought of being late even by a few seconds. As the fanfare of trumpets heralded their arrival at the Great West Door of the abbey, Philip turned to her and whispered, "Don't know who is more nervous, you or me?" adding, "Am I holding on to you or are you holding on to me?"

"I am holding on to you," the princess replied.

"The morning was brilliant," recalled Noël Coward, who attended the service, "and the crowds lining the streets looked like endless, vivid herbaceous borders." He went on in his flamboyant style, "The police were smiling, the Guards beaming and the air tinged with excitement and the magic of spring." He then changed his tone and noted, "The Queen alone looked disagreeable; whether or not this was concealed sadness or bad temper because Tony Armstrong-Jones had refused an earldom, nobody seems to know but she did scowl a good deal."

The playwright noted that Prince Philip was "jocular and really very sweet and reassuring as he led the bride to the altar," and described the atmosphere: "The music was divine and the fanfare immensely moving. Nowhere in the world but England could such pomp and circumstance and pageantry be handled with such exquisite dignity. There wasn't one note of vulgarity or anything approaching it in the whole thing. . . . It is still a pretty exciting thing to be English."

At Princess Margaret and Anthony Armstrong-Jones's Buckingham Palace wedding breakfast after the ceremony, Philip was chosen to make one of the speeches to the assembled company of 120 people in the ball supper room. As an already experienced speaker, he was able to be both witty and amusing and most important brief. He welcomed Tony as the newest member of the family, to which Tony replied equally briefly before he and Margaret cut their 6-foot-(1.8-meter)-tall wedding cake.

A year later, in March 1961, during a tour of India, the Queen and Philip took part in a tiger hunt that caused a wave of press criticism. Organized by the Maharajah of Jaipur in the Sawai Madhopur game reserve, it was no photographic safari. On the second day, the royal treasurer Rear Admiral Bonham Carter shot a tiger, while Philip—photographed by his wife from 10 yards (9 meters) away— shot a tigress. The tigress measured 8 feet 9 inches (2.67 meters) from head to tail and was skinned and cured, ready to be taken back to Buckingham Palace as a trophy at the end of the visit.

The shoot was followed by another game expedition producing a bag that included a crocodile and a Nepal rhino, whose killing apparently orphaned a calf. "The Kill" made headline news in the British press and brought protests from wildlife experts. The rhino was killed by the then foreign secretary, the Earl of Home—who had apparently missed the tigress with four shots. The Queen and Prince Philip are seen in the background of the photograph on their "howdah"—an elephant-back passenger box. This time, much to his annoyance, Philip could not take part because of an injured trigger finger. The shooting trips were intended as an honor, but unfortunately the criticism of the shoot got more coverage than all other aspects of the successful trip. Demands were made for the Queen to exclude what they called "elements of unnecessary barbarism" from future tours.

It was particularly unfortunate for Prince Philip, who was about to become involved in the World Wildlife Fund at the instigation of his old friend Peter Scott. In July, Scott took the proposals to Philip and asked him if he would become president of the British National Appeal for the World Wildlife Fund International, which would be based in Switzerland. Philip, without any apparent pangs of conscience (ten years later the tiger population of India had dropped by such an alarming rate that the WWF had to invest almost $100,000 in Mrs. Gandhi's scheme to prevent extinction), immediately started giving lectures about people killing things and saying the wildlife of the world was in crisis. He admitted he had no idea "that all sorts of wild animal species are dying out . . . man is the crux of the situation . . . we should be able to control our own involuntary actions."

Prince Philip's dislike of the press is well documented, but he had no qualms in using them to get his views across when he needed to. In November 1957, when he arrived back from a solo South American tour, he wrote an editorial in the *Daily Mirror* and told industrial leaders in London: "There is no getting away from it, at the moment we have a reputation for being rather slow and rather old-fashioned." He added that in South America people say of Britain, "You don't seem to have anything to offer now."

Relations with the once reverential press had changed, and Prince Philip was goaded into calling the *Daily Express*—the biggest-selling newspaper of the time and one that charted the royal visits—"a bloody awful newspaper." His controversial views made him an entertaining speaker. At a lunch for the Foreign Press Association in February 1964, forty-three-year-old Philip was the star of a question-and-answer session. He was asked if he thought the monarchy had found its proper place in the Britain of the 1960s and if it had found the right approach to the problems of the day.

"What you are implying is that we are rather old fashioned. Well, it may easily be true. I do not know," Philip replied. "One of the things about the monarchy and its place—and one of its great weaknesses in a sense—is that it has to be all things to all people. Of course, it cannot do this when it comes to being all things to all people who are iconoclasts. We therefore find ourselves in a position of compromise and we might be kicked on both sides. . . . I entirely agree that we are old fashioned: the monarchy is an old-fashioned institution. The interesting thing is that it is not a monopoly of old people."

Asked whether he thought fame was an asset or a liability in life, he smilingly answered: "That is rather an awkward one. Without indulging in false modesty, I think the questioner is asking the wrong person. I do not consider myself to be famous. As you know, I may be notorious . . . and whether or not it is an asset to be notorious and well known, that cuts both ways. In some cases, it is helpful and, in some cases, it is rather trying. That's as far as I can go."

It was typical of Philip, turning the question on its head and then providing the answer he wanted to give. He was a quick thinker and a modernist, and although he kept it well hidden, a surprisingly sensitive man.

A month later, on March 10, 1964, this soft caring side to Philip's normally abrasive character was demonstrated when he stayed at his wife's side while she gave birth to their third son, and he kept the medical team cheerful during the wait. Philip then telephoned the news to the Queen Mother, and Princess Margaret and Princess Anne, who was by now at Benenden School. He also telephoned Prince Charles, hoping to cheer him with the news. There were worries that Prince Charles, at the age of fifteen, was unhappy at his school on the Moray Firth. His loneliness had been made worse when he contracted pneumonia after a camping trip with a party of Gordonstoun boys on the Balmoral estate and he was obliged to spend ten days at the Walzon-Fraser nursing home in Aberdeen. Unaware at the time of the extent of his eldest son's unhappiness, Prince Philip continually wrote to him, but instead of being sympathetic to his plight, he told him to be strong and basically grow up and man up. He took Charles's reluctance to talk about his school life as a young man being secretive and decided, for once, it was not his place to interfere.

In May, a ten-day state visit to Germany provided Philip with the opportunity to take the Queen to Wolfsgarten, a former home from home for him, and they then spent the weekend at Salem with his sister Theodora and were entertained by Margarita at Langenburg. The year had been a rare family get-together for Philip, as his mother had joined him, the Queen, Charles, Anne, Andrew, and Dickie Mountbatten for a review of the Home Fleet in the Clyde and he spent most of the summer at Balmoral. "Dear Bubby-kins," his mother wrote to Philip, using her favorite term of endearment, "you don't know how happy you have made me this summer and I am so sad it was over so quickly."

On September 18, 1964, it was Philip's turn to represent the Queen, in Athens at the wedding of the young King Constantine of the Hellenes and Princess Anne-Marie of Denmark. He took Prince Charles and Princess Anne with him since Anne was to be the chief of five bridesmaids and Prince Charles a crown holder.

Although Prince Philip spent much of his life two steps behind his wife, he sometimes paved the way for her more sensitive, immediate visits, where her presence was either too politically sensitive or, in the case of disasters, could hamper any rescue efforts by deflecting attention from the immediate problems.

In January 1965, an event of great significance took place—
ninety-year-old Sir Winston Churchill, the Queen's first prime
minister, died. When he had been taken ill ten years before, plans
code-named Operation "Hope Not" were put in place for a full
state funeral. They were immediately activated, and during the
lying-in-state at Westminster Hall, the Queen, accompanied by
Prince Philip, became the first reigning monarch to pay public homage to a commoner. Together with Princess Margaret and Lord
Snowdon, as Armstrong-Jones was now known, they entered the
east door of Westminster Hall just before 8 p.m., while crowds
continued to file past the catafalque bearing Sir Winston Churchill's
coffin. All four stood in silence for about five minutes, mostly unnoticed by the crowd. In this somber moment, Philip saw it as his duty
to stand just behind the Queen and her sister and stepped slightly
back to take his place with Lord Snowdon.

On October 21, 1966, a slag heap collapsed engulfing a school in
the mining town of Aberfan in South Wales and killing 146 people, mostly children. Philip galvanized his office to get him there
as quickly as possible along with the prime minister and his
brother-in-law Lord Snowdon. Six days later he returned with the
Queen, and they spent two and a half hours with the villagers and
rescue workers. Together they climbed over broken planks, cor-
rugated iron, and poignantly shattered desktops to the top of the
slag covering the school. The Queen then placed a wreath at the
cemetery where eighty-one children had been buried, and she and
Philip walked to the house of Councillor Jim Williams, who lost
seven relatives in the disaster, to take tea and listen to his tale of the
disaster. The Queen was moved to a rare show of public distress,
especially after a little girl presented her with some flowers and she
gently took them, some say shedding a tear. Sometime later she said
it was one of her great regrets that she didn't go to Aberfan sooner,

but at the time she thought her high-profile presence at the disaster site would hinder the rescue efforts.

Philip was at his best at these kinds of occasions, which the Queen found difficult and distressing. His support was invaluable both emotionally and physically, and most important he enabled her to show royalty as caring, available, and in touch. The question of the monarchy being in touch instead of being seen as an archaic institution was always on Philip's mind. He had plenty of opposition to his ideas, particularly from his mother-in-law, the Queen Mother, who wanted to keep everything as it had been during her husband's lifetime. The Queen saw the need for change and modernization, but she also wanted to keep her mother happy, so Philip's task was not easy.

In 1968, an opportunity arose that suited Philip's ideas for popularizing and modernizing the monarchy through the medium of television. During a weekend at the Norfolk home of Lord Buxton, he was approached by Dickie Mountbatten's son-in-law, Lord Brabourne, with an idea of making a behind-the-scenes television documentary about the royal family. Philip liked the idea since he knew there was "nothing between the court circular and the gossip columns" and felt it was time for the monarchy to meet the medium of television on its own terms. When the discussions became serious, he insisted the Queen should be consulted before it went any further. Surprisingly, she was not averse to the idea on one condition to which the BBC had to agree. If she didn't like the film, the entire thing would be canned. Richard Cawston, head of the documentary department of the BBC, was suggested as director, and it was agreed the BBC were to be allowed to spend a year recording the activities of the family at home and abroad, including recording unrehearsed conversations.

It was a major breakthrough, with Prince Philip not only being part of the filming but chairing the joint BBC–ITV advisory committee set up to monitor the project. He saw the role of the film as one that would create a favorable impression of the monarchy and give the illusion of being less mysterious by merging private family life with public performances. It would also appear to allow the camera to eavesdrop on private conversations. Eventually forty-three hours of film was condensed to a one-and-a-half-hour program shown on June 21, 1969, and watched by more than half the British population.

"It wasn't a soap," Brabourne said. "It was a matter of conveying these people as human beings." To an extent it did, and it showed the Queen as quick and humorous, on the rare moments she appeared to be at ease; Prince Philip as energetic and impatient, but kind; and Charles as awkward as Anne was confident.

Prince Philip liked the result and seemed pleased with his part in getting such a groundbreaking idea off the ground. He wanted a practical rather than just a symbolic justification for the monarchy and its cost, which he knew was a bone of contention with successive governments. He believed the film helped pave the way to understanding that the monarchy was a workday business and its figurehead was just doing a job.

"I think it is quite wrong that there should be a sense of remoteness about majesty," Philip said when asked about the film. "If people see, whoever it happens to be, whatever head of state, as individuals as people, I think it makes it much easier for them to accept the system or to feel part of the system."

The film had its critics, and many to this day believe it "started the rot" by offering an intimacy never previously provided and leaving the public and the press hungry for more. Some even said the film encouraged the discarding of any remaining restraint.

"The sight of Prince Philip cooking sausages meant that after that people would want to see the dining room, the sitting room and everything except the loo," said historian Kenneth Rose, who subscribed to the "started the rot" theory. Prince Philip's opinion was if it hadn't happened, then it would have been even more difficult to control in the future, but the film was only ever shown once again.

Prince Philip's search for ways to make the monarchy more accessible and its privileges acceptable to the ordinary person had been successful, although they did not always meet with universal approval from the old guard at the palace. William Heseltine, the Queen's new, ambitious private secretary, proved an invaluable ally. During the antipodean tour in early 1970, he was the instigator of the "walkabout," a term previously used to describe the wanderings of the Australian bushmen.

The film about the royal family had done its job: to the people of Australia and New Zealand, the Queen was no longer just a lady on the postage stamp, but she drove a car, barbecued with her husband, loved dogs and horses, and was humorous. It was clearly a moment to move things forward, and on the way to Wellington's city hall for the 200th anniversary celebration of Captain Cook's voyage, the Queen and Philip took a casual and apparently unscheduled walk down the street, talking with onlookers. The famous *Daily Mail* reporter Vincent Mulchrone coined the phrase "walkabout" when describing the scene, and it became part of the royal repertoire.

The Queen, who has always found certain types of public appearances a strain due to her inherent shyness, relied heavily on Philip's support in the early days of walkabouts. Partly because he was inclined to walk so quickly, but mostly because he couldn't wait to get it over, he was never far from her in the crowds.

She relied on him again when, together with Prince Charles, they paid a visit to the ailing Duke of Windsor at his residence on the Bois de Boulogne in Paris during their 1972 state visit to France. The duke was terminally ill with cancer, and the idea of the visit was to allow the Queen to see her favorite uncle before he died, rather than a carefully crafted gesture of reconciliation, as suggested by the press. When the Queen was shown to his upstairs sitting room, she found him in an armchair, wearing a blazer, having told his doctor he wanted to see his niece "Lilibet" without what he called "the damn rigging" of needles and tubes. She chatted brightly to the dying old man for half an hour, and then she bade him goodbye and joined Prince Philip and Prince Charles in the library, where they were having tea with the duchess.

"The Duke put on an incredibly courageous performance," the doctor, who was present throughout, noted. "Between them, they carried it off in the best tradition of the stiff upper lip." Ten days later, the Duke of Windsor died.

Six days before the Queen and Prince Philip celebrated their twenty-sixth wedding anniversary on November 20, Princess Anne married Captain Mark Phillips in Westminster Abbey on November 14, 1973. At a time when the country was looking at the worst economic crisis for decades, and the royal family was being criticized for its cost, the wedding was at last some good news for the nation. Prince Philip rode with his daughter in the glass coach to the abbey, as he had done for Princess Margaret thirteen years before. According to lip readers, as he walked her down the aisle, he asked her if she was nervous, and typically, she replied, "No, of course not."

As the father of the bride, Prince Philip made the first speech at the wedding breakfast held in the ball supper room of Buckingham Palace. He struck just the right note: "Unaccustomed as I am . . . ," he began, and then after a theatrical pause, "to speaking at breakfast . . ."

*

A year before, it had been the Queen's turn to make the speech, at a celebratory luncheon given by the City of London at the Guildhall to celebrate their twenty-five years of marriage. "On such a day," she said, with Prince Philip smiling at her side, "the speech really should start with 'My husband and I.'" Everyone roared with approval.

Also at the table were the Archbishop of Canterbury and his wife, Mrs Ramsey. So, turning toward him to give her definition of married life, the Queen said: "When the bishop was asked what he thought about sin, he replied with simple conviction that he was against it. If I am asked today what I think about family life after twenty-five years of marriage I can answer with equal simplicity and conviction: I am for it."

The Queen then said that she and Prince Philip had attended the service beforehand at Westminster Abbey—the scene of their wedding—"with the spirit of real thanksgiving for our good fortune." Afterward she expressed her thanks during a walkabout with her family at the Barbican, talking to children and office workers while confetti poured down from the newly built tower blocks.

That evening there was a private party at Buckingham Palace for two hundred guests, arranged by Prince Charles and Princes Anne with the help of Lady Elizabeth Anson, the Queen's cousin. Outside it was miserable and raining, just as it had been on their wedding day, but there was still a crowd to watch guests arriving—including members of European royal families—and to give a special cheer for the Queen Mother. Inside, a classical concert opened the evening, but after dinner the dancing took over with a live band and a relatively new innovation for private parties—a disco for the younger guests.

The first jubilee of significance was the Silver Jubilee of 1977, which proved a resounding success despite the Queen and Prince Philip's initial reservations and the Queen's perpetual worry that no one would turn out to see them. At the time, the state of the British economy was the worst since the ending of the war: there were 1.3 million unemployed and the rate of inflation was at 16 percent.

Prince Philip added his voice to the controversy about the state of the nation in an article written for the *Director* magazine when he said: "People are slowly coming round to the feeling that we have been driven too far along one road; that we have got to come back a little and not concentrate so heavily on the unfortunate, the under-privileged, but try to create a situation whereby the enterprising can make their contribution." His remarks were not popular, and many considered the Prince had behaved unconstitutionally by making an intrusion into politics.

Anniversaries and jubilees are an inevitable part of royal life, and Prince Philip is not a fan of the latter. In 2002, however, during the Golden Jubilee, he would write to an acquaintance from 16 Squadron, "The Jubilee has been a most interesting experience," and "it's impossible not to be stimulated by the enthusiasm of the crowds."

So much had changed in the world, but their lives and the institution they represented had remained relatively the same. An era had gone from Doris Day and Vera Lynn to the Sex Pistols; from the age where pregnancy wasn't mentioned or shown to the age of satire and loss of deference. The reverence of the past was fading— as was the willingness to take official information about the royal family on trust.

It was not dissimilar to today: at the start of a new decade, when the Queen's family are the subject of intense criticism, she remains above all conscientious, dignified, patriotic, unaffected, and wise.

Whatever Prince Philip's feelings, he seldom lets them show. His quips and witty asides were designed to alleviate boredom, his and that of those whom he was talking to. In his younger days, he was far too considered and controlled to offend, he was just using his quick wit, and on most occasions the recipient was as amused as he was. As he got older, he cared less and could be offensive, but at the end of each day he was the only person with whom the Queen could truly share her feelings, whether they were good, bad, or indifferent. Possibly she too was the only person whose feelings concerned him. Her happiness and the respect people showed her have been supremely important to him. When an estimated crowd of a million people filled the Mall to see the gold state coach take them from Buckingham Palace to St Paul's Cathedral for the Silver Jubilee service, he knew the boredom, the frustrations, and the fatigue had been worthwhile.

Chapter 11

ANDREW AND EDWARD

Like his father, Prince Andrew was outgoing, curious, confident, and competitive as a child. Prince Philip's relationship with his second son was complex and sometimes difficult, perhaps because they were superficially so similar.

According to the late Gina Lady Kennard, Prince Andrew's godmother, "The Queen and Prince Philip were good parents. Always interested in their children and always actively involved. He used to read them stories, play with them go fishing—the lot." By modern standards, that doesn't say much, but they were considered good parents at a time when children of the aristocracy were still consigned to the care of nannies and only saw their parents when it was convenient to them.

The Queen and Philip had been married for almost twelve years when the Queen became pregnant with Prince Andrew. It can hardly have been planned because the crucial second and third months of her pregnancy coincided with an exhaustive tour of Canada in the summer of 1959.

As Philip once said: "People want their first child very much.

They want their second almost as much. If a third comes along they accept it as natural, even if they haven't gone out of their way to try for it."

Against all advice, the Queen insisted the tour should go ahead (in the late 1950s pregnancy was looked upon very differently than it is today), and the only precaution she took was to take an extra seamstress to let out her clothes should it be necessary. She was dutifully determined to do everything the Canadians had asked of her and attended function after function, flying from St. John's to Gander, Gander to Deer Lake, Deer Lake to Stephenville, Stephenville to Schefferville, becoming increasingly tired in the process.

Prince Philip was worried about his wife and he became ever more belligerent. When one journalist reported that the Queen looked "tired and strained," Philip sought him out and berated him in no uncertain terms. Philip's anxiety about his wife made him more aggressive and outspoken than usual, and he criticized Ontario's "obsolete and old fashioned" liquor laws and took it upon himself to lecture the Canadian Health Association on the state of the "sub health" he said existed in Canada. Not surprisingly, neither comments were well received.

Philip's anxieties were better understood by the traveling royal physician, Captain Steele-Perkins, and after a serious discussion the two men agreed to put pressure on the Queen to alter the schedule. She finally agreed and canceled a planned trip to Dawson City, letting Philip go alone. He then went on to Yellowknife and Uranium City while she remained in bed. In the 1950s, royal pregnancy was still a very personal matter, and the royal couple decided not to divulge any information as to why the Queen was so tired. When they eventually arrived home, royal physicians Lord Evans and Sir John Weir ordered the Queen to rest before she traveled to Balmoral for the summer break.

A brief official announcement was made, saying only that the

Queen would be undertaking no further public engagements in the foreseeable future.

In the early evening of February 18, 1960, the Queen retired to her bed in the Belgian suite overlooking the lake at the back of Buckingham Palace. Prince Philip, playing the dutiful husband, canceled his evening engagement so he could be close at hand if the baby was born. The two of them had a light supper—Philip from an old-fashioned trolley by the bed and the Queen from a tray—and he went to bed early.

At about ten o'clock Philip went upstairs to the royal apartment and told his valet, "I think we'll get another good night's rest tonight." He was right—it wasn't until 3:30 p.m. the following afternoon that the baby was born. Philip was in his study, not at the Queen's bedside, when Lord Evans brought him news of the birth. He was euphoric and ran downstairs to see his wife, calling to anyone who cared to listen, "It's a boy!"

The new Prince was christened Andrew Albert Christian Edward after his grandfather Prince Andrew of Greece, his great-grandfather King Edward VII, and his great-great-grandfather Christian IX of Denmark. Most important to Philip, he was the first child to have the surname of the royal family—Mountbatten-Windsor. Shortly before Andrew was born, the Queen, in recognition of the valuable service of Prince Philip as consort and head of the family, decreed, "While I and my children shall continue to be styled and known as the House and family of Windsor, my descendants shall bear the name Mountbatten-Windsor."

As a father, Prince Philip wasn't quite the severe paternal taskmaster he is sometimes painted as, and he did not impose his views on any of his children.

"It's no good saying, do this, do that, don't do this, don't do that," he said. "It's very easy when children want to do something to say no immediately. I think it's quite important not to give an unequivocal answer at once. Much better to think it over. Then if you eventually say no, I think they really accept it."

There were not many noes in Andrew's young life. As with most parents, the Queen and Prince Philip's theories about bringing up children had been tempered by experience, and Andrew enjoyed a far more carefree infancy than either Charles or Anne had.

He was also spared the public appearances the elder children had had to endure. In a conscious reversal of the policy they had adopted with Charles and Anne, Prince Philip persuaded the Queen not to pander to the public's seemingly insatiable appetite for information about the young prince. At Andrew's christening, his own father took the photographs with his newly acquired Hasselblad camera. Then there was one session with Cecil Beaton, when Philip once again used his own camera, much to the irritation of Beaton, who described Philip's continual interference as "maddening." There were no other photo calls, and apart from appearing in the official photographs to mark the Queen Mother's sixtieth birthday, Andrew was rarely seen.

That in itself presented a problem. As Philip later explained, in reference to Andrew and Edward: "You cannot have it both ways. We try and keep the children out of the public eye so they can grow up as normally as possible. But if you are going to have a monarchy you have got to have a family and the family's got to be in the public eye." Because Andrew wasn't, the more scurrilous of the Continental press concluded that he must be disabled in some way. He wasn't, of course, but he was excused the formative pressures of constant public exposure.

Philip found fatherhood for the third time around more enjoyable than he had before, and "Andy Pandy," as the staff called Andrew, after the popular children's TV character of the time, was an endless source of entertainment. Philip could relate to him in a way he hadn't been able to with Charles, and although Andrew could be a mini hooligan, he was more biddable around his father. Philip taught Andrew to swim in the palace pool around the same time he taught Anne to drive a car around the royal estates and Charles how to handle a gun and swing a polo mallet. He was a fun father, delighting them with practical jokes, joining in their games, and playing football with them along the long corridors of the palaces. Andrew recalls his parents divided their responsibilities toward him equally:

"Compassion comes from the Queen, and the duty and discipline comes from him [Philip]. I think our mother probably put a bit more effort to make sure there was time for us as children, bearing in mind she was Queen when we came along. We used to see her in the afternoons and in the evenings the usual standard bath time sort of routine. And father would usually read us a story or we would read to him—the *Just So Stories*—all sorts of things like that."

Philip also told all his children stories he had improvised himself. Extremely well read, Philip drew his inspiration from endless children's tales, from witches to dragons to the classic fairy tales from the pen of the Brothers Grimm. There was also Heinrich Hoffmann, the German psychiatrist whose original work *Struwwelpeter* was published in Victorian times. Hoffmann wrote cautionary tales for children, warning them not to torment animals, suck their thumbs, play with matches, or fidget at meals, which Andrew loved, but also ignored.

Despite his reading skills, Prince Philip's appearance in the top-floor nursery filled nanny Mabel Anderson with apprehension, as it had Nanny Lightbody before her. It was usually a prelude to tears, as Andrew often became overexcited when playing with his father, leaving the nanny to sort out the mess—though not before Philip collected a black eye in the rough-and-tumble on one occasion, and on another got chocolate all over the front of his dress shirt from Andrew's sticky fingers. Philip made play time a learning time too, and lured his aging widowed mother, Princess Alice, to join in when she was staying at the palace. She would bowl a soft ball to little Andrew in the long corridors while he attempted to use a hearth brush as an improvised cricket bat.

It was an interesting experiment in royal child-rearing—and one fraught with hazards. Andrew was cosseted in a palace with an indulgent mother, a devoted nanny, a retinue of servants to command with the snap of his tiny fingers, mixing only with the most carefully selected of playmates, and without the continuous steadying authority of his father, who was often absent. When his older brother and sister were away at school, he was virtually an only child, spending his time in the nursery with nanny Mabel Anderson, assistant June Waller, and a nursery footman. It was not surprising that Andrew's natural high spirits frequently crossed the boundaries into high-handedness. He was not always popular with the palace staff, who sometimes saw him as an arrogant nuisance. It was a judgment that was to dog him into adulthood and irritate his father, who could be equally as rude but in a more intelligent way.

If Philip had to defer to the Queen in public, his private influence over her was immense. Major decisions, such as where their children were to be educated, were left to him, which in turn gave him considerable influence over the shape of the monarchy itself.

When Prince Edward was born on the evening of Tuesday, March 10, 1964, Prince Philip was at the Queen's bedside. It was the first time he had seen one of his children born. The Queen, for whom having children had been an impelling dynastic duty, was determined to enjoy the experience, and she wanted her husband to share it with her. How quickly social mores had changed. Prince Philip had been barred from the birth of Charles, Anne, and Andrew. The idea of having him there with her would have been incomprehensible if not distasteful in an age so decorous that it forbade any photographs of the Queen during pregnancy and never officially acknowledged that she had delivered her first born by cesarean section. But now even the Queen had caught the change in mood and decreed that Philip would attend the birth—the first time, in modern history, that any royal father had been allowed to see his progeny born. He had drawn the line at attending the Queen's private prenatal classes with the late Betty Parsons, whose relaxation techniques and no-nonsense advice helped thousands of women deal with the concerns of childbirth, but when Betty arrived at the palace the morning the Queen went into labor, it was Philip who ushered her into the delivery suite, before the medical team of five doctors and two midwives could lock her out.

The Queen did not have what today would be called a "natural" childbirth, though by the standards of the time it was regarded as very straightforward. The anesthetist administered gas and oxygen as necessary, and she also had pethidine, a pain reliever with properties similar to morphine. This was popular at the time. Prince Philip did his bit by keeping the anxious medical team happy. The baby was a week premature, and the process was slower than they might have hoped, so they were understandably anxious.

"It's a solemn thought that only a week ago General de Gaulle was having a bath in this very room," he said as he walked into the bathroom of the Belgian suite, which had been converted into the delivery suite. It was typical of Philip, but for once his jesting proved invaluable and helped ease the tension.

By comparison to his siblings, Edward was a small child, weighing in at just 5 pounds 7 ounces (2.47 kilograms). The Queen had convinced herself she was going to have a girl, and so nobody had bothered to think of any male names before Edward's arrival. He was finally named Edward Antony Richard Louis after his godfathers Lord Snowdon, Richard Duke of Gloucester, and Prince Louis of Hesse, prefixed by the old royal name of his great-great-grandfather Edward VII. The selection of names was not officially announced until twenty-four hours short of the forty-two-hour deadline, and he was christened on May 2 in the music room of Buckingham Palace.

With the birth of their third and fourth children, the Queen and Prince Philip took a different approach to parenthood. Philip, older by then and less driven to seek compensation for his disappointments, was less demanding of Andrew and Edward than he had been of Charles. He may have attended Edward's birth, but he was no new man in the making, and two days later and without thinking too much about it, Philip flew to Athens to attend the funeral of his cousin, King Paul of the Hellenes. He saw it as a royal duty to be there rather than at his wife's bedside.

The Queen would spend more time with Edward than she had with her elder children, and his childhood was marked by an informality that would have been out of place in Charles's and Anne's day. But there was still an order, a seemingly immutable routine to life in the nursery. And, as always, presiding over everything were not the children's parents, but the royal nannies.

Philip had been very close to his own English nanny, Emily Roose, and he much preferred Mabel Anderson, who came into royal service in 1948, to the senior Nanny Lightbody, whom he thought over-cosseted Prince Charles and who was eventually "retired." While forty-year-old Mabel still ran the nursery in the traditional royal way, which was according to a strict regime, she had the good sense not to challenge Prince Philip openly, knowing he did not like his orders questioned.

Prince Philip, Mabel said, "was a marvelous father. He always set aside time to read to them or help them put together those little model toys." From the kits popular at the time he helped Edward build plastic model ships, which would adorn his Buckingham Palace bedroom.

"I remember my mother would look after Edward and me in the evenings at the place, alone quite happily. It was a proper family," Andrew said. In fact, it was not quite as he remembered: when it was nanny's evening off, the Queen would go upstairs with a footman, who provided a gilt chair for her to sit on while she gave her children their bath. The footman would remain in attendance to hold the towels.

In the autumn of 1968, the French magazine *Paris Match* published a series of family snaps of Edward as a newborn baby, propped up in bed with his mother, his brother Andrew on the old-fashioned counterpane beside her and Anne and Charles at the bedside. Philip took the photographs. They were delightful, informal—and stolen.

It was not until a year later that it was discovered that a free marketeer in the commercial processing laboratory where the film had been sent for developing had made an extra set of prints to sell to the Continental press. This loophole in royal security was immediately closed. By then, the photographs had been seen by millions. *Life* magazine in America had bought them. In Britain, the *Daily Express* had plastered them across its broadsheet front page.

The royal family were appalled, especially Prince Philip, who had taken most of the snaps with his Hasselblad camera. Princess Anne had taken some too, in which Philip and Charles are kneeling on the floor beside the Queen's bed. It was a violation of their privacy, a gross intrusion into their family life, and it was believed by many inside the palace that photographs of the Queen in bed would detract from Her Majesty. Despite Philip's protestations, it was decided not to sue. It was 1968, and the royal family was not prepared to exercise its legal muscle, preferring to hide behind the legal illusion that for some unspecified reason it could not "answer back."

The bedrock of deference upon which the royal family had rested for most of the twentieth century was being replaced by the kind of fickle adulation more appropriate to the entertainment industry. The publication of the Edward photographs was symptomatic of that trend. The public were starting to claim the right to know anything and everything they wanted about the royal family. They were aware of this change in attitude and unsure about how best to react to it, but this was not an intrusion they cared for. When Philip talked about having his family "in the public eye," he meant only at times and in circumstances of their own choosing. The firm was used to stage-managing public interest; it was understandably disconcerted when the audience started to direct the show.

It was partly in order to bring the situation under control that the Queen, encouraged by Prince Philip, agreed to allow television cameras to look into their lives with the sympathetic and carefully made documentary *Royal Family*, first screened in 1969.

Prince Edward as a five-year-old was acknowledged by some as stealing the show in the film. It was a poignant comment on his young life that this was the only show he was allowed to steal for some time to come.

It was Philip, still a dynamic fifty-year-old, who mapped out the overall strategy for Andrew and Edward's education, just as he had with Charles and Anne. But this time around he left the practicalities to his wife. Experience had done much to leaven the Queen's attitude. Only twenty-five years old when she inherited the throne, she had been overwhelmed by the responsibility and, under the stress of her office, had somewhat lost touch with her maternal priorities. By the time Edward made his appearance, however, she had reigned for more than a decade. She was confident in her position and determined to make the most of what would certainly be her last venture into motherhood.

In the early days of parenthood, it was Philip who was the more tactile parent. He could be brusque and severe, but if he was in residence, he would never sit down to dinner without first going to the nursery to say good night. When he was going out on an official engagement with the Queen, Nanny Anderson would take the children to a nearby window overlooking the garden entrance to wave goodbye. Before she got in the car, the Queen, resplendent in evening gown and tiara, would look up at the two small faces pressed against the windowpane and give a discreet little wave. Philip, on the other hand, would always blow a kiss.

At first glance, Edward, whose youthful looks, as everyone remarked, were almost feminine in their delicacy, had seemed the very antithesis to his hearty, gruff father. But Edward was not as delicate as he looked—and nor was Philip as harsh—and as he grew up, Edward enjoyed a close rapport with his father.

"Prince Philip was always great fun," recalled Marina Mowatt, Princess Alexandra's daughter, who always spent Christmas with the Queen and her family. "He would snap at his children as any father does, but he certainly wasn't cold. And he'd never not have time for them. He was one of those people who got annoyed if you didn't concentrate; if he was trying to teach you something, he wanted you to concentrate. Like with me for instance he gave me a lot of time driving a couple of ponies and if I started giggling, he got very annoyed. That could be quite scary, but if you got around that, there was a lot of charm underneath."

When it came to shooting, Philip found a willing pupil in Edward. A keen shot himself, he started to teach Edward the skills of marksmanship at an early age. "He began by shooting rabbits when he was quite tiny—about seven or eight," Marina recalled.

Andrew had only the vaguest interest in field sports. For him it was little more than a matter of royal form—field sports are part of the rural routine of royal life. Edward, on the other hand, became a genuine enthusiast.

A high point of Edward's stays at Sandringham was getting up before first light to go duck shooting with his father on the marshes of the Norfolk coast. Unhampered by the trappings of royalty and quite alone, father and son would crawl for hours among the tall reeds, something Philip also later enjoyed with his first grandson, Peter Phillips.

During the summer, Edward, Andrew, and other members of the royal family would frequently spend their days at Holkham Beach, part of which was—and still is—designated as a nudist area. The naked sunbathers came under the closest of royal scrutiny, and Marina Ogilvy recalled: "We all used to have a good look through our binoculars. It was very funny and the Queen Mother's remarks were always the naughtiest."

Not every holiday was given over to youthful pleasure. When Edward was fourteen, he was diagnosed as having too many teeth for his jaw and had to have several removed. It was a painful process, followed by a year wearing a brace to slowly and painfully close the gaps and draw his teeth together again. Prince Philip and the Queen did not usually reward their children, but on this occasion they had the teeth mounted in gold settings and made into chain-linked cufflinks, which they presented to him in recognition, they explained, of his "pluck." Edward's daughter Lady Louise, who looks very like her father, has similar dental problems, although today braces are far more comfortable than they were in the 1970s. Louise is a talented equestrian and, like Marina Mowatt, was taught the rudiments of carriage driving by Prince Philip, coming third in a competition in the 2019 Windsor Horse Show, much to his delight.

*

Although Andrew and Edward, with a four-year age gap, were not especially close, they followed the same educational path—Heatherdown Preparatory School and then Gordonstoun. It was the Queen who had opted for Heatherdown because it was close to Windsor Castle and because so many of her friends and relations sent their sons there. She took pleasure in the practical minutiae of first Andrew's and then Edward's school life.

"She knew their faults and their shortcomings—she really did know them terribly well," said James Edwards, the headmaster of Heatherdown. "Some parents who give their children over to nannies sometimes hardly know their children at all. But she did. Prince Philip appeared, but not as much as the Queen. She determined and controlled their early education. I discussed their school reports with her rather than him."

More than 65 percent of Heatherdown's boys went on at thirteen to nearby Eton College. Both the Queen and her private secretary, Sir Martin (later Lord) Charteris, the future provost of Eton, felt that Britain's most famous public school might best suit the young Edward. The Queen Mother certainly thought so. But Philip would have none of that. He took the view that what had been good enough for him was good enough for his sons.

Underlying that seemingly straightforward explanation were substrata of resentment and frustration. Philip had never been accepted by the establishment, which regarded him—not without reason—as a pushy interloper with disturbingly radical ideas for streamlining and modernizing the monarchy.

Philip, for his part, held the old-fashioned power structure of British society in barely disguised contempt. He believed that people should be judged on what they achieved rather than who they were. He regarded the old-fashioned public schools, which Eton epitomized, with suspicion. To him they smacked of unearned and all too often unwarranted privilege—the breeding ground for an elitist old boys' network of which he was not a member. He believed that Gordonstoun—now coeducational and far more comfortable than it had been in Charles's time, but still with its accent on individual development and community service rather than team sports and classics—provided a more rounded education. New masters had come in, fired with an enthusiasm to get back to the principles that Hahn had originally espoused, but tailored to meet changing social expectations.

Philip visited Andrew and Edward at school and in Edward's first year watched him in the house play, a revue of Peter Shaffer's *Black Comedy*. Prince Charles, accompanied by the then Lady Diana Spencer, to whom he had just become engaged, came to see him in the Feydeau farce *Hotel Paradiso*, which Edward produced as well as starred in. It was an open-air production staged under the walls of the school chapel. The weather had been fine for the previous night's performance, but it started to rain—as Edward had predicted it was bound to—when his brother and future sister-in-law arrived. The stage became very slippery. Everyone was slipping and sliding and the audience was laughing in all the wrong places.

It was Charles's first visit to the school since he had left to go to university. It was Diana's one and only visit to the school, which she would later refuse to allow her sons to attend. Back then, however, the couple were in the first enthusiastic flush of their relationship, and both Charles and Diana appeared to enjoy the evening, crouched under umbrellas, watching the young Edward skidding across the stage.

When Edward appeared in Noël Coward's *Hay Fever*, the Queen and Prince Philip made the three-hour car journey across the Grampians from Balmoral. Seats had been reserved for them: Edward had written labels and stuck them on the back of two chairs in the front row. They read, "Mum" and "Dad."

Hay Fever was performed in the services center. Just as the performance started, the lights began to play up. In a loud whisper, which could be heard several rows away, Philip remarked to the Queen, "I think they are doing *Black Comedy* again." The remark, so typical of Prince Philip, luckily produced a ripple of laughter from the audience. "It was all very good-natured and lighthearted," James Thomas, one of the masters recalled.

In spite of Prince Philip's occasionally embarrassing behavior, he was always fair. He believed in letting his children make their own mistakes, and when they asked for paternal guidance, he would give it to them. This was illustrated when Prince Edward decided to leave the Royal Marines. The popular account was that Prince Philip had been furious with Edward for quitting, especially as he was then captain general of the Royal Marines himself.

The truth was somewhat different, as was revealed when the *Sun* newspaper published a letter from Prince Philip to Sir Michael Watkins, Edward's commanding officer. In the letter, printed on January 7, 1987, Prince Philip expressed his regrets, but made it very clear that the final decision had been Prince Edward's alone. The letter also stated that Prince Philip felt that Edward would now face a very difficult period of adjustment. Two days later, Prince Philip ordered an inquiry to find out who had leaked the information and began proceedings for breach of copyright over the private letter. Eventually the *Sun* had to pay an undisclosed sum to one of Prince Philip's charities. On January 13, 1987, Buckingham Palace issued an official statement confirming that Prince Edward was indeed resigning. "Prince Edward is leaving the Marines with great regret but has decided that he does not wish to make the service his long-term career."

"Everything that had been planned for me ceased," Edward told me. "You see the railway tracks were there and I was trundling down them and, OK, I'd gone off here and there and done other things, but basically that is where I was going. Then suddenly I had actually gone off the tracks. Right off the tracks—I was literally off into the bundu.

"Everybody said, what's the point in stopping if you don't know what you are going to do? I said I would prefer to do that than carry on doing something that I knew instinctively was not going to go anywhere."

It was exactly as Prince Philip had feared. That summer, there was worse to come when Edward produced the charity TV show *It's a Royal Knockout*, in which members of the family dressed in period costume as captains of four teams in a celebrity tournament at Alton Towers theme park.

It was undignified, and to make matters worse, Edward was in a truculent mood at the ensuing press conference. He lost his temper and flounced out after the media made it clear they didn't think much of it all. It was such a disaster that it is still talked of today as one of the greatest PR gaffes the royal family have ever made.

"I was annoyed," Edward told me later. "I had given them [the media] the opportunity to get their knives in. It was an experiment. I did make a million for charity, but I seemed to have lost everything and gained very little."

As Philip was so close to his son, it seems odd that he didn't step in to stop it before the idea took off, but according to his friend General Sir Michael Hobbs, who worked with him for many years as chairman of the Duke of Edinburgh's Award scheme, that was not Philip's way of doing things.

"It was not in his nature or that of the royal family at the time to discourage or stand in the way of anything. There was, if you like, a sort of inspired policy of drift, of laissez-faire. I don't think Prince Philip would ever have said, 'over my dead body,' I don't think it's in his nature."

For all their superficial differences, Philip's relationship with his youngest son is based on genuine respect on Edward's part and equally genuine affection on Philip's. The duke is not a demonstrative man, but in private he will affectionately put his arm around his son's shoulder—he calls him Ed—and give him a kiss. It was Philip, for instance, not the Queen, who came to see Edward receive his degree on graduation from Jesus College, Cambridge. That Philip should take such an interest in his youngest son is perhaps unexpected. After all, it was Andrew who followed in his father's footsteps by going to the Royal Naval College, Dartmouth, and eventually joining the Royal Navy, going on to serve his country in the Falklands War. But Philip's relationship with his youngest child is conducted on a level of easy familiarity, which he had to a lesser extent with Andrew but certainly not with Charles.

When it came to ladies in his sons' lives, Prince Philip started off with a fair degree of optimism, especially if they were pretty, which they usually were. He would happily sit next to them at candlelit black-tie dinners or transport them to the picnic lunches in his Land Rover with its specially converted picnic trailer. One girlfriend of Andrew's whom Philip liked was American actress Koo Stark. Although he only met her once or twice, he was captivated by her petite beauty, but he doubted the relationship could ever work.

"I was single, he was single," Koo recalled many years later, when she talked about her romance with Andrew. "We had every reason to be carefree and no reason not to be. When Andrew comes into your life there is no room for anyone else. He takes up all the space."

When the Falklands War was announced in April 1982, Prince Andrew was attached to the frontline carrier HMS *Invincible* as a Sea King search-and-rescue pilot, and had to leave London immediately to join his ship. During the conflict, when he was copilot aboard a Sea King helicopter flying to decoy the Exocet missiles the Argentinians were determinedly launching at HMS *Invincible*, Koo was able to stay in touch with her lover through the occasional ship-to-shore call and they wrote long letters to each other. His most harrowing moment was watching from the air the sinking of the supply ship *Atlantic Conveyor* by an Exocet intended for HMS *Invincible*.

"It was horrific," Andrew remembered. "At the time I saw a 4.5 shell come quite close to us. I saw my ship *Invincible* firing her missiles." The prince's Sea King rescued three survivors.

On June 14, the Argentinian forces surrendered. Two days later, Andrew landed in Port Stanley. He was one of the lucky ones and he knew it—out of the 28,000 Britons who had sailed into action, 255 had died and 777 had been wounded. Koo recalled the day Andrew's ship arrived back in Britain from the Falklands and he disembarked in Portsmouth from HMS *Invincible* with a rose between his substantial teeth.

"It was the day he became irresistible to the press," Koo said wistfully. "He was a Royal romantic hero—so, everyone wanted to know, who was his girlfriend? All hell broke loose."

The pair traveled to Balmoral separately and spent the days on the moors and in the evenings playing "parlor games, doing jigsaws and pretending the dog hasn't farted," Koo recalled. "Suffice to say I had a memorable time—but relaxing as it is en famille, even when the family are the Royals, what we really wanted to do was to go on a beach holiday."

So, under the names of Mr. and Mrs. Cambridge, they flew off to Princess Margaret's holiday home Les Jolie Eaux on the Caribbean island of Mustique. While they were there, some "screen grabs" from *Emily*, a semi-erotic film Koo had made in the early 1970s, were published. It was the beginning of the end for Andrew and Koo. She recalled, "But what I could never know, during that idyllic but eventful holiday, was how a film role I played years earlier was about to come back to haunt me . . . and change the course of my life, and my relationship with Andrew, forever."

The popular myth is that it was Prince Philip who persuaded his son to end his romance. This was not true—it was not Philip's style. He knew to his personal cost that the story would not die until the media had claimed a victim. It had attempted—and failed—to ensnare him all those years before with Pat Kirkwood and Hélène Cordet, but although he escaped, they were forever labeled as his possible lovers. Now it was his son's turn. Andrew could walk away—he was a prince of the realm. Koo Stark could not. She was hounded and is still branded as Andrew's ex.

When the Queen saw the headlines in the *News of the World* saying, "Queen bans Koo," Koo and Andrew were having tea with her at Windsor Castle. According to Koo, all the Queen said was that she wished the press would call them by their proper names— Andrew and Kathleen, instead of Andy and Koo. Prince Philip was more vocal, albeit privately, but he never insisted Andrew should stop seeing Koo. He was well aware of the potential problems of being a member of the royal family and marrying an actress who had appeared in what was considered a soft-porn film. But he left it at that. He knew the stress of the massive publicity surrounding the romance would eventually kill it. He was right.

When Sarah Ferguson came on the scene in the summer of 1985, Philip had no reason to doubt his son's choice. Her father, Major Ronald Ferguson, had once been his polo manager and a "mucker," and subsequently Prince Charles's polo manager. The Fergusons knew the royal family well enough to be invited to stay for shooting weekends at Sandringham, and Sarah was what the Queen called "one of us," a term she had also applied to Diana. Sarah was a friend of the Princess of Wales. Her great-aunt Jane had married

Sir William Fellowes, a longtime land agent at Sandringham, and Sir William's son Robert, later the Queen's private secretary, had married Diana's eldest sister, Jane.

For all her connections, Fergie found the restrictions of her royal role difficult, but made every effort to integrate herself. Philip taught her how to carriage drive, and when she gained her pilot's licence, he was pleased. He knew his son was arrogant and had experienced problems at Gordonstoun by throwing his royal weight around. Andrew had made it clear he knew who he was and let everyone else know it too. One fellow pupil called him "a poor little rich kid who didn't know if he wanted to be a Prince or one of the lads." Another called him "the boy with a fat bottom who laughed at his own jokes." He became head boy of his house, Cummings House, but he was never made head boy (or "guardian," as it is officially called) of the school, as his father and both his brothers were.

Philip thought Fergie would knock the arrogance out of Andrew. When questioned about his son's choice of bride, he was—for him—quite effusive. "I'm delighted he's getting married, but not because I think it will keep him out of trouble because, in fact he's never been in trouble, but because I think Sarah will be a great asset."

Sarah *was* a great asset. People responded to her charm and humor, and to the way she seemed determined to get on with things without surrendering her personality to the strictures of royal life. Yet her very success in continuing to be herself was the seed for her later troubles. She appeared to be having too much fun and was accused of reveling in her position, taking too many skiing holidays, for instance. Worst of all, she was called "a parasite."

Part of the problem was that, because of his job, Andrew was away more than he was at home. He told the Queen and Prince Philip that Sarah couldn't deal with the long separations. They asked if they could move into married quarters but were flatly refused. Sarah pleaded that it was very difficult being without her husband.

According to Sarah, Prince Philip replied: "The Mountbattens managed, and so can you. Stiffen that lip, old girl." And the subject was closed.

Instead of the ally he had once been, Philip became more and more irritated with Fergie and what he described as her "antics." He took every opportunity to criticize her and disliked what he considered her informality with the staff. Like others before her, she became tongue-tied in his presence. When she did try to make polite conversation, he let his contempt be known. He didn't reserve it solely for Fergie, but also goaded Andrew, picking on him at every opportunity for some perceived weakness or other. Ever-loyal Fergie found this so insulting, she told me, that it gave her the courage to admonish Philip when he attacked Andrew over dinner. She told him in no uncertain terms that he couldn't speak to Andrew like that.

It was the death knell for their relationship. Philip simply doesn't like being challenged by someone whom he considers his intellectual inferior.

In 1992, the Queen's "annus horribilis," Sarah and Andrew separated after six years of marriage. Their meeting with the Queen and Philip was brief and painful. Andrew muttered words like "mutual incompatibility." Sarah apologized for her behavior, which she agreed had been a long way short of what was both expected and required. The Queen, as always, clung to the delusion that time would heal the breach. Philip, once an outsider himself who had to learn the exigencies of royal life, was able to take an objective view of its requirements and regarded his daughter-in-law's behavior as selfish and reprehensible declared: "If she wants out, she can get out."

When it comes to issues of behavior, he is rigid. During the summer of 1992, when Fergie was staying at Balmoral in order that the Queen and Prince Philip could see their grandchildren, photographs appeared of her topless in the South of France with her supposed financial advisor John Bryan nuzzling her toes. The Queen was furious. She did not scream or shout. That is not the Queen's way. Rather, she was cold and abrupt as she berated her semi-detached daughter-in-law for exposing the monarchy to ridicule.

Some years later, Sarah told me that Prince Philip had likened her to Edwina Mountbatten, whose morals had long been a source of embarrassment to the royal family. He had said to her: "You belong in a nunnery—or a madhouse."

It was not until twenty-six years later that the two met again, at the wedding of Princess Eugenie and Jack Brooksbank in October 2018. It may not have been the most auspicious of reunions, but it paved the way for a better relationship between them—so much so that in 2019 Sarah and Andrew were invited to dine with the Queen and Philip at Windsor Castle, as if the problematic years of the 1990s had not existed. Sarah even joined Andrew at Balmoral that summer, but left abruptly once Prince Philip arrived, to go on holiday with Andrew in Spain. Andrew's predicament over his disastrous friendship with convicted pedophile Jeffrey Epstein, who subsequently killed himself, refused to go away, and Sarah was determined to be at his side to lend support.

There is no official record of what Prince Philip thought about his son's difficulties, but it would be out of character if he had not expressed some extremely volatile opinions. He would have been infuriated that the disgrace heaped upon his son reflected so badly on the monarchy.

Chapter 12

SPORTS AND
OTHER INTERESTS

When Philip was born, aviation was in its infancy. He was six when Charles Lindbergh made the first nonstop transatlantic flight and nine when the jet engine was invented. When Spitfires took to the skies in 1938 and later became the most famous plane of the Second World War, Philip had just left school and enrolled as a cadet at the Royal Naval College, Dartmouth. Given his natural interest in technology, it's not surprising that Prince Philip has always been fascinated by flying. "I really wanted to go into the Air Force," he said. "Left to my own devices I'd have gone into the Air Force without a doubt."

If Philip had had his way in 1939, instead of going to Dartmouth, he might well have become a fighter pilot in the Battle of Britain in 1940, one of "The Few," as Winston Churchill christened them. For many years, Churchill was adamantly against any of the royal family taking to the air; an interesting attitude given that Churchill had himself learned to fly in the First World War and in 1919 was made secretary of state for air.

Although Philip did not begin his flying training until 1952, flying became a passion not only because it enabled him to get from A to B in the shortest possible time, but because it gave him a degree of freedom and control he could not enjoy when on the ground. He lived a crowded life; wherever he went an entourage of security officers, equerries, secretaries, courtiers, and servants accompanied him. In his public appearances, he was dogged by the press and mobbed by the crowds. As a pilot with perhaps only a copilot beside him, he answered to nobody but himself. As he put it, "I fly because it's useful for getting about but I also enjoy the intellectual challenge of it all, if that is the right word." The challenge for Philip as a pilot includes being familiar with the characteristics and instrumentation of many types of aircraft, being aware of weather conditions and visibility for every flight path, and having knowledge of the destination aerodrome for landing.

Prince Philip began his flying training on November 12, 1952, at White Waltham, his instructor being Flt. Lt. Caryl Ramsay Gordon. His wish to qualify as a pilot was reported by the secretary of state for air, and it met with the coolest possible response from the prime minister. "In view of his public position and responsibilities," Churchill declared, "His Royal Highness should not expose himself to unnecessary risks."

Churchill's anxieties are revealed in documents released at the Public Record Office in London, which show that the cabinet in the 1950s discussed the worrying matter of Philip's aeronautics no fewer than eight times. The papers reveal not only the caution of a generation of ministers brought up for the most part in a world without airplanes, but also the quiet determination with which

Philip got his way. He was determined to qualify as a pilot before the coronation in June 1953. After initial training on the de Havilland Chipmunk, he continued on the faster North American Harvard. He was awarded his "wings" (a badge awarded to members of the RAF upon their completing flight training) by Chief of the Air Staff Marshal Sir William Dickson at a private ceremony at Buckingham Palace on May 4, 1953.

One week before the coronation, Philip took a ride in a navy helicopter from the gardens of Buckingham Palace to inspect some Commonwealth troops who had been stationed at various barracks around the country. When Churchill heard of the helicopter trip, he summoned Philip's equerry Mike Parker to 10 Downing Street. "Is it your intention to destroy the entire Royal Family in the shortest possible time?" he thundered. Eventually, Churchill came around to helicopter travel himself.

Philip earned his helicopter wings with the Royal Navy in 1956, and in 1959 he gained his private pilot's licence. He took the controls of many different aircraft at every possible opportunity, eventually clocking up 5,986 hours flying in fifty-nine various types of aircraft, before his last outing as a pilot in 1997. Although Philip was never permitted to pilot the Queen on his own, he has flown other members of the royal family, including taking Prince Charles back to school at Gordonstoun.

It was through flying that the Middleton family became known to Philip years before Kate Middleton was born. In 1962, Philip embarked on a two-month tour of South America, visiting British factories, traveling on the British-built railway in the Andes, and sightseeing at Machu Picchu and Lake Titicaca. He elected to pilot the tour jet on many of the journeys during the tour with Captain Peter Middleton, Kate Middleton's paternal grandfather, as copilot. Peter Middleton, who was first officer throughout the tour, was a Mosquito fighter-bomber pilot during the Second World War whose job was to nudge V1 rockets aimed at London into a harmless tra-jectory. He died in 2010, a year before his granddaughter married Prince William.

From 1952 until 2002, Philip was grand master of the Guild of Air Pilots and Air Navigators. He is also patron of the British Gliding Association. He was introduced to the sport of gliding by Sir Peter Scott, of the World Wildlife Fund, and used to appear at the annual National Gliding Championships.

But his great interest in the technology of flight and of space travel went beyond flying planes. He was an early subscriber to the *Flying Saucer Review* and has made several visits to different NASA estab-lishments in the United States. In 1991, at NASA's headquarters in Texas, he was put in the command seat of a space capsule simulator in which he had to dock the capsule with the International Space Station. When asked what it was like, he said, "It was like a bloody great mechanical copulator." After the Apollo 11 moon landing, Philip entertained the three astronauts at Buckingham Palace. He also talked to British astronaut Timothy Peake after his six-month stint on the International Space Station in 2016. In 1966, three years before the first moon landing, Philip gave the centenary address to the Royal Aeronautical Society, in which he said: "The first hundred years of aviation have seen some spectacular developments but I do not believe even these will compare with the developments in aero-nautics during the next hundred years . . . and the challenge of space is the most exciting and daunting which mankind has ever faced."

It is said that pilots should not fly fixed-wing aircraft and heli-copters on the same day because the skills and disciplines involved are so different. However, Philip was able to jump from one to the other without a pause. He thought nothing of flying himself down from Scotland to an aerodrome near Windsor and, having landed, walking across the tarmac to a helicopter to fly himself to Smiths

Lawn for a game of polo. This was long before carbon emissions became an important factor in climate change, and he was not then criticized for doing so.

Many years before Philip took up polo as his principal sporting activity, cricket was his game of choice. In his school days, he was captain of the First XI at Gordonstoun and would have made the first team at Cheam had he not been sent away to Salem, where cricket was unknown. As soon as he moved to Windlesham Manor, his first matrimonial home, he turned the grass tennis court into a cricket pitch and put together a team made up of his detective, his chauffeur, the gardeners, and a few friends to play against local teams. His equerry Mike Parker was recruited as wicketkeeper for the Windlesham team. As a player, Philip was an all-rounder, being both a proficient spin bowler and, according to Don Bradman, Australia's greatest ever batsman, perhaps somewhat obsequiously, "possessing perfect technique as a batsman."

He turned out many times for celebrity matches to raise funds for charity, in particular for the National Playing Fields Association, for which he was the main fundraiser. He also played for the Thursday Club cricket team, which included the actors James Robertson Justice and David Niven as well as Baron Nahum, the official photographer for the royal wedding in 1947. Philip retired from cricket as a player in 1958 but remained involved with the sport for the rest of his life. At Royal Ascot, when the Queen was watching the racing, he would go into the back of the royal box and watch the cricket on television.

He was twice president of the Marylebone Cricket Club, then the sport's ruling body, and served as patron and twelfth man of the Lord's Taverners, based at Lord's cricket ground since their formation in 1950 until the present day. The Taverners charity serves as the leader in supporting youth cricket players and those with disabilities. When asked if he would like to be president of the Taverners, Philip claimed it would be too much work. He created the role of the twelfth man, a job in every cricket team that involves keeping the team's equipment in order and serving refreshments. In the preface to the book on the history of the Taverners, Philip wrote, "Scientists may one day discover what controls the homing instinct of fish and birds but I hope they never try to analyse the urge of the Taverner to return to Lord's." When asked during an interview on *Test Match Special* how cricket could be improved, he said, "I only wish to God that some of their trousers fitted better."

Horses featured in the Queen's life from a very young age. She had her first riding lesson in the private riding school at Buckingham Palace Mews in January 1930, when she was just three years old, and was given her first pony, the Shetland mare Peggy, by her grandfather King George V on her fourth birthday. She has remained passionate about horses for the whole of her life. In contrast, Philip did not become involved in equestrian sports until much later in life. Philip's first recollection of riding is from 1928, when as a seven-year-old he would ride along the Black Sea beaches with his cousin King Michael of Romania. Horse riding did not feature in Philip's school days nor during the war years when he was in the Royal Navy.

Philip's interest in playing polo started in earnest during his stay in Malta between 1949 and 1951 while serving in the Royal Navy. He was encouraged to play by his uncle Dickie Mountbatten, who was commanding the 1st Cruiser Squadron there. To begin with, Philip showed little interest in polo, preferring navy cricket and deck hockey matches, but he soon realized that Princess Elizabeth would far rather watch a game of polo than a cricket match. Mountbatten, whom the polo players nicknamed Marco Polo, was an expert polo player and had written a book published in 1931 called *An*

Introduction to Polo, by "Marco," which has become the classic reference book to the sport. To get him started, Mountbatten loaned Philip a couple of polo ponies in Malta, and before long Philip was hooked and polo became his passion for many years.

"He was looking for an active sport to get out his frustrations and energies," Lord Patrick Beresford, who played with Philip for almost ten years, recalled. "He tried cricket, but it was too slow, and it was Lord Cowdray, who provided him with three polo ponies at Cowdray Park in Sussex, who really got him into polo."

Together with two former naval officers and Col. Alec Harper, Philip formed a team called the Mariners at Cowdray Park. As Cowdray Park was some distance from Windsor, he eventually moved his ponies to the bottom yard of the Mews at Windsor and formed the Windsor Park team with Lord Patrick Beresford. Polo has handicaps that start at -2 for beginners and go to 10 for the very best professionals, and Philip was considered good for someone who wasn't a professional. "Prince Philip had a very good eye for the ball," Beresford remembers. "He was a five-goal player, which is very good for an amateur. He was very fit. When he played, he rode hard and was as competitive as anyone, but once the game was over, he switched off and we all had a drink together. Win or lose he looked forward to the next match."

Always impatient, Philip could be pretty vocal on the field. On one occasion, when Algernon Ferguson, Fergie's grandfather, was umpiring a match in which Philip was getting irate with both the players and his own horse, he told Philip if he carried on "he would be sent off." This did not go down well. Philip is not used to being chastised in public, and he sarcastically reported the incident to Col. Gerard Leigh, the then chairman of Guards Polo Club.

Lord Patrick Beresford never remembered Prince Philip shouting on the polo ground, but others did, especially at Prince Charles when they played together. "He is inclined to give a running commentary, even while watching a match, but did not scream at anyone," Beresford insisted. "In August 1966, we all went to the Commonwealth Games in Jamaica and Prince Charles joined us on his way back from Gelong Grammar School in Australia. We played several matches as the Windsor team. We then flew back on the royal flight. Prince Philip was cautious about this as he could not be seen to be using it as a private conveyance, but it was acceptable as he had Prince Charles with him."

Prince Philip became one of the top eight amateur British players of his time. Polo is an expensive sport. As polo ponies are restricted to the number of chukkas (periods of seven minutes) that they can play in a match, it was necessary for a keen player like Philip to maintain a string of seven or eight ponies, albeit most of them were given or lent to him. These ponies had to be housed and fed and looked after by several grooms. The expense of playing polo was used as a reason for successive governments not to give Philip an increase in his pay from the Civil List, it being said that if more money was needed Philip should cut back his polo. Speaking in 1969 in the United States on the royal family's finances, Philip said: "We go into the red next year. . . . I may have to give up polo." This remark caused Philip much criticism in the press at home. Given his desire to bring the monarchy into the modern era and ensure that it was seen to move with the times, it shows just how committed he was to the sport that he was not worried about opening himself up to criticism because of it.

In 1955, with Philip as president and the Queen as patron, the Guards Polo Club was founded in Windsor Great Park with ten polo pitches at Smiths Lawn. Philip was instrumental in building the popularity of polo as a spectator sport, with many thousands of spectators attending every time he played in a match. Polo can be dangerous and Philip had his fair share of injuries. Press photographers were always on hand to capture the moment when Philip took a fall. Once, when he cut his chin on a bridle buckle during a game, he turned to the photographers saying, "Bad luck! I'm not dead!"

When Philip turned fifty in 1971, he retired from polo as arthritis had affected his wrists so badly that he could no longer play properly. "He tried every remedy, but nothing worked," Beresford recalled. "He knew people came to watch him play and he cared about that as it promoted the game. It was a blow when he had to give it up. But polo's loss was carriage driving's gain."

After giving up polo, Prince Philip explained in an interview for *Majesty* magazine in 1992: "I was looking around for something else to do. As I was president of the FEI [Fédération Equestre Internationale] I got involved in writing rules for international carriage-driving competitions." He persuaded the Windsor Horse Show to hold the European Championships, in which he took part in 1973, the beginning of an interest that was to last him the rest of his life.

Five years after becoming FEI president in 1964, he formed a committee with a view to making carriage driving an FEI sport. He created the rules for competitive driving, at which he quickly proved a remarkably proficient exponent. Rules for carriage driving are based on the ridden three-day event. Drivers and their horses are a team in singles, pairs, or a four-in-hand. Competitors are first marked on a round of dressage that also includes a presentation of tack and horses. The second phase is the marathon, testing speed and endurance and finally driving around cones for accuracy and obedience. For practice, Philip had access to plenty of antique carriages, horses, grooms, and land. In 1973, in his first competitive event, he recalled, "I came in not quite last, but very nearly."

"It's fascinating. You spend much more time practicing and training than you would at playing polo, where you can only knock about for a limited amount of time and training a polo pony is a skill for professionals. But with the driving, as I knew nothing about it, I was training myself as well as the horses and I've just got on with it.

"It's great fun. The thing about any sport is that people become enthusiastic. It's not only with sport, but any interest—they forget about backgrounds, origins, standing, and nationality and, of course, we've got something in common. You meet each other at hazards [while walking the course], then you call upon them in their stables. It was very dangerous to call upon the Hungarians because the moment you went near them, they pressed barack, a peach brandy, on to you. You got away an hour later cross-eyed."

Later in his career, Philip represented Great Britain in three European and six world championships. In the introduction to his book on driving, *Thirty Years On and Off the Box Seat*, he wrote: "I think the experience of playing polo gave me a certain advantage when transferring to driving. I got to know about the temperament of horses, their management, and the almost endless list of diseases and conditions to which they are liable."

The book details how, after being asked as president of the FEI to help compile rules for the increasingly popular sport, he found himself hooked. He relates how, to get started, he borrowed five Cleveland Bays from the Royal Mews, along with a set of neck collar harnesses and a big wooden carriage called the Balmoral dogcart, and off he went. The book reveals a different side to Prince Philip's character. It is written from his notes and scrapbooks in great detail, including weather conditions, but reveals him at his happiest among his fellow competitors who treat him as an equal. His energy and enthusiasm to combine his competitive carriage driving with his royal duties requires the kind of split-second military timing he loves.

"I knew it was going to make for a very complicated weekend," he said, referring to competing at the Farleigh Wallop estate in Hampshire during Royal Ascot week in 2003. He continued: "The only way I could walk the obstacles was to drive to Farleigh Wallop from

Windsor on Thursday morning and back to Windsor for lunch before going racing, and then drive over again after tea in the royal box at Ascot and back again to Windsor for dinner." He then drove back to the Farleigh Wallop estate after the obligatory tea at Ascot on Friday to do his dressage, stayed the night before the marathon on Saturday, but had to get back to Windsor that evening for his grandson Prince William's twenty-first birthday party. The next morning, he had to go back to Farleigh Wallop again for the cones. At the age of eighty-two, it was a pretty incredible physical and mental feat and illustrated perfectly that his duty to be at the Queen's side during Royal Ascot was of paramount importance, regardless of what else he was doing.

As with every sport, there were teething problems, most notably getting his horses to cross water, an essential requirement for competitions that comprise a tough schedule of dressage, precision driving through cones, and a cross-country marathon obstacle course. "It must be remembered these were ceremonial horses and their only experience of water was limited to avoiding puddles in London streets," he said.

Having personally designed a water crossing for the Home Park at Windsor, he got them across by shaking sugar lumps on the other side. At the "grand old age of sixty-five" and finding himself "the oldest competitor on the international circuit," he sent his horses back to the Mews and press-ganged the Fell ponies at Balmoral into active service. Having spent the stag-hunting season lugging carcasses, they arrived south "round as barrels and extremely hairy"—a slight drawback in the dressage stakes. Many years later, he was still as passionate about and as successful as ever with his ponies.

He also published two other books on the subject of driving. He greatly improved the design of carriages for driving, replacing

THE

Tatler

& Bystander 2s.6d. weekly 25.July. 1962

THE
SOCIAL
RISE
OF
POLO

The sporting prince: never one to waste a moment, Philip is pictured sketching while waiting his turn to compete during a carriage-driving event. When arthritis forced him to give up polo, he took up carriage driving with gusto. He did much to popularize both sports, and the *Tatler* chose him riding for his Windsor Park team for the cover of their July 1962 issue.

In a Hawker Siddeley Andover of the Queen's Flight in the late 1960s. Philip learned to fly fixed-wing aircraft in 1952 and, he has said, if he had had his own way, he would have preferred to go into the Royal Air Force rather than the Royal Navy.

Philip has always loved photography, and when he embarked on a four-month voyage on HMY *Britannia* in 1956, he had with him his Hasselblad reflex camera and a telephoto lens. By good chance HMY *Britannia* was equipped with a darkroom.

Prince Charles leading his father from the Viking aircraft in which the duke arrived home from Malta with aide and friend Mike Parker. Two-year-old Charles greeted his father at London Airport while his mother was at Ascot to watch the Festival Stakes. The duke had just handed over his command of the frigate HMS *Magpie*.

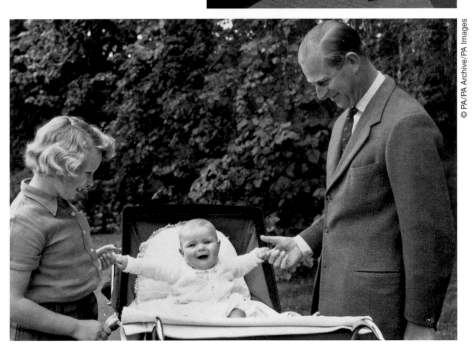

Prince Philip has always been good with young children and knows how to keep them entertained. Here he holds hands with seven-month-old Prince Andrew alongside ten-year-old Princess Anne at Balmoral in September 1960.

With Queen Elizabeth the Queen Mother, who was almost a hundred years old, at the June 2000 Derby meeting at Epsom. Philip did not always agree with his mother-in-law, but he admired her strength of character and enthusiasm for life.

Prince Philip joking with grandsons Princes William and Harry at Sandhurst Royal Military Academy after the Sovereign's Parade marking the completion of Prince Harry's officer training in April 2006.

Prince Philip and his youngest son, Prince Edward, watch the Vulcan fly-past at the Royal Ascot Spectacular in aid of the Prince Philip Trust in July 1984.

Prince Philip jokes with the Duchess of Cambridge at the St. George's Chapel wedding of Princess Eugenie and Jack Brooksbank on October 12, 2018. The Duchess of Sussex, standing next to him, was just about to announce her pregnancy.

The Princess of Wales and the Duke of Edinburgh after the wedding of Lady Sarah Armstrong Jones to Daniel Chatto in July 1994. Prince Charles and his estranged wife arrived and left separately, and Prince Philip looked after the princess while she waited for her car.

A sharply dressed Prince Philip, aged ninety, ever the charmer, talks to Gwyneth Paltrow at the Arts Club in Mayfair, where he was hosting a party to celebrate its reopening on October 5, 2011.

Prince Philip at the Field of Remembrance at Westminster Abbey just before Armistice Day in November 2012. Here he is providing amusement for another glamorous lady, a Chelsea Pensioner, distinctive in her scarlet coat and tricorn hat.

Two of the original great conservationists of this century, the Duke of Edinburgh and Sir David Attenborough, at the Order of Merit luncheon at Windsor Castle in May 2019.

Philip's very last official engagement before retirement was as Captain General of the Royal Marines in the forecourt of Buckingham Palace on August 2, 2017. The pouring rain did not dampen the spirits of the ninety-six-year-old duke.

wooden parts that were liable to break with lightweight metal components. Although no longer driving in competitions, Philip still takes the reins and was seen in his ninety-eighth year driving his carriage in Windsor Great Park and on the Sandringham estate. Not only did Philip have an enormous influence over making carriage driving what it is today, but it enabled him to have a completely independent lifestyle, traveling around both the UK and Europe from one grand country house party to another for competitions, often with a glamorous lady riding with him.

It was Philip who encouraged Penny Romsey (now Countess Mountbatten) to take up carriage driving. She expressed an interest in what she called "this driving thing" and asked him whether it might be possible to teach her daughter's pony to pull a trap. He lent Penny his head groom Micky Flynn to teach her and persuaded her to start competitive driving, although she had no idea what she was letting herself in for. What it did mean for Philip was that together with his loyal friend and private secretary Brian McGrath, who loved the sport and always traveled with him, he had an attractive companion to share the endless competitions and house parties associated with the sport.

In 2002, he also persuaded Sophie Wessex to have a go at driving and said she obviously enjoyed it, did well, and he "hoped she was hooked." He said she had considerable talent and had shown keenness until she fell pregnant with his granddaughter Lady Louise Mountbatten-Windsor, who now competes herself. Both Sophie and her daughter competed at Windsor Horse Show in 2019, and Sophie is now vice president of the show.

"Carriage driving is always great fun," Philip said in 2004. "When I started driving, I used to try to find people I could stay with so that I could drive. I now drive so that I can go and stay with people." Among them was his good friend Sebastian de Ferranti, who built his own stately home, the neo-Palladian Henbury Hall in Cheshire, where Prince Philip and the Queen frequently stayed. Philip persuaded Sebastian to give up hunting and take up carriage driving and lent him one of his ponies, Carrick, to get him started. Like Philip, he became fanatical about the sport and eventually adapted part of his parkland to host competitions where the guest of honor was, of course, Prince Philip.

Philip admits that his thoughts turned to retirement from time to time. When he was eighty-two, his old green horsebox and trailer needed replacing, and that would be an "excellent excuse," he thought. "But then I thought, perhaps unreasonably, that I would be damned if I was forced to give up just because the horsebox and trailer had run out of puff." He continued: "You may well wonder why I have continued to compete for quite so many years. The simple answer is that I have enjoyed every moment of it, or, more accurately, almost every moment of it. It gets me into the fresh air and it keeps me reasonably fit."

Another thing he has done that serves him well today is adapt a range of clothing that would keep him warm during the winter months, especially at Sandringham, where the east wind comes straight off the North Sea. It occurred to him that motorcyclists managed to keep out the cold and wet, so he acquired a "reasonably discreet" Gortex jacket with a zipped-in padded inner jacket. He wore this with a lightweight pullover and a heavy Scandinavian jersey, and it kept him warm even in the most arctic of conditions. Always inventive, he then acquired from the police a pair of padded Gortex overtrousers, which he wore over moleskin trousers and a pair of "moon boots" from China. He used three layers of gloves— electrically heated under gloves plus so-called waterproof gloves over a pair of surgical rubber gloves—and topped off the outfit with a deerstalker hat to keep the rain from going down his neck. "I may well look like Inspector Clouseau in cold pursuit of the Pink Panther in the Arctic," he admitted, "but it is effective."

Philip has had more influence than anyone on the way international equestrian sport has developed. He was presented with the FEI award for dedicated and distinguished services to equestrian sport in 2001. Among his many achievements in the post of president were the creation of equine passports for international competitors, contributing to a hugely expanded international calendar, and welcoming endurance and driving under the FEI umbrella. On the domestic front, he was the driving force behind the creation of the Pony Club Mounted Games for the Prince Philip Cup, the finale to a season-long series of competitions in which thousands of children across the country compete in equestrian events.

In his capacity as president of FEI, Philip attended five Olympic games over twenty years to oversee the equestrian events of show jumping and dressage. He found it a duty rather than a pleasure. As he put it: "I am not really a talented spectator, frankly. Yes, it is quite fun to watch but it is not the be-all and end-all. I've had enough of it. I did something like five Olympic Games when I was just standing around watching things. I'd rather do something."

He has very strong views on opening and closing ceremonies. Interviewed for the *Daily Telegraph* in 2006, he said: "Olympic opening and closing ceremonies ought to be banned. Absolute bloody nuisances. I have been to one that was absolutely appalling, awful. I was suddenly told at Munich I think it was—that we couldn't have the main arena for show jumping because it had to be prepared for the closing ceremony. What is the Olympics about, the competition or the closing ceremony?"

Philip's views on the opening of the 2012 Olympics in London, when a stand-in for the Queen was seen to parachute into the stadium in a James Bond sequence, are not recorded, but he was dubious about his wife getting involved. It was left to the princess royal and the director of the ceremony, Danny Boyle, to persuade her to appear with James Bond actor Daniel Craig in a recorded cameo sequence. According to her dresser, Angela Kelly, she was very amused by the idea as long as she was able to deliver the iconic line, "Good evening, Mr. Bond."

Philip once said: "A lot of weird things have been written about the Olympic Games. It's much more important to come away from the games with a good reputation and having made friends with everybody there than to come back with a bagful of medals. On the other hand, I have no objection to doing both."

It was during his school days at Gordonstoun that Philip first became interested in sailing. That interest, coupled with a lifelong love of the sea, stayed with him for many decades.

When Philip arrived at Royal Naval College, Dartmouth, such was his seamanship that he was one of only two cadets in his year who were allowed to captain the college's cutters and whalers. His years in the Royal Navy furthered his ability to read charts, to feel the wind, and to understand the tides and the sea to the extent that sailing became second nature to him.

After Philip's marriage in 1947, Cowes Week, the oldest and largest annual sailing regatta in the world, became an annual fixture in Philip's diary. Cowes Week originates from King George IV's passion for yachting, and the first race was held on August 10, 1826. The event is held on the Solent, which is the area of water between Southern England and the Isle of Wight, and the early twentieth century saw the regatta continue to grow in strength and popularity. Philip became a friend of the legendary boat designer and Cowes native Uffa Fox, with whom he often raced during Cowes Week.

One of Uffa's most popular designs was the Flying Fifteen. *Coweslip* is the most famous of the Flying Fifteen keelboats, having been given to Princess Elizabeth and Prince Philip as a wedding present by the people of Cowes in 1949. Philip frequently sailed on *Coweslip* with Uffa, and together they had great success sailing competitively, including winning the Britannia Cup in 1952. They also had their mishaps: in 1962 at Cowes, *Coweslip* nearly sank when she was hit by a gust of wind and capsized, throwing both Uffa and Philip into the water. Press photographers drove Philip to distraction when sailing. They would follow in a flotilla of small boats hoping to get a picture of Philip up to his neck in water.

Philip and Uffa also sailed together in the Dragon class yacht *Bluebottle*. In 1961, Philip agreed to become commodore of the Royal Yacht Squadron for a period of six years. As is his wont, Philip saw room for improvement in the organization of Cowes Week, which had previously been run by seven local sailing clubs, each with their own particular rules. Philip oversaw many reforms, combining all seven sets of club rules into one and fixing the starting point of all Cowes races at the Royal Yacht Squadron line. He has remained admiral of the squadron during his life and is also patron of the Royal Southern Yacht Club in Hamble.

During Cowes Week, Philip based himself on the royal yacht HMS *Britannia*, which became a fixture in Cowes until 1997, when *Britannia* was decommissioned. In 1962, Philip purchased the 63-foot (19-meter) ocean racing yacht *Bloodhound*, which he raced at Cowes. He also took *Bloodhound* on the royal family's annual holiday, sailing around the Western Isles of Scotland, where he taught both Prince Charles and Princess Anne to sail.

In Uffa Fox's 1950 book *Handling Sailing Boats*, he praised Philip's seamanship when he wrote: "Prince Philip is a great seaman, and in one race, when our next mark was so far away that it was under our horizon, he continually looked back at the mark we had rounded and by keeping this steady on the land steered such a straight and steady course that we gained four places and never had to alter the trim of our spinnaker or mainsail."

Through his work with the Royal Yachting Association, which is the national body for dinghy, yacht, and motor cruising, all forms of sail racing, sports boats, windsurfing, and personal watercraft, Philip has encouraged young people to take up sailing. In 2006, the fiftieth anniversary of the Prince Philip Cup was held in Cowes. The cup has attracted some of the island's finest sailors, including Uffa Fox, whose name is engraved several times on the trophy. Philip continued to appear at Cowes every year until his retirement from public life in 2017.

As a teenager, Philip spent time in the school holidays on the extensive country estates of his brothers-in-law in Germany. There he was introduced to the country pursuits of deerstalking, hunting wild boar, and fly-fishing for trout. It was not uncommon for fifty wild boar to be bagged in a day. In later years, after the Second World War, Philip would make secret private visits to Germany to take part in the sport.

It was not until his father-in-law King George VI gave him a pair of Purdeys, the best shotguns in the world, as a wedding present that he took up shooting in earnest. The King was a crack shot and Philip was a fast learner and soon became an expert himself. Christmas holidays at Sandringham would find him shooting four days a week on the 20,000-acre (8,000-hectare) estate, sometimes bagging thousands of pheasant. In August at Balmoral, he would be in the butts on the grouse moors. His valet John Dean recalled acting as Philip's loader so that Philip didn't waste time in reloading his guns and the bag could be maximized by carrying two guns. Forty or fifty soldiers from the Highland Regiment that provided the guard at Balmoral would act as beaters, driving droves of grouse toward the guns. Deerstalking is another activity Philip enjoyed at Balmoral. He became expert at tracking a stag over miles of heather and then dropping it with a single shot to the heart.

In his day, Philip has shot deer, rabbit, hare, wild duck, snipe, woodcock, teal, pigeon, partridge, and pheasant in vast numbers. For many years he has been patron of the British Association for Shooting and Conservation, formerly called the Wildfowlers' Association. Unlike grouse and pheasant shooting, which are social activities built around shooting parties, wildfowling is a more solitary sport. It has been described by Wentworth Day in terms that would appeal to Philip: "The true philosopher of the gun is the wildfowler, for he must have the sensitive eye of an artist, a love of solitude and lonely places. He measures beauty by the flash of a bird's wing, by the glint of dawn on sliding waters, by the march of slow clouds."

Philip has always found it easy to reconcile his love of blood sports with his position as president of the conservation charity the World Wide Fund for Nature (WWF, previously the World Wildlife Fund). Because he was tired of so many people questioning his stance, a standard reply was printed. Philip's stated view is that keeping the numbers in balance is good husbandry and good for the preservation of the species. However, while it may be necessary to cull deer to keep the numbers down and to promote healthy stock, it is harder to justify rearing many thousands of pheasant chicks for the sole purpose of shooting them as adult birds.

The Queen often accompanied Philip on pheasant shoots. She is an expert dog trainer and handler and organized the dogs to pick up and retrieve the downed birds. On one occasion, when they were both staying at Lord Dalhousie's estate in Scotland, she was behind the guns picking up birds when she saw one of the two figures at Philip's butt fall. For one awful moment she thought it was the duke and ran as fast as she could to where the men were. It was actually his loyal valet Joe Pearce, who was loading for Philip when he had a heart attack and dropped dead. Philip was fond of Joe, who had worked for the family for years and had been the Queen's personal footman when she was still Princess Elizabeth. A memorial service was arranged for him later, which Prince Philip attended.

The royal passion for shooting has not escaped a new generation. Prince William is said to prefer shooting to any other sport, while Prince Andrew took his daughter Beatrice on a shoot when she was six. Prince Harry, an excellent shot, has been persuaded by his wife, Meghan, to slow down on his slaughter of game birds. During a weekend shooting party with his close friends in 2018, Harry and Meghan were the guests of honor and arrived in time for dinner before shooting the next day. At exactly 9 a.m. all the guns were waiting at the door to move off, but no sign of Harry. They didn't quite know what to do so they waited and waited until Harry eventually appeared at the door in his dressing gown looking very sheepish. His embarrassed explanation was that Meghan did not want him to go out with the guns, which was extremely awkward as he was guest of honor. Prince Philip would never have put up with such behavior, and in the days when Princess Margaret was married to Tony Armstrong-Jones, he would rudely leave his hand on the horn when Tony was late, which he inevitably was.

Philip had to give up shooting after he had a stent inserted in his heart in December 2011. The fear was that the recoil of the gun when it was fired might dislodge the stent. Since then, he has been obsessed with fishing, and it has become his main outdoor activity after carriage driving. He goes out for hours with just a ghillie and only stops for meals. He has been out in all weathers, and if he has caught some brown trout, he loves to cook it over a barbecue.

Philip has always kept active. From swimming and waterskiing to squash at Buckingham Palace and deck hockey and competitive rowing in the Royal Navy, he has always kept himself fit. Even at the age of ninety-eight, he maintains physical fitness with a daily routine of air force exercises he has been practicing for years. He believes if his body is flexible, he is less likely to fall—and he is still able to stand up remarkably straight for a man of his age.

Outside of sport, he has a keen artistic bent. He has always been an avid photographer. His book *Birds from Britannia* captures many birds in flight as well as photographs of Galápagos wildlife and whaling in the Antarctic. Although Prince Charles is better known than his father for his watercolors, Philip enjoys painting both in watercolors and in oils. He has painted landscapes at Balmoral and in Australia as well as floral still lifes and an intimate portrait of the Queen at breakfast that includes a pot of marmalade on the table and a Stubbs equine painting on the wall.

He is extremely knowledgeable about art and is one of the few who know all the artworks in the royal collection. He also has a talent for design, having created several pieces of jewelry for the Queen, including her engagement ring and a bracelet for their twenty-fifth wedding anniversary. After the fire at Windsor Castle in 1992, when a blaze devastated much of the castle's state apartments and burned the private chapel to the ground, Philip played a key role in the five-year restoration project and designed a stained-glass window for the new private chapel.

Philip has always shown an interest in food and cookery. This has been evident from his very early days in the galley of the Gordonstoun ketch, where he was renowned for his scrambled eggs, to brewing cocoa in the Royal Navy, which earned him a mention in 1940 in HMS *Kent* first lieutenant's log: "It rained most of the morning watch. Luckily had Prince Philip as the snotty and he makes the best cup of cocoa of the lot."

As a married man, Philip acquired an electric frying pan, which he used to cook bacon and eggs for breakfast, until the Queen complained that the smell of cooking lingered until lunchtime. The frying pan went everywhere with him on his travels. Having been presented with a breakfast banquet by renowned French chef Regis Crepy in 2002, Philip announced, "The French don't know how to cook breakfast."

Philip has an extensive library of cookery books and has always asked the chefs at home to try out new dishes from recipes he collected on his travels abroad. Now he is at home much of the time, he loves to watch cookery programs on television; Mary Berry is one of his favorites. She has said: "I am very lucky to have had lunch with the Queen. I was seated next to the Duke, a delightful man who talked about barbecuing. He said that he took his game birds at Sandringham and stuffed them with haggis but put in more breadcrumbs to absorb the fat. I could see that he knew what he was talking about." Philip would himself pluck, clean, and prepare for cooking all manner of game birds that he shot, snipe being his favorite. Being a highly skilled barbecue chef, he designed a portable barbecue that would fit into the back of a Range Rover so he could take it out onto the moors at Balmoral.

Given the extent of his official duties as consort, the constant public appearances, his regimental duties, and the countless dinners and speeches, Philip has been left with limited leisure time. Therefore it is all the more remarkable that in his day he has been a very good cricketer, a world-class polo player, a race-winning yachtsman, and a world-champion carriage driver, and that he has flown thousands of hours in many types of aircraft. Not only has he participated in many sports, but he has also reorganized, improved, and promoted them for the benefit of future generations.

Chapter 13

CONSERVATION

Fifty years ago, on February 9, 1970, Prince Philip gave an address to a conference in Strasbourg for European Conservation Year. "Between them, technology and mankind have created a vast network of road, rail, and air transport systems along with a problem in refuse and waste disposal which has completely defeated our efforts to control it," he said. "Meanwhile, increasing leisure has released millions of people into the mountains and on to the beaches. Now we are facing a crisis situation. We must decide how much pollution of the air, the land and the water we are prepared to tolerate. The fact is we cannot postpone decisions any longer. Time is fast running out and it remains to be seen whether those in political authority can shoulder their responsibilities in time and act quickly enough to relieve a situation which grows more serious every day."

These words might well have come from the 2019 Global Environmental Outlook compiled by the United Nations and endorsed by 130 countries, including the United States, Russia, and China, setting out a framework for halting what has been dubbed the sixth mass extinction of life on earth, from insects to plant life and fish.

It is the strongest call for action ever by global scientists. Prince Philip's grandson Prince Harry took up the cause in September 2019 when he said he felt "impassioned" to help when he saw the damage tourism had inflicted on the environment. "Sometimes when we appreciate the world's beauty, we heighten its fragility. It's a paradox," he said, "but in our enthusiasm, we can put a great strain on the natural wonders we travel to see, as well as the communities that call these places home."

When Prince Charles launched his Sustainable Markets Council in January 2020 at Davos, he described "global warming, climate change and the devastating loss of biodiversity" as "the greatest threats humanity has ever faced." He spoke for future generations when he said his grandchildren's generation are "standing up and saying, 'What are you doing? We can't go on like this.'"

Prince Philip, who watched his son on television at the Davos summit with a degree of satisfaction, had become aware of the potential dangers to the earth's biosphere and all wildlife many years before the term "global warming" came into popular usage. He drew attention to the dangers to the entire world arising from acid rain, the destruction of the ozone layer, and the "greenhouse effect" caused by too much carbon dioxide in the atmosphere well before they were acknowledged as serious problems. In the early 1990s, he told his biographer Tim Heald: "The whole business of the conservation of nature has had a significant influence on my life and thought." He had one of the first electric cars of its time, a Metrocab, which according to legendary anthropologist David Attenborough "made no noise whatsoever," and then exchanged it for a more eco-friendly runaround in 1999 that ran on liquified petroleum gas. As long ago as 1994, at Philip's behest, combined heat and power plants were installed at Windsor Castle and Buckingham Palace to generate electricity and provide heating and hot water, and in 2001, a Buckingham Palace "energy saving committee" was formed to explore ways of reducing energy consumption. They decided to drill a 500-foot (150-meter) borehole in the Buckingham Palace garden to provide water to cool the Queen's gallery and to flush the visitors' lavatories, which at Prince Philip's instruction were adapted to save water. Hydroelectric schemes now partly power both Windsor Castle and Balmoral.

So how did Philip come to take up an interest in conservation in its widest sense—that is, relating to all forms of life, both animal and vegetable, on earth, in the air, and in the seas, and make it one of his lifelong passions?

By his own admission, Philip had little or no interest in the natural world as a schoolboy and during his days in the navy. While on two long world tours on the HMY *Britannia* during the second half of the 1950s, it was his interest in photographing seabirds that led to him thinking about conservation. Prior to that time, as we have already seen, his only contact with nature was through field sports, including shooting, stalking, and fishing. His German brothers-in-law had extensive country estates where he witnessed the hunting of wild boar and shooting of game birds. As an engagement present, King George VI gave Philip a pair of Purdey twelve-bore shotguns and then coached him in the finer points of shooting. After his marriage, Philip became active in the field sports that his father-in-law enjoyed so much, namely shooting pheasant at Sandringham, grouse at Balmoral, and stalking stag on the hills.

Philip has no problem reconciling his love of field sports with his passionate interest in conservation. He has said that experienced hunting sportsmen have for generations practiced conservation by observing the close season, ensuring that there is always sufficient stock for the following season, and holding the welfare of their prey in high regard. In the introduction to the book *Wildlife Crisis*, Philip has written:

"Stalking deer and shooting game birds was so much a part of the life of my relations that it has never become a moral problem as far as I am concerned, although I realize it can raise strong emotions in others. I came to conservation through shooting and bird-watching. To anyone with a conventional view of pleasure, the idea that there might be any thrill in wildfowling or rough shooting must seem too painfully ludicrous to be considered. Yet this is the stuff of natural history, this is a certain way to arouse an enthusiasm for conservation."

Philip, who is patron of the Wildfowlers' Association of Great Britain, is content to go wildfowling in the Norfolk fens, where the object of the sport is to kill as many ducks as possible with a single shot from the massive gun mounted on the bows of a punt. At the same time, he also takes delight in spotting any rare birds or creatures.

Philip has long had an interest in photography, and his office contains dozens of neatly filed and titled photograph albums. When he embarked on a four-month voyage on *Britannia* to open the Olympic Games in Melbourne in 1956, he had with him some expensive pieces of equipment—his Hasselblad reflex camera and a telephoto lens. By good chance HMY *Britannia* was equipped with a darkroom for developing film. Until that time, he had never consciously taken a photograph of a bird. In all his years in the Royal Navy, in home waters and in the Indian and Pacific oceans, he said that, apart from game birds like pheasant, he thought that all birds came into three categories: sparrows, seagulls, and ducks.

The voyage was intended to take in some island communities and outposts of the commonwealth that are too small to be visited by air, as well as to meet up with Sir Vivian Fuchs and the Commonwealth Trans-Antarctic Expedition in New Zealand. Starting from Mombasa, HMY *Britannia* sailed to Melbourne via the

Seychelles, Ceylon, and Malaya. After Melbourne, *Britannia* sailed eastward from New Zealand across the South Pacific and around Cape Horn toward the Falkland Islands, a distance of 3,800 miles (6,115 kilometers) of open sea, with seabirds being the only living things to observe from the decks of the royal yacht. This was the start of Philip's lifelong fascination with ornithology and resulted in the publication in 1962 of his book of photographs *Birds from Britannia*. The expedition's official artist, Edward Seago, was on board HMY *Britannia*, and he painted a picture of Philip on deck seated in front of his easel with brush in hand as he tried to capture the seascapes. He also gave Philip lessons in painting.

On the voyage were Philip's equerry Mike Parker and a team from his office that issued news bulletins from time to time. Parker expressed disappointment that the press at home did little to report on the job that Philip was doing in visiting far-flung outposts of the Commonwealth like Tristan da Cunha, the most remote inhabited archipelago in the world, with its colony of rockhopper penguins. The expedition only made headlines when on *Britannia*'s return via Portugal, Mike Parker resigned his post as Philip's private secretary and equerry because he was embroiled in divorce proceedings.

HMY *Britannia* made a stop at Norfolk Island, where the descendants of the mutineers from HMS *Bounty* had been settled after leaving Pitcairn Island. Philip records meeting Fletcher Christian's descendant as well as seeing a number of bird species native to the island. The expedition also paid a visit to the British Antarctic survey team in South Georgia, which provided an opportunity to photograph penguins. Philip referred to the overpowering odor of the penguin rookeries, which can contain many thousands of birds, as being so unpleasant that they should only be approached from upwind. In order to visit the British bases within the Antarctic Circle, Philip went aboard the icebreaker *John Biscoe* for a few days. One of the passengers had brought along a couple of tennis rackets and some balls. So, with great solemnity and not a little hilarity, the only recorded game of tennis in the Antarctic was played on the ice outside one of the bases.

Philip devoted several pages in his *Birds from Britannia* book to whaling and included some of his photographs of whaling ships. Inside the Antarctic Circle he went on board the whale factory ship *Southern Harvester* that acted as a depot for fifteen to twenty whale catchers. He gave a graphic and detailed description of the harpooning and stripping of the carcasses of sperm whales and blue whales, which was then a major industry. He said that whale factories both ashore and afloat have a smell all of their own that has to be experienced to be properly appreciated.

The section in his book on whaling is included as a matter of general interest, and Philip makes no mention of the conservation of whales. By 1982, however, things had changed: in the intervening years there was a growing realization about the harm being done. In a speech to the Council for Environmental Conservation Conference in London, Philip said, "As far as whales are concerned, conservation and welfare act together because the species are in danger." Things are very different today with Greenpeace leading the global condemnation of whaling.

To commemorate their Antarctic adventure—and the honorary membership of the Order of the Red Nose for sailors who have crossed the Antarctic Circle—Edward Seago and Philip designed a linocut certificate featuring an amusing image of Philip himself with a red nose, wrapped up against the elements, with a seal and penguin looking on. Philip inked and printed the linocuts himself. Seago wrote in his diary at the time: "Prince Philip has really done the design for it although the wardroom asked me, but I must admit his idea is better than what I had in mind! I am amazed at his keenness and energy."

To quote from *Wildlife Crisis*, a book published in 1970 and coauthored by Philip, he said: "Simply as a pastime I tried to take photographs of birds. That did it; from then on, I was hooked. I had to know what each species was called. I had to try and get a reasonable picture of every species that came anywhere near the yacht." He continued: "It is only a matter of a short time of birdwatching and photography before the question of survival of species begins to dawn on the mind."

Philip was soon able to recognize the many varieties of seabird in the southern Pacific. He noted seeing sooty, wandering, black-browed, and shy albatrosses; gray-faced, white-headed, and stormy petrels; prions, shearwaters, fulmars, and mollymawks. Philip made a second long voyage in *Britannia* in 1959, representing the British Association for the Advancement of Science at meetings in Delhi and Karachi; he then visited Borneo, the Solomon Islands, and Christmas Island (so named because it was discovered by Captain Cook on Christmas Day 1777) and continued through the Panama Canal to the Bahamas and Bermuda to celebrate the 350th anniversary of the island being a colony to the Crown. Although there was less opportunity to photograph birds on this voyage since Philip had a full program of engagements ashore, he said even the gardens of the government houses sometimes yielded an interesting specimen or two.

On one of these *Britannia* voyages, Philip invited the US ambassador, who was also a keen bird-watcher, on board. One day they were scanning the seas with their binoculars looking in vain for signs of birdlife. The ambassador eventually said to Philip that there seemed to be a remarkable lack of ornithological activity that day. Philip thought for a moment, then said, "You mean there are no bloody birds."

Back in London in 1961, Philip became friendly with Sir Peter Scott, the renowned ornithologist, conservationist, and artist. An ex–navy man, Scott was the son of the Antarctic explorer Captain Scott and had won a bronze medal for Great Britain's sailing team at the 1936 Olympic Games in Berlin. He thus had several interests in common with Philip. He was knighted in 1973 for services to conservation. At the time, in 1961, Scott was in the process of setting up the World Wildlife Fund with Prince Bernhard of the Netherlands. Prince Bernhard was consort to Queen Juliana, and Philip—being in the same number two position as Bernhard with no constitutional rights—had sought his advice on the position of consort to Queen Elizabeth.

The WWF was set up as a campaigning and fundraising arm of the international conservation movement, including the International Council for Bird Preservation. Scott designed the panda logo for the WWF based on Chi Chi, the giant panda living in London Zoo. He recruited Philip to become president of the British National Appeal of the organization and invited him to contribute a couple of chapters and some of his bird photographs to the book *Wildlife Crisis*, which was sold to raise funds for the WWF. Luckily for Scott, Philip had injured a leg in a polo accident and as a result had to cancel several weeks of engagements, thus freeing him up to do some writing. In the end he contributed three long chapters written out in long hand.

The World Wildlife Fund was founded in 1961 by a group of mainly British naturalists. It was established as a Swiss foundation with offices in Zurich, and the deed of foundation specified among the purposes of the organization that the WWF aims to "stop the degradation of the planet's natural environment and to build a future in which humans live in harmony with nature." In 1985, the WWF formally re-registered its name as the World Wide Fund for Nature to try to escape the preservation of animal species image and reflect a broader view of global conservation.

Prince Philip has been closely associated with the WWF ever

since its foundation. Not only was he that year the first president of WWF-UK—a position he held for twenty years—but he was also president of WWF International between 1981 and 1996, when Prince Bernhard was forced to step down after being involved in a bribery scandal with the Lockheed Aircraft Corporation in his home country. On his retirement, Philip became the WWF president emeritus—a position he still holds today. Under Philip's leadership in the 1990s, the WWF revised its mission statement: "To stop the degradation of the planet's natural environment and to build a future in which humans live in harmony with nature, by conserving the world's biological diversity; ensuring that the use of renewable natural resources is sustainable; and promoting the reduction of pollution and wasteful consumption."

In an interview to mark the fortieth anniversary of the WWF in 2001, Philip declared: "If nature doesn't survive, neither will man." But, he warned, the survival of both depended on human attitudes. "We can't make the Earth any bigger and we can't squeeze any more out of its natural resources without changing its whole character and damaging its systems."

Over the decades, much of Prince Philip's work with the WWF has been behind the scenes, often with heads of state or government. This helped bring about the creation of national parks, the protection of endangered species, and the introduction of stronger environmental laws around the world. As Philip said himself, it would be foolish to deny that a title always looks good at the head of a charity. Government ministers, company chairmen, presidents, and even popes take notice when in receipt of a communication from Prince Philip.

To mark the occasion of Philip's ninetieth birthday, the WWF throughout the world paid tribute to him, saying that his contribution to nature and the environment, and to the WWF in particular, had been immeasurable. "His farsighted and passionate commitment to conservation will benefit countless people for generations to come," said James Leape, director general of WWF International. "His work for us over the years has been highly effective, and we send him our warmest greetings on his ninetieth birthday."

For many years before conservation and the environment became global issues, Philip warned of a dire crisis and that time was running out. Fifty years ago, politicians would not listen. At the 1970 Conservation Year Conference in Strasbourg, both Philip and Prince Bernhard spoke passionately about the need for action. Labour cabinet minister Anthony Crosland, who was at the conference, expressed the view that people in privileged positions should be more concerned about substandard housing than worrying about endangered species like giant pandas. Many politicians of the day shared his views.

Philip has held the view that the inexorable growth of the world's population is at the root of the problems faced by conservationists. As early as 1962, in an address to the WWF in New York, he referred to "the human population explosion which, together with the technological explosion, is the origin of the most direct threat to the survival of much of the natural environment. Which is it to be? The unfettered right of people to have as many children as they like without any concern for the consequences. Or is it acceptable to suggest voluntary restraint for the sake of the survival of many other life forms?"

The ever-increasing world population is a subject which Philip revisits time after time. It is noteworthy that he offers no solution and studiously avoids the subject of population control and family planning. Perhaps this is as well coming from the father of four children. It was his duty to provide an "heir and a spare" to ensure the continuity of the royal line but, having done so, to have two additional children hardly sets a good example to be followed. In a

1987 address in London, Philip said: "To make any comment about human population is just about as dangerous as going for a Sunday afternoon walk in a minefield. I do believe however that human population pressure—the sheer number of people on this planet—is the single most important cause of the degradation of the natural environment, of the progressive extinction of wild species of plants and animals and of the destabilisation of the world's climatic and atmospheric systems."

At the time Philip was writing, the world population was about 4.5 billion; it has since increased to nearly 8 billion and is growing fast. Today global warming and the degradation of the biosphere is blamed on heavy industry, carbon emissions, plastic pollution, and a host of other causes, but little is said about the "human population explosion" as Philip has called it. One of the few outspoken voices on this subject is that of Sir David Attenborough, who is patron of Population Matters, a charity set up in 1991 to influence policy-makers, communities, and individuals to make positive changes for a sustainable human population. He has said: "All our environmental problems become easier to solve with fewer people, and harder—and ultimately impossible—to solve with ever more people. In the long run, our population growth has to come to an end." He attributed population growth partly to increases in life expectancy: "people like me are living longer than we did," Sir David told a BBC interviewer in 2018, and our rate of increase is "alarming."

During his years with the WWF, Philip spoke often of the need to control the free-for-all exploitation of the seas, particularly regarding the maintaining of fish stocks and the taking of whales for meat. Typical of his speeches was the Fairfield Osborne lecture given in New York in 1980, when he said: "The whole of the North Sea was thrown open to the members of the EEC just at the time that fishing techniques were becoming increasingly efficient. In consequence, it was overfished and there is now a severe restriction on the taking of most species of fish and much unemployment among fishermen."

Under his auspices, the WWF launched a campaign called "The Seas Must Live," and among its aims were establishing sanctuaries for calving whales, the conservation of coral reefs, and the protection of a number of endangered species, including the Indus dolphin, the Mediterranean monk seal, and the narwhal with its long single tusk.

During the 1980s, as we will see, Prince Philip became increasingly interested in religion and its relationship with conservation. His views on conservation became something of a religious crusade, which he termed "the moral imperative." Speaking in 1982, he said: "All plants and creatures, including man, were created or caused to be evolved by the Almighty and therefore we have a moral obligation as His final creation to protect and conserve all our fellow living beings and organisms. If we are to exercise our responsibilities so that all life can continue on earth, they must have a moral and philosophical basis."

And on another occasion, he expressed: "If God is in nature, nature itself becomes divine and from that point it becomes reasonable to argue that reverence for God and nature implies responsibility not to harm it." He went on to say that this moral imperative is recognized by all the great religions. Philip quoted from the book of Genesis to support his belief in the moral imperative.

In 1986, the year of the WWF foundation's twenty-fifth anniversary, Philip organized an event to forge an alliance between conservation and five of the world's great religions. He invited the leaders of the religious authorities representing Buddhism, Christianity, Hinduism, Islam, and Judaism to gather at the Basilica of St. Francis in Assisi. These leaders produced the Assisi Declarations, theological statements showing the spiritual relationship between their followers and nature, which triggered a growth in the engagement of those religions with conservation around the world. Each of the five religions published a declaration on nature, typical of which is: "What is needed today is to remind ourselves that nature cannot be destroyed without mankind ultimately being destroyed itself."

More recently, in 2016, the Declarations of Assisi were reinforced when the WWF held an audience with Pope Francis, resulting in the issuance by His Holiness of an encyclical, or message. It provides an unprecedented moral call to the world to act on behalf of future generations to prevent growing inequality and catastrophic climate change. Pope Francis's message added a much-needed moral approach to the climate debate, which is increasingly a moral and ethical issue. The encyclical was closely followed by expressions of solidarity from representatives of other faiths from all over the world.

More than fifty years have elapsed since Philip first warned of the dangers of "the greenhouse effect" arising from the increase in carbon dioxide in the atmosphere as a result of the burning of fossil fuels and the destruction of rain forests, which together has led to global warming. In 2019, the United Nations issued its direst warning yet of the consequences of this warming. The catastrophic effect of the melting of the polar ice caps with the resulting rise in sea level could bring about what the UN calls the sixth great extinction when all life on earth would be threatened. Philip was a man many years before his time. His warnings, unheeded at the time, have now become central issues for the whole world.

In his last interview, given on BBC radio in 2016, before his retirement from public life, Philip was not entirely pessimistic. He concluded that it is engineers who could hold the key to the future of humanity and its ability to thrive on the planet. He said, "Everything not invented by God is invented by an engineer." He continued that engineers could play a vital role by helping to solve the issues that arise as a result of the world's increasing population.

Philip holds out some hope for the future of the earth, saying: "The human population of the earth is growing and is occupying more space. It's got to be accommodated somehow or another. And I think most people would like to see that it accommodates a certain amount of the natural world and everything we require to keep it going. Somehow or other that balance, to try to fit as many people on to this globe as comfortably as possible without doing too much damage, I think ultimately it's going to be engineers that decide that."

Chapter 14

THE PHILOSOPHER PRINCE

As a child and a young man, Philip had a thirst for knowledge about all things. His brothers-in-law remembered being pestered with endless questions, and his teachers have spoken of his inquiring mind. During his life, his range of interests has been vast, including philosophy and psychology, science and technology, conservation and the natural world. He even took an interest in flying saucers: he was a subscriber to the *Flying Saucer Review* and wrote to Timothy Good, the leading authority on unidentified flying objects, "There are many reasons to believe they exist." His interest in space travel remains to this day. In 2016, the following message was sent by the Queen to British astronaut Tim Peake: "Prince Philip and I are pleased to transmit our best wishes to Major Timothy Peake as he joins the International Space Station in orbit."

Early in his married life, Philip began to establish himself as a public speaker. As he took on the presidency of more and more charitable organizations and professional societies, accepted university chancellorships and freedoms of cities, and took part in foreign tours, his range of speaking subjects became wider and wider. On his own admission, he did not have a special knowledge of any particular subject, but he was expected to have something suitable to say whatever the occasion. Several books of his speeches on an extensive range of subjects have been published. It is noteworthy that for many years his speeches were more of a practical and scientific nature and not in the least philosophical.

Philip did not share his mother's religious fervor during his childhood, and it was not until much later in life that he discovered he wanted to explore the meaning of the obsessions that had driven her. He began to talk and write about religion and theology, the meaning of life, the origin of the species, and the presence of God. Unlike the Queen, who is devoutly religious and enjoys church services, Philip described himself as an ordinary Christian, going to church on Sundays. He was baptised into the Greek Orthodox Church. but according to Dr. Fisher, the then Archbishop of Canterbury, he always regarded himself as an Anglican. There were chapel services on Sundays at school and short Sunday services on board ship during his navy days.

He has no patience with sermons, mainly because he loves an argument and sermons give no opportunity to the listener to reply and discuss. As soon as he had the authority to do so, he imposed a strict limit of twelve minutes for the sermon whenever he was going to church. On the subject of sermons, he is reported to have said, "The mind cannot absorb what the backside cannot endure." In 1957, when giving the speech at the annual dinner of the Royal Army Chaplains' Department, he took the chaplains to task when he said: "The tables are turned with a vengeance this evening. I cannot think how many hours I have spent at your mercy. Now it is my turn, although I would admit that the sitting is not quite the same."

Within the walls of Windsor Castle is St. George's House, a series of buildings that form part of the fourteenth-century foundations of the College of St. George. At the heart of the college is St. George's Chapel, the home of the Knights of the Garter, the most exclusive order of chivalry in the country, where every day prayer is offered for the nation. King Edward III established this tradition of prayer in 1348.

St. George's House was founded in 1966 by Prince Philip and Robin Woods, the newly appointed dean of Windsor, as a place where members of the clergy could stay for periods to increase their learning and where people of influence and responsibility in every area of society could come together to explore and communicate their views and analysis of contemporary issues. As the college is hidden away within the castle walls, it is particularly attractive to people in positions of leadership within government, industry, commerce, and the churches as a place for discreet discussions of mutual and national interest. Its stated objective is to effect change for the better in our society by nurturing wisdom through dialogue.

According to Woods, initially Philip had no particular interest in the religious or theological aspects of St. George's House. He was more interested in the annual St. George's House Lecture, at which he took the chair and whose speakers have ranged from the princess royal to the chief rabbi Jonathan Sacks and the playwright Sir Tom Stoppard. Philip said that he found the whole process of developing the structure and program for St. George's House "entirely satisfying." As time went by, it became customary for Woods to join Philip for a drink and an informal discussion whenever the royal family were in residence at Windsor. These discussions continued to take place with successive deans of Windsor after Woods moved on to become bishop of Worcester. To begin with, the subjects for discussion were mainly of a practical nature relating to the running of St. George's House.

When Michael Mann was appointed dean in 1976, the discussions became more philosophical and abstract. Philip struck up a relationship with him that resulted in the publication of several philosophical works by both Philip and Mann during the 1980s. Prior to his call to the Church, Mann had been a Guards officer and had a degree from Harvard Business School. He was also a military historian with several books to his name. Philip was particularly drawn to his style of preaching as Mann limited his sermons to seven minutes in the belief that if he could not get his point over in that time he never would.

Philip's writings with Michael Mann center on such questions as: What are we doing here? What is the point of existence? Is there anything beyond this life? Was the world created by a supreme being? Is everything that has happened since the creation part of His plan or is it all a matter of chance? These are questions that Philip has said men have been asking ever since they discovered speech.

Mann established a close rapport with Philip through a series of letters, published in book form in 1984 as *A Windsor Correspondence*. In the introduction, Dean Launcelot Fleming described the letters as revealing the duke's questioning mind and deep concern about religious issues, and he described Philip as having the frank and able response of a sympathetic theologian. Prior to this publication, the first of what might be called Philip's philosophical views appeared in a book published in 1982 called *A Question of Balance*. It comprises a selection of lectures given by Philip to general audiences rather than to a specifically religious group of listeners. Mann collaborated with Philip in the selection of material for this latter book and also edited the content.

In opening the introduction to what became the first of several slim volumes with philosophical content, Philip somewhat self-deprecatingly stated, "I make no claim to being a philosopher," which belies the description on the jacket that the book looks at some fundamental human issues and examines Philip's own beliefs.

There is a common theme that runs through the contents, which is Philip's view of the importance of the individual and the crucial part that human nature plays in every aspect of communal life. There is a theological slant to his views as seen from the introduction: "Whether it is also partly due to what I learned about Christianity as I grew up or whether I learned more about Christianity from the discovery of individualism I really could not say. However, I am quite certain that the two are linked together and . . . I am very much inclined to believe that religious conviction is the strongest and probably the only factor in sustaining the dignity and integrity of the individual."

The importance of the individual is at the cornerstone of Philip's philosophy. He has written: "I do not believe there can be any real satisfaction of any kind unless the individual can come to see a purpose in his own individual existence and recognises that the only thing which can make life tolerable for his fellow beings, as well as those who will come after him, is the responsibility he takes for his own attitudes and his own actions. . . . It seems to me everything begins with the individual and it is people who decide what sort of communities they are going to live in." In *A Question of Balance*, Philip went to great lengths to destroy Marxist theories that do not allow for individuality and freedom. Philip's own deep interest in philosophy is apparent from his references to Plato and Keynes and to Marx's manifesto *Das Kapital*.

Philip maintained that if we are to exercise our responsibilities so that all life can continue on earth, they must have a moral and philosophical basis. Simple self-interest, economic profit, and absolute materialism are no longer enough. It has been made perfectly clear that a concern for any part of life on this planet—human, plant, or animal, wild or tame—is a concern for all life. A threat to any part of the environment is a threat to the whole environment, but we must have a basis of assessment of these threats, not so that we can establish a priority of fears, but so that we can make a positive contribution to improvement and ultimate survival. Philip stated: "It is an old cliché to say that the future is in the hands of the young. This is no longer true. The quality of life to be enjoyed or the existence to be survived by our children and future generations is in our hands now."

One of the chapters in the book is on the subject of truth and underlines Philip's interest in science. He wrote: "Finding the truth is the purpose of all science. . . . The way that you search for the truth is really the most important factor. . . . The scientific method—and life in general for that matter—requires three things: technical knowledge, personal observation and judgement, and moral standards. . . . Without absolute honesty and objectivity in the approach for the search for truth, the results will be misleading, which is worse than not finding anything at all."

Another chapter, called "Clashes of Interest," links two of Philip's favorite subjects, namely conservation and the dangers of the human population explosion. He wrote: "The greatest threat to the future of the earth is the unchecked human population explosion . . . a classic case of conflict of interest between parents who feel entitled to have as many children as they please and the world at large which patently will not be able to support a natural world as well as feed and house a vastly inflated human population." Since this was written, the world population has increased from 4 to 7.7 billion.

Never afraid to speak his mind, Philip, at the launch of the US National Appeal of the World Wildlife Fund in 1962, got into diplomatic hot water for suggesting that a certain country with a vast and rapidly expanding population (China) did not really need the assistance of the products of rhinoceros horns for certain natural functions. He also upset the French while discussing a European population policy in 1970 at Strasbourg when he suggested that they might like to start sneaking contraceptives into their baguettes.

Coming from someone who had fathered four children, this did not go down well.

The final chapter in the book, titled "Satisfaction and Contentment," was taken from a speech Philip made at the opening of the 1980 Commonwealth Study Conference. It is clear that by then Philip had established some firm philosophical and Christian views. He started the chapter by quoting Shakespeare's Caesar: "Men at some time are masters of their fates; the fault dear Brutus is not in our stars, but in ourselves." Philip then wrote that there is nothing wrong with this world that cannot be cured by people. Almost nothing will be put right by theories, systems, and organizations by themselves.

The chapter ends with another reference to the importance of the individual in society: "In the end civilised standards still depend absolutely on the way people treat each other as people . . . in the final analysis only individuals can find satisfaction and contentment which are created by the relationships between one individual and another at work, in the community and in the home. You do not have to be a practising Christian to see that human rights begin with Christ's teaching—'Always treat others as you would like them to treat you.' "

A Windsor Correspondence came into being when Philip sent Michael Mann a copy of a lecture titled "Evolution from Space," given by eminent astronomer and mathematician Sir Fred Hoyle in 1982 at the Royal Institution. Hoyle—who coined the expression "the Big Bang," which he later debunked—challenged a number of Darwin's theories on the origin of man and maintained that the evolution of species as described by Darwin was mathematically impossible. He insisted that there were too many permutations in the natural world for everything to have come into being through evolution and natural selection. He did not specifically refer to God but what he called cosmic intelligence. It was Hoyle's belief that life must be of frequent occurrence in the universe, something that Philip had considered in his younger days when he became interested in flying saucers. Hoyle argued that the primeval molecules from which life evolved on earth had been transported from elsewhere in the universe. This assertion clearly piqued Philip's interest and he invited Mann to comment on it.

There followed an interchange of letters between Philip and Mann, some eighty pages long, in which they argued about the origin of man, the purpose of life on earth, and the relationship of science and Christianity. Mann asked the rhetorical question "What is the point of human life. Is death the end? If it is, then, as St Paul says, 'We are of all men the most miserable.' The only theory that has satisfied me is that God became Man in Jesus Christ who conquered death and gave us the hope of eternal life."

Philip's response was that the point of life is to make it more tolerable and more civilized for the generations we have every reason to believe will come after us, rather than to secure a better deal in the afterlife. Philip went on: "Whether God became man in Jesus Christ is a philosophical question; what is a matter of fact is that Jesus tried to show us how to live so that the world would become a better place." Mann did not accept Philip's assertion. In his response he said: "The belief that God became man in Jesus Christ is not in the Christian view a philosophical question; it is a matter of faith." Mann defined faith as the belief in things that cannot necessarily be proved in the scientific sense.

More than once Philip brought up what he called "his hobby horse," namely the need to reconcile science and theology, which in some respects appear contradictory. Mann said scientific truth and religious truth are complementary not opposed, and he believed that science and Christianity were moving closer together. Philip stated that the breach between science and theology will remain just as wide as long as the Bible is used as the authority for the explanation of natural phenomena that is at variance with scientific fact. Both Philip and Mann agreed that science and theology were moving closer together.

Philip summarized by saying: "Prosperous and civilised communities do live in peace and justice and that this is achieved because they are inspired by a moral and religious philosophy. . . . Certain however is that God is very necessary to influence human behaviour as human behaviour is likely to continue to have the same potential for good as well as for evil."

It is clear from this correspondence that Philip must have spent a considerable time pondering the central issues discussed, such as evolution and morality, the need to reconcile science and theology, and the question of life after death. It demonstrates his inquiring mind and how over time religion has become more important to him.

From the foundation of St. George's House in 1966 to the publication of *Survival or Extinction* in 1989, Philip's output of philosophical writings, debates, lectures, and ideas was prodigious. All this was achieved while he maintained an extraordinarily busy schedule of plaque unveilings, state banquets, after-dinner speeches, foreign travels, and military commitments at the same time as carrying out his duties at what he considered his principal job—that of supporting the Queen.

In spite of all Philip's commitments, he still managed to find some time for his sporting and leisure interests. He said: "I must confess I am as interested in leisure in the same way that a poor man is interested in money—I can't get enough of it. Furthermore, I have no problem whatever what I do is good or wise or likely to improve my character or to help me to become a 'whole man.'" Somehow, he has managed to find time in his later years for some contemplative philosophizing.

*
Survival or Extinction: A Christian Attitude to the Environment, another book coauthored by Philip and Mann, was published five years later, for St. George's House. While *A Windsor Correspondence* is largely concerned with abstract theology and provides an insight into Philip's own philosophy, this book deals with the more practical issues regarding the environment and conservation. In it Philip asked the question "Just how much battering can earth's natural system absorb?" Much of the book is centered on the subject of saving planet earth for future generations, which Philip terms "a moral imperative," and other related issues, which are dealt with in the chapter on conservation. However, there are some theological passages from which it can be seen how Philip's religious views have come into focus over a period of years. As Philip is the coauthor of the book, it is reasonable to suppose that the beliefs expressed are his own. These include:

> The beginning was a Big Bang

> The creation of the universe was an act of God and still depends on God

> Man has a moral obligation to care for our planet earth

> We have a moral duty not to put at risk the chances of survival of other species by our own actions

> Every species is an inherent part of God's Creation to which we owe a sense of responsibility

> The Christian has a moral obligation to strive for justice and salvation which is not restricted to humanity but which includes the whole of God's Creation

In addition to his role as dean of Windsor, Michael Mann became domestic chaplain to the Queen, and in the late 1980s, on her instructions, he arranged an important meeting at Windsor between leaders of diverse faiths. He was also registrar of the Order of the Garter and chairman of St. George's House. He carried out a particularly difficult task for Prince Philip after the death of his mother, Princess Alice, at Buckingham Place in 1969. Philip was anxious to fulfil his mother's last wish, which was to be buried alongside her aunt Elizabeth, known as Ella, the widow of Grand Duke Serge of Russia.

Ella was recognized as a saint for her charitable work in Russia and was Alice's inspiration for setting up an order of nuns in Greece. The Bolsheviks murdered Ella by throwing her down a mine shaft during the Russian Revolution in 1918. Her remains were later taken to Jerusalem. Michael Mann took on the difficult task of arranging for Alice's reburial in the Garden of Gethsemane, near Ella. The task involved eight years of protracted negotiations with the religious authorities and several governments and, after permission had finally been granted, a long day of standing masses and requiems in Jerusalem.

Not all of Prince Philip's philosophical considerations were directed toward religion or the state of the planet; some were much nearer to everyday issues, as shown by his stated philosophy behind the Duke of Edinburgh Awards scheme: "The philosophy is neither very profound nor very complicated. It is simply this: 'A civilised society depends upon the freedom, responsibility, intelligence and standard of behaviour of its individual members, and if the society is to continue to be civilised, each succeeding generation must learn to value those qualities and standards. . . . Above all, it depends on a willingness among the younger generation to find out for themselves the factors which contribute to freedom, responsibility, intelligence and standard of behaviour.' These are abstract concepts, so the Award has attempted to bring them down to earth; to give individual young people the opportunity to discover these ideas for themselves through a graduated programme of experience."

This philosophy is echoed in a collection of Philip's views and opinions, published in 1984 with the title *Men, Machines and Sacred Cows*, in which he stated that the clue to the reform of society is the development of individuals into decent and responsible citizens, each trusting the others to do their best with whatever talent and opportunities they may have. This is not something that can be imposed on people. Only people who have discovered a purpose in their lives and see the virtue of decency can do it, and they need to be willing to help others by example so that people can go out and make these discoveries for themselves.

Philip's standards are high, his dissatisfaction sometimes considerable. He would frequently like to be things he isn't or cannot be. But in his quest for perfection he has used his position of influence to help bring about those changes he considers important.

Chapter 15

A LADIES' MAN

In 2018, *The Times* newspaper published an obituary of Commander Keith Evans, who died on June 26 at the age of ninety-eight. Evans first met Philip when they were based at HMS *Royal Arthur*, the officers' training school at Corsham. Evans got to know the future Duke of Edinburgh well in the months before he married Princess Elizabeth. Philip gave Evans the nickname "Scratch," navy slang for a clerk, as Evans had previously been a captain's secretary. Some seventy years later, Evans and Philip met again when the Queen and Philip visited Pangbourne College, the naval school, to mark its centenary. Evans was present as the oldest living old boy of Pangbourne. When questioned by journalists about Philip's time at Corsham in 1947, he described him as "a bit randy," hastily adding "but you had better not put that down." After a few minutes' reflection, Evans relented and allowed the journalists to use his quip on condition that his description of Philip as "a bit randy" was upgraded to "very randy." The *Oxford English Dictionary* defines "randy" as "eager for sexual gratification," a description that in all probability could have been applied to most young, unmarried officers at Corsham at the time.

Philip's earliest encounters with the opposite sex occurred at the end of the 1938 summer term at Gordonstoun, when he traveled to Venice to stay with his aunt Princess Aspasia of Greece and Denmark and mother of his cousin Alexandra. In her biography of Philip, Alexandra described him as "very amusing, gay, full of life and energy and a tease." He reminded her of "a huge, hungry dog; perhaps a friendly collie who never had a basket of his own and responded to every overture with eager tail-wagging. . . . Blondes, brunettes and redhead charmers, Philip gallantly and, I think, quite impartially squired them all."

One girl in particular, Cobina Wright, caught his attention. She was named "most attractive and talented New York girl of the 1939 season." Her first meeting with Philip was at Harry's Bar, and Cobina later recalled that on seeing Philip, her mother had "shoved" her into his arms. Over the next three weeks, Philip escorted Cobina around Venice, spending "passionate evenings in gondolas on the Grand Canal," before following her back to London. Although nothing more came of their romance, when interviewed by the American *Town and Country* magazine in 1973, Cobina revealed that in her bedroom she kept photographs of the three loves of her life, one of them being Philip.

Cobina Wright's place was taken by Osla Benning, a beautiful Canadian-born debutante with "dark hair, alabaster white skin, an exquisite figure and a gentle loving nature," according to her friend Sarah Norton, later Baring. She and Philip met in late 1939 when they were both eighteen, while Osla was living with Sarah, who was Dickie Mountbatten's goddaughter. They went out on the town together in London, dancing at the 400 Club in Leicester Square or at the Café de Paris. Osla's friend Esme Harmsworth remembered having lunch with her at Claridge's. "I noticed she was wearing a naval cipher as a brooch. They're jeweled and not the sort of thing you scatter around. 'Oh', I said. 'What's that? Who is it?' She blushed and ummed and ahhed and eventually said, 'Well, he's called Philip.' 'Philip who?' 'Well, he doesn't have another name . . . actually he's Philip of Greece.' I'm sure it was a serious thing as far as Osla was concerned."

"It was obvious that he was Osla's boyfriend in a simple, nice way, so to speak; it was not a full-blown affair. I can tell you that right away," said Sarah Baring. "We just didn't think of that at all. We just weren't brought up to it. We were brought up to what my mother used to call 'behave nicely' . . . I mean the boys never even asked you to. You could kiss on the cheek, but not much more. We were allowed to hold hands in taxis—that was considered quite daring." During the war years, Philip and Osla kept in touch when Osla was recruited to work at Bletchley Park as a multilinguist in the naval section. After a night's dancing in London, Philip would take her in the early hours to Paddington Station to catch the milk train back to Bletchley.

"I do know that he was her first love," her daughter Janie Spring said. "She never told me about him for years. She just said, 'I fell in love with a naval officer.' Then I found a wonderful picture of Philip, very young looking with his hair all tousled, quite curly. . . . I could see why they got on. They were both very much outsiders with no roots in the English milieu in which they moved. Probably unconsciously, they recognized this similarity in each other and this is what gave them a special bond."

By Christmas 1943, with "nowhere particular to go," as he nonchalantly put it, Philip went with his cousin David Milford Haven to stay at Windsor Castle. Princess Elizabeth, now seventeen, was animated in a way "none of us had ever seen before," wrote her governess Marion Crawford. By the following year Philip's correspondence with the young Princess Elizabeth had progressed to the point where they had agreed to exchange photographs.

Another early girlfriend was Georgina Wernher, later Lady Kennard, whom Philip had met during the school holidays while staying with the Wernhers at Thorpe Lubenham. They used to go out dining and dancing in London at places such as Quaglino's, which was patronized by the Prince of Wales and the Mountbattens. Throughout the years, royalty continued to favor Quaglino's; a table was permanently reserved for Princess Margaret, and it was the first public restaurant ever visited by a reigning monarch when the Queen and Prince Philip had dinner there in 1956. Lady Kennard said that Philip's mother would have been very happy if she had married him. She recalled: "We were both too young and he never asked me. It was a tremendous friendship—he was my best friend in the world. I thought he was marvelously clever and amusing and I loved being with him. Good-looking? He was astronomical, but I was terribly naive and disciplined and we all behaved in those days. Girls certainly did."

Things were very different in 1944–45 when Philip and Mike Parker, both first lieutenants with the Pacific Fleet, spent several shore leaves in Melbourne and Sydney. Girls then were very free with their favors, particularly when it came to handsome young officers in naval uniform. The ever-present threat of death or injury in combat brought about a degree of promiscuity not seen again until the emergence of the birth control pill in the 1960s. Mike Parker was at great pains to insist that nothing of a sexual nature ever took place when he and Philip were on leave. Although he admitted to "armfuls of girls," he said that nothing serious happened. He said: "We were young, we had fun, we had a few drinks, and we might have gone dancing and that was it." Years later, Parker added: "I was with him for fifteen years and the affairs were zero. He had plenty of opportunities during the war and nothing happened."

In spite of Alexandra's description of Philip in her biography as "with a golden beard, [he] hit feminine hearts first in Melbourne and then in Sydney, with terrific impact," Parker said Philip went to some lengths to avoid being compromised. Parker reported, "He always seemed to have one eye over his shoulder." With his iron self-control, it is quite plausible that Philip was ever mindful of Uncle Dickie's advice not to do anything to compromise his relationship with Princess Elizabeth.

Biographers, investigative journalists, and anyone seeking to write about Prince Philip and women face an uphill task. After more than seventy years of marriage, not one iota of hard evidence of his supposed affairs has emerged. No female has come forward saying that her relationship with Philip was anything other than platonic. No employee, member of crew, or security detective, by whom Philip was surrounded, has broken silence on the subject of affairs. Even those biographers who insist that he has had affairs have been unable or unwilling to produce any corroboration to the rumors of his affairs with married aristocratic ladies, actresses, and showgirls.

What remains is a combination of speculation, innuendo, and pure invention, with one example being in the Netflix television series *The Crown*. In an attempt to add a degree of credibility to the series, the writer and producers added to the storyline an affair in 1957 between Philip and a real person, Galina Ulanova, one of the greatest ballerinas of the twentieth century. She was the prima ballerina of the Bolshoi Theatre for sixteen years. However, Philip is not known for his love of the ballet, and there is no evidence that he ever met Galina. Furthermore, she was eleven years older than Philip, but it is said in *The Crown* that she gave him a photograph of herself that he was foolish enough to carry around until his wife came across it—a most unlikely scenario.

The Crown also seeks to link Philip with wild parties thrown by Stephen Ward, a key figure in the Profumo affair in 1963, a sex scandal that rocked the British government. At its center was Christine Keeler, a cabaret dancer and model who was introduced by Ward to John Profumo, the then secretary of state for war, with whom she had an affair. At the same time, Christine Keeler was engaged in a relationship with an attaché in the Soviet Embassy in London, giving rise to speculation about a possible breach of security. The scandal caused Profumo to resign in 1963, and Prime Minister Macmillan followed suit later that year.

The series attempts to establish a connection between Ward and Prince Philip on the basis of a drawing Ward made of Philip. Ward was put on trial for living off immoral earnings. As he had no money to pay for his defense, he gave his lawyer David Jacobs a collection of his drawings as security for the costs of the case. After Ward's suicide while awaiting sentencing, the drawings were seen to include portraits of several well-known people, including Prince Philip, none of whom had sat for Ward. In reality there was nothing to connect Philip with Ward or to suggest that he ever attended any wild parties organized by Ward.

This is not to say that Philip led a life of monastic quiet. "He is like his father was," the late Hélène Cordet once said. "Of course he likes women. What the hell can he do to have a decent reputation? If he doesn't look at women, they say he likes men. He likes women. So what. It's a good thing."

A fellow member of the Thursday Club, James Robertson Justice, the actor who played Sir Lancelot Spratt in the *Doctor* series of films (*Doctor in the House*, *Doctor at Sea*, etc.), became a close friend of Philip. Together they went wildfowling on the Norfolk

Broads, and Justice instructed Philip in the art of falconry. Justice owned a house in Scotland, at Spinningdale, about an hour's drive from Inverness, where from time to time he organized parties that were attended by Philip. The house was in a beautiful location, with views down to Dornoch Firth, and was hidden from the main road by gardens and trees.

A statement was obtained from a retired police officer who lived a few miles from the house and used to be employed on royal protection duties whenever the royal family were in Scotland. He stated: "I do recall my late Detective Superintendent relating stories to me as a young police officer, I think as a detective, being posted to the gate of the drive leading from the main road to ensure that nobody uninvited got past while wild parties ensued at Spinningdale House with the key VIP guest being HRH [Prince Philip]. Certainly, the parties there were not that infrequent and it was a duty he did several times. He recounted to me of what he termed 'floozies' being taken in by road from the south for the events—no doubt the party set of the time but certainly they were young women and not local. There is of course a reluctance by Highland people to discuss such things even though JRJ was not particularly well liked." While this statement is hearsay, there is no reason to doubt the police officer, but there is also no indication of what exactly took place at the parties.

There are several women whose names have been linked with Philip romantically, although without exception there has been no evidence of any serious entanglement. The problem is that the stories get repeated regularly both in the press and in books, so much so that after a while people are inclined to think there must be some truth in them.

A prime example of this is Philip's alleged relationship with the actress Pat Kirkwood, who in the 1950s was the highest paid performer on the musical stage in London. In 1948, Pat was dating

Philip's photographer friend Baron. One evening Baron took Philip and his equerry to meet Pat in her dressing room after her performance in the revue *Starlight Roof* at the London Palladium. Later they all went out to Les Ambassadeurs Club for dinner, followed by some dancing at the Milroy Club, where Philip was seen to monopolize Pat on the dance floor. The evening ended with Baron making scrambled eggs for everyone at his flat. Philip and Pat never met again socially, although they met once more in 1960 when Pat was in the receiving line of the cast presented to Philip at a charity concert at the Theatre Royal in Drury Lane.

On the basis of their single social evening, a myth has existed for more than fifty years that Pat was Philip's mistress. In 1988, after yet another outing of the same story in the press, Philip wrote to Pat from Balmoral: "I am very sorry indeed that you have been pestered by that ridiculous 'rumour.' The trouble is that certain things seem to get into journalists' folklore and it is virtually impossible to get it out of the system. Much as I would like to put a stop to this and many other similar stories . . . we have found that short of starting libel proceedings there is absolutely nothing to be done. Invasion of privacy, invention and false quotations are the bane of our existence." Kirkwood reportedly went on to tell one journalist: "A lady is not normally expected to defend her honour. It is the gentleman who should do that. I would have had a happier and easier life if Prince Philip, instead of coming uninvited to my dressing room, had gone home to his pregnant wife on the night in question."

In the 1950s, there was a convention among Fleet Street editors that the British press would not publish salacious stories about members of the royal family. The American press, however, respected no such convention. In 1957, the *Baltimore Sun* caused a furor when it ran a story with the headline "Report Queen, Duke in Rift Over Party Girl," in which the prince was alleged to be "romantically involved with an unnamed woman whom he met on a regular basis in the West End apartment of a society photographer."

This article appeared shortly after Philip had been away for four months on HMY *Britannia* visiting some far-flung outposts of the British Empire. The long absence from his family, coupled with the *Sun* story, caused questions to be raised about Philip's conduct, and allegations were made about wild parties on board during the voyage. As *Britannia* had a complement of two hundred crew and twenty officers, nothing of the sort could have taken place without it becoming public knowledge. In a break from the rule that Buckingham Palace never comments on rumor, the Queen authorized an official denial, and the royal press secretary stated, "It is quite untrue that there is any rift between the Queen and the Duke." According to Parker, "Philip was incandescent. He was very, very angry and deeply hurt."

Philip has also been linked to other artistes, including Hélène Cordet, Merle Oberon, and Anna Massey. Hélène Cordet was a childhood friend of Philip's. He often spent summer holidays with her family in Le Touquet, and her stepfather gave some financial help to Philip's family in Paris. When Philip was seventeen, he gave Hélène away in her marriage to her first husband. Some years later, after she was divorced, Hélène had two children out of wedlock. Because Philip became godfather to the children and helped with Hélène's son's school fees at Gordonstoun, it was rumored that he was the father of the two children. Hélène called the paternity gossip ridiculous and said her children were fathered by French fighter pilot Marcel Boisot, whom she later married. Hélène was a cabaret artiste who appeared frequently at her club the Saddle Room in London's West End. Hélène claimed that she asked Philip what she should do about the rumors concerning her relationship with him, although they certainly did no harm to her career. Philip said: "If you like, you can sue them, but I don't think it is worth it. On the contrary it will just stir up more trouble." Hélène remained friends with Philip for many years and went to his fiftieth birthday party.

There is one thing on which all biographers are agreed and that is Philip's enjoyment of the company of beautiful women. The girls in his office have always been attractive, with good figures. If Philip enters a room or appears at a reception, he will make a beeline for the most attractive female in the room and engage her in conversation. He is an excellent dancer and thinks nothing of dancing with other men's wives all evening at a party. One of Philip's close lady friends said: "He has got terrific rhythm, he can dance close or apart, he can even do a bit of rock. When you dance with someone attractive, you get quite close to them and Philip certainly gives you a lot of attention. . . . He's accused of having had all these affairs, but on the basis of my own experience, I believe him when he tells me he hasn't."

There are a number of women with whom Philip has remained on very friendly terms for many years. They have all been younger than Philip, very attractive, and members of the aristocracy. Philip made sure that the guest lists at Sandringham and Balmoral always included at least one female he found attractive. The Queen was tolerant of the girls he had to stay. It is possible that she simply ignored the allegations surrounding her husband. We don't know if she even acknowledged that he might have been behaving indiscreetly, because the Queen was very, very discreet and very buttoned up in those days—and she might not have even said anything. The Queen would have turned a blind eye to his indiscretions. She was confident in his love, and she sort of said, "Well men will be men." That was her attitude. It doesn't mean she was not hurt, but she wouldn't show it.

*

The Queen's cousin Princess Alexandra was one of Philip's first close friends. She is fifteen years his junior and daughter of Marina Duchess of Kent, whose hospitality at her home Coppins was so welcome when Philip was courting the young Princess Elizabeth. The tall and elegant woman was a bridesmaid at Elizabeth and Philip's wedding. Unlike the Queen, who had little interest in sailing and did not go to Cowes, Alexandra enjoyed sailing. When Philip invited her to join him aboard HMY *Britannia* for Cowes Week she was delighted to accept. Alexandra effectively stood in for the Queen as hostess for Cowes Week on an annual basis.

As well as the sailing, Cowes Week involves a round of parties, dances, receptions, and fun to be had with the likes of Uffa Fox. In 1963, Alexandra married Angus Ogilvy, the son of the 12th Earl of Airlie, and at the Queen's invitation the newlyweds spent their honeymoon on the Balmoral estate. It was there that Alexandra had her first taste of scandal, when a photographer caught her romping with Angus in the heather. The highly revealing images of the amorous couple became legendary among those editors who saw them, but in the more deferential climate of the time toward the royals they were never published.

Philip and Alexandra developed a close friendship, and before long rumors began circulating that they were having an affair. While they had a deep friendship, which lasted for many years and which is said to have caused a rift with her husband, Angus Ogilvy, the rumors of affairs have never been substantiated. Alexandra became one of the hardest-working royals, putting in hundreds of public appearances every year. She is patron of more than a hundred organizations and has been carrying out duties on behalf of the Queen for more than six decades. The claim that she had an affair with Philip is especially far-fetched—the Queen has continued to lavish honors on her cousin, including the Order of the Garter and Dame Grand Cross of the Royal Victorian Order, which would be highly unlikely if there was anything untoward in her relationship with Philip.

Sacha, Duchess of Abercorn, who was twenty-five years younger than Philip, was another close friend. They were third cousins, related through their Russian ancestry, and he had known her since she was a child as he was a good friend of her parents, Harold and Georgina Phillips when they lived at Luton Hoo. Sacha, who died in 2018, was the founder of the Pushkin Prizes promoting art therapy for young people. She was appointed an OBE (Order of the British Empire) in the 2008 Birthday Honors for her work with children in Northern Ireland, her family home.

During her London years, she trained as a counsellor and developed a strong interest in the Swiss psychologist Carl Jung's ideas. In the early 1980s, she helped to organize seven "consultations" run by Prince Philip and Michael Mann, who was the dean of Windsor and the chairman of St. George's House in Windsor, a college for clergy and laity. When the duke asked her, "Could you get some of your Jung people to come to a consultation," she introduced a group and participated herself, thereby instilling in Philip an interest in Jungian philosophy.

Rumors of a relationship began circulating in 1987, when a newspaper published a photograph of Philip, wearing only a towel around his waist, with his arm around the duchess, who was in a swimsuit—even though her husband was also in the picture. Sacha once explained, "The Queen gives Philip a lot of leeway." Her father told her, "Remember he's a sailor. They come in on the tide."

In Gyles Brandreth's book *Philp and Elizabeth: Portrait of a Royal Marriage*, Sacha admitted that she had had a passionate friendship with Philip for more than twenty years. "It was certainly not a full relationship," she said. "I did not go to bed with him. It probably looked like that to the world. I can understand why people might have thought it, but it didn't happen. It wasn't like that. He isn't like that. It's complicated and, at the same time, it's quite simple. He needs a playmate, and someone to share his intellectual pursuits." When asked if she thought Philip had slept with any of his other playmates, she said: "I doubt it very much. No, I'm sure not. But he's a human being. Who knows? I don't. Unless you are in the room with a lighted candle, who knows?"

Sacha went on: "Philip is always questing, exploring, searching for meaning, testing ideas. He asks the difficult questions and that's what drew me to him. . . . He is practical, unsentimental and logical, but also emotional and intuitive. He is deeply sensitive. His senses are so supercharged."

Sarah Bradford, the highly respected biographer whose works include the lives of Disraeli, King George VI, Princess Diana, and the Queen, told Brandreth: "The Duke of Edinburgh has had affairs—yes, full-blown affairs and more than one. He has affairs and the Queen accepts it. I think she thinks that's how men are. Philip and Sacha Abercorn certainly had an affair. Without a doubt." Sarah Bradford's opinion is just that—an opinion, which she has chosen not to support with any evidence.

Philip's more recent playmate has been the former Penny Romsey, now Countess Mountbatten of Burma. Blonde, slim, and still strikingly beautiful, Penny, who is thirty-two years younger than Philip, has been his partner in carriage-driving competitions since 1994. When the duke was still driving competitively, they would travel the country together to participate in competitions. This was after Philip befriended her when her life began to fall apart following the death of her five-year-old daughter, Leonora, from kidney cancer in 1991. Philip encouraged her to take up carriage driving and supported her when her husband, Norton, his godson, left her in 2010 for a fling with Nassau-based fashion designer Eugenie Nuttall. Penny eventually took Norton back, but insisted he moved into a converted barn while she remained in Broadlands and ran the estate. The Queen and Philip admired Penny for her indomitable spirit, dignity, and grace and made sure she was included in their lives as much as possible—so much so that Penny acquired the nickname "and also" as she was frequently a guest at Windsor Castle for weekends. More recently, she spends time with Philip at Wood Farm on the Sandringham estate and is credited with persuading him to give up his driving license after his 2019 accident. Despite his great age, she still acts as a confidante and they share a boisterous sense of humor. Philip also gives sound advice on the running of the Broadlands estate, and they have the ability to cheer each other on even in the direst of circumstances.

When I saw Philip and Penny gliding around the dance floor at the Royal Yacht Squadron Ball during Cowes Week, neither of them gave a damn who saw them or what anyone might say. I noticed that Philip, an excellent dancer, was completely in rhythm with the beautiful Penny. He's undoubtedly close to her and is a supportive friend and mentor. In 1996, at the height of what was dubbed "the war of the Waleses," the snooping radio ham Neville Hawkins taped a mobile phone call made by Philip to a "plummy-voiced" woman, in which they discussed the bitter battle between Charles and Diana. The plummy voice turned out to be Penny's. But, at one point in the conversation, she handed the phone over to her husband, thus rather destroying any illusion of a clandestine affair.

Since 1975, when she was first introduced to Prince Charles, Penny has been popular with the royal family, but it is her lively mind, as well as her beauty, that's turned this former meat trader's daughter into a central figure at the heart of royal life. She provides a touchstone to the outside world and tells both Philip and the Queen about what's going on. They even persuaded her to go on the countryside march in 1998 so she could report back to them on its progress.

How the Queen feels about it all, we will never know. Philip has always liked to flirt and make suggestive remarks, and the Queen is the first to make jokes about his lascivious nature. Equally, she'd never let on if she'd been hurt by rumors of her husband's supposed dalliances. Quite possibly, she may even have resorted to her usual trick of burying her head in the sand and pretending nothing was happening.

"As far as I'm concerned, every time I talk to a woman, they say I've been to bed with her—as if she had no say in the matter," Philip told TV presenter Jeremy Paxman when he was eighty-five. "Well I'm bloody flattered at my age to think some girl is interested in me. It's absolute cuckoo."

Cuckoo or not, the rumors persist and will always do so, because royal protection officers are not always there in private homes and often stay in a local pub, so there are opportunities in spite of Philip's insistence that he always has someone with him. Whether they are there or not, protection officers are always the souls of discretion as they are in the delicate position of being able to witness family secrets. For twenty years, Prince Philip's protection officer was Chief Inspector Brian Jeffrey, who sadly died of cancer, but nowadays royalty protection is less personal and PPOs, as they are called, are there to do a job, not to become confidants.

There are and always will be stories of different ladies alleged to have had affairs with Prince Philip. The list of candidates continues with the beautiful actress Sally Ann Howes, who is nine years younger than Prince Philip and played Truly Scrumptious in the film *Chitty Chitty Bang Bang*, and with the oil heiress Olga Deterding, who was supposed to have conducted a clandestine affair with Philip in a company apartment in Cumberland Terrace, Regent's Park. The company chairman's wife witnessed the comings and goings at Cumberland Terrace and noted the unusual late-night visits and dawn departures. She claimed Olga's visitors included Prince Philip and also broadcaster Alan Whicker.

Oxford-educated Olga was born in 1926, the daughter of a White Russian (Belarusian) and the Dutch billionaire Sir Henri Deterding, the founder of Royal Dutch Shell Oil company. When he died, Olga was only ten and he left most of his estimated £65 million fortune to her. Not surprisingly, she became a wild adventuress and socialite, the darling of the gossip columns. She eventually became engaged to broadcaster Alan Whicker but broke it off and had a long affair with Jonathan Routh, of *Candid Camera* fame. Olga had been living in the Ritz Hotel, but at the age of twenty-seven she abandoned the high life and went to work in Dr. Albert Schweitzer's leper colony in West Africa for a year, then lived in Tahiti and Beirut before returning to London. She tragically died at the age of fifty-two in a nightclub in New York after choking on a sandwich.

When the late Diana Princess of Wales was at the height of her hatred of Prince Philip shortly before her death, she claimed that he had several illegitimate children and was determined to find out who they were. One of the Queen's closest friends also claimed he was "always having a rummage." And when I interviewed Eileen Parker in 1995, she told me a story of how Philip used to rendezvous with a certain girl by getting messages delivered to her at a London club. On one occasion the message was left at the wrong club and was never picked up by the recipient, causing all kinds of problems, but no names were ever mentioned. Eileen also told me she had received a very unpleasant missive from her former husband, Mike Parker, who died in 2001 at the age of eighty-one, telling her to stop talking about Prince Philip and never reprint her 1982 book, *Step Aside for Royalty.*

In spite of all the rumors, not a shred of evidence of a physical relationship between Philip and any of his playmates has ever come to light, but—like his gaffes—the stories will never go away.

Chapter 16

HUMOR AND WIT

In 1983, Philip attended a dinner in Geneva as president of the Fédération Equestre Internationale (FEI) with his private secretary Brian McGrath. The purpose of the meeting was to discuss venues for the equestrian events at the 1984 Olympic Games to be held in Los Angeles. Everybody at the dinner had identification badges giving their names and countries except for McGrath as he was there simply as Philip's secretary.

McGrath recounted: "Philip and I went into the dining room together, and having been in the wine trade most of my life, I wandered across to inspect the line of promising-looking bottles that had been put out for the meal. Suddenly, to my astonishment, two large security guards moved up on either side of me and said that they did not think I was meant to be there. I replied it was quite all right because I was there with Prince Philip. 'Oh yeah,' said one of them. 'Well we have just asked His Royal Highness who you are,' and he said, 'It's a funny thing you should ask because I was wondering myself. We came in together but I don't think I have ever seen the man before.'" As McGrath was propelled out of the room, he caught sight of Philip bursting himself with laughter. Luckily, they bumped into the secretary general of the FEI, who put the security men straight. McGrath said later, "That was when I realized that life with Prince Philip was going to be great fun, if a little unpredictable."

Prince Philip's first private secretary, Mike Parker, recalled another more elaborate practical joke. On one occasion during a Royal Air Force fly-past over Buckingham Palace, Philip and Parker telephoned the Air Ministry and played a tape recording of a Battle of Britain dogfight complete with machine guns blazing; then they shouted: "Help! Help! We are being attacked! One of your pilots has gone berserk and is strafing the palace." Parker shook with laughter at the retelling of this story and denied that it prompted criticism from the old guard at the palace. "The younger generation always thinks the older generation are a bunch of twerps. It's quite normal. But we were never silly enough to ignore the establishment. After all, we had to learn from them."

These two stories are typical of Philip's undoubted sense of humor and his puerile love of practical jokes, something he shared with his late father, Andrew, whose four brothers were all practical jokers. Like his father, Philip used to wait until a situation was conducive and then amuse everybody by having some fun at their expense. The late Stephen Barry, Prince Charles's then valet, recounted an amusing tale that illustrates Philip's quick wit. One morning Prince Philip said to Joe Pearce, his valet at the time, that he had not seen one of the footmen for a while.

"I'm afraid, sir, he was fired," Pearce reported.

"For what?" the frowning duke demanded to know.

Pearce lowered his voice as he explained, "I'm afraid they found him in bed with one of the housemaids."

"And they fired him for that?" exploded the duke, who has been known to grumble about the number of gays around the palace. "The man should have been given a medal!"

From an early age, Philip always had a sense of fun about him. Kurt Hahn wrote on Philip's arrival at Gordonstoun: "His laughter was heard everywhere and he created merriness around him." In one of his letters from school to his cousin Alexandra, he wrote about the practical jokes played on one of the masters by sewing up his pajama trousers and filling his shoes with water. Hahn described his conduct as "naughty but never nasty." Many years later his grandsons Prince William and Prince Harry used to put balloons full of water on the top of a half-opened door so when someone entered, the balloon burst all over them. This is not everyone's idea of a joke, but members of the royal family all have a rather infantile sense of humor, perhaps because everyone is so willing to laugh in the right places.

When they were first married, Princess Elizabeth was very young and very shy. Philip was able to put her at her ease, particularly on formal public occasions, with a few jocular words. When her first Christmas speech was recorded for television, as we have seen, the producer had great difficulty in getting her to relax; it was Philip, with a few gestures and a silly joke, who managed to get the Queen smiling for the cameras. While the couple endured countless formal photographic sessions, it was Philip who relieved the tension with a jocular attitude—as in a photo session with royal photographer Cecil Beaton, who in his diary described Philip "as he stood by making wry jokes."

Being something of a photographer himself, Philip had little patience with professionals who took hours to get through a session. During a photo call at the RAF Club, while posing for pictures with Second World War veterans to mark the seventy-fifth anniversary of the Battle of Britain, the prince lost patience and commanded the photographer, "Just take the fucking picture." The resultant video went viral. After Princess Eugenie's christening at Sandringham in December 1990, cockney photographer Terry O'Neill was trying to organize the christening group for the official photographs. As usual Prince Philip was tetchy and impatient. "Haven't you taken enough?" he kept saying. "I can't believe anyone can take so long just to take a few boring photographs. If you haven't got the photos you want by now you are an even worse photographer than I thought you were." O'Neill, one of the great British photographers, took no notice, and although tempted to answer back, he just ignored the insults and kept snapping.

Given how intrusive the press has been with his family, Prince Philip's sense of humor has never been extended to them, for whom he has nothing but contempt and rude words. On a visit to Gibraltar, where Philip was feeding the resident Barbary apes in the presence of a crowd of reporters, he questioned: "Which are the apes and which are the reporters?" In 1992, Philip said he had frequently been misrepresented. He said: "I find a lot of it very unpalatable. . . . You cannot take quotations in a newspaper seriously. It so happens that it is perfectly legal to put anything in a newspaper in quotation marks, and there is nothing you can do about it." In 1966, on a visit to a Caribbean hospital during a malaria outbreak, Philip made an insensitive comment to the matron: "You have mosquitoes. I have the press."

When in 1951 Princess Elizabeth and Philip toured Canada in the place of King George VI, who was recovering from an operation, they covered the length and breadth of that country by train. On the 10,000-mile (16,000-kilometer) journey from the Atlantic to the Pacific and back, Philip kept the young princess entertained with practical jokes and amusing stories. Philip's valet at the time, John Dean, was a fan of joke shops and he tells of the pranks Philip played with items Philip borrowed from him. One joke was an imitation tin of mixed nuts from which a toy snake sprung out when the tin was opened (a popular joke in the 1950s). Another was a device that delivered a mild electric shock when touched. John Dean said he often heard screams of laughter coming from the royal carriage.

Later during the tour, when they crossed into the United States, while looking over the shoulder of a reporter who was scribbling wildly on his notepad, Philip remarked, "If you took that page to a chemist, he would make up a cough mixture from the prescription." On a later tour of New Zealand, where lamb was on the menu rather too often, Philip watched an exhibition of sheep shearing on a farm. When he was invited to try his hand at shearing a sheep, he said, "No thanks. I might nick it and we have already had enough mutton."

It is Philip's sense of humor that has helped the Queen through some of the more difficult periods of her life, and they have often been photographed enjoying a private joke together. The Countess of Wessex once said of her in-laws: "They make each other laugh— which is, you know, it's half the battle, isn't it?"

In her 2017 Christmas broadcast, the Queen spoke of Philip's humor when she said: "Even Prince Philip has decided it's time to slow down a little—having, as he economically put it, 'done his bit.' But I know his support and unique sense of humour will remain as strong as ever, as we enjoy spending time this Christmas with our family and look forward to welcoming new members into it next year."

State banquets at Buckingham Palace are awe-inspiring occasions with elaborate table settings for one hundred guests, each place set with half a dozen glasses and solid-gold cutlery. Ranks of liveried footmen stand behind the seated guests. The wife of the visiting head of state was always seated next to Philip. If she seemed a little nervous or lost for words, Philip would break the ice by studying the long and elaborate menu, which is always printed in French, and then exclaiming, "Ah, good—fish and chips again."

For many years, Philip was an honorary life clown of the Variety Club of Great Britain, whose fundraising for the National Association of Boys' Clubs was important to him. He was a great Tommy Cooper fan, and the late comedian genuinely doubled him up with laughter. Cooper performed many times in front of Philip and even entertained him and the Queen at Windsor Castle. Avoiding putting his own feelings across, the Prince said, "Tommy Cooper is the Queen's favourite comedian." After one Royal Command Performance, Cooper asked the Queen, "Do you mind if I ask you a personal question?"

"No," replied the Queen, "but I might not be able to give you a full answer."

"Do you like football?" asked Cooper.

"Well, not really," said the Queen.

"In that case," said Cooper, "do you mind if I have your Cup Final tickets?"

Besides the Variety Club, Philip was a companion rat of the Grand Order of Water Rats, another society with many comedian members. He is also an honorary member of the Saints & Sinners and has been a guest at their lunches and dinners (where they always have the crème de la crème of amusing speakers), and he has hosted dinners and a cricket match at Windsor for the club. He enjoyed the company of comedians, including Flanagan and Allan of the Crazy Gang. After Bud Flanagan was awarded an OBE, Philip addressed the Variety Club, saying, "If that particular member found his way to Buckingham Palace there is hope for all of you." When the Variety Club wanted to organize a greyhound race in Philip's name, he suggested a silver lamppost as a suitable trophy for the winner.

*

Like Prince Charles, Philip was a fan of the BBC radio program *The Goon Show*. He formed a friendship with the star and writer of the show, Spike Milligan, with whom he conducted an amusing correspondence. Spike was one of the few able to address Philip informally—he addressed letters to him opening with "Dear Skipper." In 1970, Spike wrote to Philip saying that a certain person who had worked with the World Wildlife Fund should be considered for an award in the Birthday Honors. Philip's witty reply was as follows: "If you think he should get a gong, I am quite prepared to take your word for it. Fortunately, or unfortunately depending how you look at these things, this is a parliamentary democracy which means the chief incumbent at number 10 Downing Street is Gong Distributor-in-Chief aided by a doubtless extremely efficient administrative string of machinery. Regrettably the incumbents of the Palace are denied both the pleasure of pulling the strings and of influencing its operation in any way." In fact, Spike's friend did receive an OBE in that year's honors. Spike replied to Philip: "I don't know if as a result of my letter to you, you had a hand in this, if you did thank you very much. If you didn't, I shall never play Prince and the pauper with you again."

In 1954, a Lagonda 3-litre Drophead coupé was made to order for Prince Philip, winning Aston Martin its first Royal Warrant. Much to Philip's delight, the car had one of the earliest radio-telephone systems. Philip enjoyed making prank calls through the switchboard to Buckingham Palace. When he was put through, he'd disguise his voice when speaking to Prince Charles and Princess Anne so they had no idea who he was, and they would squeal with excitement at the funny voices he put on.

Along with Mike Parker and Philip, other members of the Thursday Club included assorted men about town who enjoyed good wine and conversation laced with plenty of humor. "We have been given the reputation of being wild," said Parker, "but the truth is we enjoyed fun and going around with people who knew what was going on. People got merry but never drunk. As far as being wild, not guilty. As far as hanging around women, not guilty." Parker enjoyed high jinks and practical jokes as much as Philip did, and for them both the club was an escape from the stuffy courtiers and staid atmosphere at Buckingham Palace.

Another member of the Thursday Club was Sir Reginald Bennett, a member of parliament and yachtsman who founded the Imperial Poona Yacht Club, which exists to this day. The club was founded as an antidote to the very serious gentlemen's clubs of the day and the more serious sailing clubs like the Royal Yacht Squadron. Many famous yachtsmen were members and they enjoyed regular convivial dinners called "tiffins." When Philip heard of the club at Cowes, he joined immediately. He was given the nom de plume of the Maharajah of Cooch Parwani, which means "Leader of Very Little." When one of the American members won the America's Cup, Philip sent him a telegram reading: "Poona is proud of you. Cooch Parwani."

It was at Cowes that Philip became good friends with Uffa Fox. Uffa was a brilliant yachtsman and designer who often sailed small boats with Philip. In Cowes Week, his home was notorious for rowdy parties with much drinking and singing of sea shanties. Like Philip, he enjoyed the timeworn practical joke of hiding a bulb motor horn under a cushion and roaring with laughter when the unsuspecting guest sat on it. In 1955, as president of the Royal Society of Arts, Philip gave a speech as he handed out the annual awards, one of which went to Uffa as a yacht designer. Philip said: "Uffa must find it just as difficult to see me as President of this society as I do to see him as a fellow of the Royal Design Institute. That is not meant as any reflection on his work, it is just that when sailing together in small boats personality counts before trappings."

*

As he grew older, Philip's sense of humor did not desert him, but it changed. The juvenile pranks and schoolboyish practical jokes gave way to a more mature, wry, and sometimes caustic sense of humor. Collectively, Philip's jokes, asides, and insults have come to be known as his "gaffes."

Much has been made of his so-called gaffes. Books of collections of them have been published. In reality, they are politically incorrect jokes usually made to relieve the tedium of foreign tours and other formal occasions. Philip has received much criticism from the press for continually putting his foot in it. He has clearly enjoyed making waves with these off-the-cuff comments. He even invented a word for it. When he addressed the General Dental Council in 1960, he said: "Dontopedalogy is the science of opening your mouth and putting your foot in it, a science which I have practised for a good many years."

The gaffes are a combination of genuinely witty remarks, insensitive comments, and sometimes outright rudeness. On occasions, innocuous asides have been blown up by the press as if they were international incidents. The most reported incident has been when Philip was in China in 1986 chatting to a group of English students and he was heard to say: "If you stay here much longer, you will go home with slitty eyes." The Chinese, who commonly refer to Westerners as "round-eyes," took no offense at the remark, but the British press had a field day. The headline in the *Sun* newspaper referred to Philip as "The Great Wally of China."

A subject that Philip has studiously avoided commenting on is politics. He did make an oblique reference to the very high rates of income tax under the Labour government in 1974, which ranged from 83 percent to as much as 98 percent on unearned income, when he remarked, "All money nowadays seems to be produced with a natural homing instinct for the Treasury."

Philip is outspoken, and insensitive to any hurt that his remarks might have caused to the recipient. He is not above issuing gratuitous insults, safe in the knowledge that he will not get an answer back, either because of the victim's fear or deference for royalty. This kind of verbal bullying cannot be described as humorous but is often quoted in collections of Philip's gaffes. At the annual Royal Variety Show, where the cream of British comedians, actors, and singers give their services for good causes, the stars of the show are presented to the royal party after the show. In 1969, Philip asked the Welsh singer Tom Jones, "What do you gargle with, pebbles?" It was not only Tom's voice that Philip found objectionable. Referring to his material, Philip said, "It's difficult to see how it's possible to become immensely valuable by singing what are the most hideous songs."

Clearly Tom's enormous success became something of an obsession for Philip. Commenting on Britain's economy at a time when money was hard to come by, Philip said: "What about Tom Jones? He's made a million and he's a bloody awful singer." Tom was not the only singer at the receiving end of Philip's contempt. At another Royal Variety Show in 2001, when Elton John came on to perform, Philip said he wished Elton would turn the microphone off. Always up for mocking celebrities, Philip told Elton: "Oh, it's you that owns that ghastly car is it? We often see it when driving to Windsor Castle." Elton had had his Aston Martin painted in the colors of Watford football club, of which he was the owner.

Madonna also caught some flak. At the premiere of the James Bond film *Die Another Day*, when Philip was told that Madonna would be singing the theme song, he said he hoped he would not need earplugs. In the same vein, at a Buckingham Palace dinner for the Duke of Edinburgh's Award World Fellowship, the acclaimed English tenor Russell Watson performed the hymn "Jerusalem," after which Philip said to him: "That was magnificent but why do you need a bloody microphone? They could have heard you in outer space." Television producers are not immune to Philip's insulting comments. When he met Sir Michael Bishop, the head of British TV's Channel Four, at a film premiere, Philip greeted him with "So you're responsible for the kind of crap Channel Four produces!"

In Philip's defense, it must be said that things were very different fifty or more years ago. The term "political correctness" did not come into common usage until the 1980s. Philip's sense of humor has not changed since that time. It is still stuck in an era when co- medians could make jokes about people of different race, sex, or color without the threat of losing their jobs. In his time, Philip has been indiscriminate about which race or nation to insult, and some of his more offensive jokes have appeared in the current century. In 2002, Philip shocked the aboriginal nation when at the Aboriginal Cultural Park in Queensland he asked their leader William Brin, "Do you still throw spears at each other?"

During a tour of a Scottish factory in 1999, he inspected an elec- trical fuse box and commented: "It looks as though it was put in by an Indian." He later tried to excuse himself by saying that he meant to say cowboy instead of Indian. The drinking habits of the Scots were highlighted when Philip asked a Scottish driving instructor, "How do you keep the natives off the booze long enough to pass the test?" In 2004, oblivious to the sensitivity of the Irish question, Philip asked a couple of students where they were from. When both answered Northern Ireland, Philip exclaimed: "At last we have two Irishmen in the same room who agree on something."

On a visit to Papua New Guinea in 1998, Philip came across a backpacker who had been trekking through the rain forests of that country, and asked him, "You managed not to get eaten then?" In 2009, at the G20 summit for world leaders, the Queen and Prince Philip joined the leaders of the G20 nations in an official photo call marking the end of the summit. Mr. Berlusconi was heard to bellow, "Mr. Obama!" at the US president, who was standing behind him. Barack Obama politely replied, "Mr. Berlusconi," in a far quieter voice. The Queen appeared to bristle at Mr. Berlusconi's booming voice and said, "What is it? Why does he have to shout?" Her remark prompted laughter among the other leaders. Philip's answer to the Queen's question was "He is Italian. How else would he sell his ice creams?"

Philip is not averse to some below-the-belt humor. At a World Wildlife Fund gathering in 1993, he asked fashion writer Serena French, "You're not wearing mink knickers, are you?" A similar question was asked of the then Scottish Conservative leader Annabel Goldie in 2010, when discussing a tartan designed for the upcoming papal visit: "That's a nice tie. Do you have any knickers in that material?" In today's politically correct world, only Philip could get away with saying to a pretty young blonde in a red dress in 2012, "I would get arrested if I unzipped that dress."

Philip's insensitivity to people's feelings reached new heights as he entered the twentieth-first century, particularly when dealing with the handicapped or disabled. At a tree-planting ceremony in Hyde Park in London in 2002, the Queen and Prince Philip met army cadet Stephen Menary, who lost an arm and most of his sight in an Irish Republican Army bomb attack. When the Queen asked Stephen how much he could see, Philip interrupted with, "Not a lot judging by the tie he's wearing." In his younger days, Philip would never have made such a gratuitous and hurtful comment.

When touring the Caribbean in 2000, Philip remarked to a group of deaf children who were in the proximity of a steel band, "Deaf? If you're near there no wonder you are deaf." To Susan Edwards in her wheelchair and accompanied by her guide dog in 2002, Philip said, "Do you know they have eating dogs for the anorexic now?" These asides were made nearly twenty years ago, and even for Prince

Philip they would never be acceptable in today's climate, where these kinds of tasteless jokes are unacceptable regardless of who you are. Unlike his son Prince Andrew, who has a complete inability to understand how things appear to the ordinary person, Prince Philip knew exactly what he was saying. I can only think it amused him to try and see how many of his so-called gaffes were picked up by the media and reported. The Queen must be very grateful he is no longer in a position to go out and about practicing them.

Before his retirement, Philip called himself the world's most experienced plaque unveiler; he could add that he is one of the world's most experienced after-dinner speakers and that he has addressed countless societies and organizations. Philip is renowned for writing his own material, and over the years several books of collections of his speeches have been published. He has an extensive library, mainly consisting of books on the subjects that interest him, such as the navy, ornithology, religion, and cookery. He has more than two hundred volumes of humor, including cartoon annuals in which he frequently figures. He wrote the foreword to *Parkinson's Law*, containing the words "You can get away with the most unpalatable truth if you make it appear funny." During his life he has delivered thousands of speeches on numerous subjects, and as the author of those speeches he has said he always tries to inject some humor.

"I don't think I have ever got up to make a speech of any kind, anywhere, ever, and not made the audience laugh at least once," he admitted. "It is my invariable custom to say something flattering to begin with, so that I shall be excused if by any chance I put my foot in it later on." In a speech given in Ghana in 1959, Philip described a sense of humor as "God's greatest gift to mankind."

Many of his speeches or toasts contain genuine witticisms. Proposing the toast to "The Common Health" at the British Medical Association dinner in 1959, he said: "It's almost as if I'd proposed a toast to pedestrians at the Society of Motor Manufacturers or to teetotallers at the Licensed Victuallers Association." Speaking to the Royal College of Surgeons of Edinburgh, of which Philip was the patron, he said: "I ought to give an immediate undertaking not to attempt to practise the craft of surgery. I understand that James IV sometimes used to have a go at members of his household. Mine are quite safe. I value their assistance and friendship too highly to take that sort of liberty with them."

Philip's grandson Prince William has claimed it's the way that his grandfather looks at life that makes him humorous. His one-liners, his waspish wit, and his disregard for political correctness are all part of what has made him the satirist he is. Humor is what keeps him sane, and although his remarks can be hurtful, he just gets fed up with the way people seem to see him, but he has admitted that misconception has its usefulness. It has left him free to be whatever he wants, according to how the mood takes him, and to form complicated relationships with interesting people. He has used his wit as a weapon, and it has allowed a release for his anger that would otherwise fester inside him. In answer to his gaffes, he said, "I sympathise with ageing politicians. They trip up over quotations they have long forgotten."

Chapter 17

DIANA

The relationship between Prince Philip and Lady Diana Spencer, whom he first encountered as a young child in the 1960s, evolved from affection to disappointment to total antipathy. This may not be surprising when considering how he would have seen her behavior as rocking the very foundations of the institution that he had sacrificed so much to support.

When Lady Diana Spencer was first mooted as a potential bride for Prince Charles, both Prince Philip and the Queen were delighted. "She's one of us," the Queen confided to friends. Diana was eminently suitable, being the granddaughter of an earl and the daughter of Viscount Althorp, who had been an equerry to the Queen's father, King George VI, as well as to the Queen for the first two years of her reign. In June 1954, the Queen and Prince Philip had attended Viscount Althorp's wedding to eighteen-year-old Frances Roche in Westminster Abbey, and Johnnie Althorp—as he was known—had traveled with them on part of the lengthy Commonwealth tour of 1954.

Park House, part of the Sandringham estate, had been leased

to Diana's maternal grandfather, the 4th Baron Fermoy. He was the local member of parliament and George VI's friend, and his daughter Frances Roche was born there. After the teenage Frances married Viscount Althorp, they moved into Park House the following year. All their children were born there including their youngest daughter, Lady Diana, in July 1961. As Diana grew up, she mixed with the royal children from the "big house," as Prince Andrew was almost the same age. She frequently went to tea at Sandringham and watched a film show in the ballroom, where the minstrels' gallery houses a film projector. Together with Prince Andrew and Prince Edward, the young Diana and several other children whose parents were part of the royal household watched films, their favorite being 1968's *Chitty Chitty Bang Bang*, based on a book written by Ian Fleming for his son. If the Queen or Philip was around, they would sometimes pop in to see how things were progressing before the nanny gave the children their tea. It was how it worked in the 1960s and '70s, when royal children rarely mixed with anyone outside their parents' social circle or the royal household.

Originally Lady Diana was not considered as a match for Prince Charles as he was more than twelve years older than her, but she possibly was for Prince Andrew. Diana was sweet and naive and she loved country life and rural pursuits and had all the attributes necessary in those days to make what was considered an extremely good marriage. She was also a virgin and unsullied by any past scandal, which as a bride for a future king was considered important in the UK back in the 1980s. For her part, Lady Diana was immensely proud of her Spencer heritage and considered the aristocracy—especially her family, who could trace their lineage back to the fifteenth century—to be philanthropic and relevant. She changed her tune in later life, but at the time of meeting the royal family she was the traditional English rose with impeccable connections and lineage.

*

When Diana married Prince Charles, the whole family, in particular the Queen Mother and Woman of the Bedchamber Ruth Lady
Fermoy, who was Diana Spencer's grandmother, were delighted.
Prince Philip was also of the opinion it was the right thing for his
son to do and had championed the union from behind the scenes. He
had seen his son fall for a number of beautiful girlfriends whose past
made them unsuitable to be the wife of a future king. In the early
1980s, finding a girlfriend who had never had a previous lover from
among the daughters of the British aristocracy was still important,
but it was not easy.

Some of Charles's friends, including Nicholas Soames and Norton and Penny Romsey (later Earl and Countess Mountbatten of
Burma), were not so pleased. They surmised, correctly, that Diana
had not given it enough serious thought and was marrying the
prince, not the person. Unable to accept his own naivete in marrying
a girl twelve years younger whom he hardly knew, Prince Charles
blamed his father for pushing him to ask for Diana's hand in marriage before he was ready to do so. He was very fond of Diana and
thought she was refreshingly sweet, lively, and fun, but even in the
beginning he had serious doubts about their compatibility.

Instead of following his instincts, part of Charles still clung to
his deep-rooted childhood desire to please his father. However over-
bearing and impatient Philip could be, he had tried to guide his son
in the way Charles wanted to go. It was Philip who chaired the 1965
education committee, which also included Lord Mountbatten and
Dean of Windsor Robin Woods, to ease his son's path to Trinity
College Cambridge and then into one or more of the armed services. Where Prince Charles's future was concerned, Mountbatten
was never short of advice, but on this occasion Philip was equally
enthusiastic in applying himself to his son's military career and did
not want Mountbatten to interfere. He wrote to Prince Charles

with details of his own meetings with the top brass, in particular First Sea Lord Admiral Sir Varyl Begg. After a formal meeting with both the Queen and Philip, it was agreed that Charles would enter the Royal Navy for at least three years. Philip agreed that Charles should consult his great-uncle Dickie, who should not be allowed to intervene directly.

Philip conducted most of the planning with his son by memorandum or letter in a factual, abrupt tone. They seldom saw each other except at the traditional family house parties at Sandringham or Balmoral, where no one broached anything controversial or morally challenging. There was a distinct gap of communication between Charles and Philip, and his father was more likely to criticize him than offer any praise. When he was eventually pondering on whether or not to ask Lady Diana to marry him, he was also acutely aware what a disappointment he was to his father. Part of him was anxious to heed his father's advice, which he considered all the more valuable because it came from a perspective so different from his own. He therefore decided proposing to Lady Diana was the right thing to do. Prince Philip had not intended to push his son into marriage, but just to warn him he could not postpone a decision for much longer without damaging Diana's reputation. She was already being regarded as "the one" by the press and was subject to an enormous amount of media interest, which she found difficult to deal with. Diana's mother, by then divorced from Johnnie and married to Peter Shand Kydd, even wrote a letter to *The Times* newspaper appealing to editors to stop their journalists harassing her daughter. "Is it fair," Frances wrote, "to ask any human being regardless of circumstances to be treated this way?"

When Diana first joined the royal family, she felt they had little understanding of what she was like—and she was right—but as time passed, she felt able to admit they had tried to be fair with her. She had a great respect for the Queen and admired her for giving her whole life to duty, sacrificing personal pleasures and even her family life to fulfill what was required of her. Diana admitted she would have never been able to do the same, but had she been older and more experienced she felt she would have been better equipped to face the problems she encountered.

In the early days of her courtship, such as it was, she opened up her heart to Prince Charles, telling him in copious letters how her spirits lifted when they were together, how she was head over heels in love with him and got butterflies in her stomach when she was with him. And most important how she was looking forward to spending the rest of her life with him.

As the wedding approached, however, she started to have misgivings. She found out very early on about Prince Charles's friendship with Camilla Parker Bowles and became fixated about her. She convinced herself that because of Camilla, Charles's heart wasn't really in the marriage. The night before the wedding she lay in bed at Clarence House and thought about calling it off. If she had been more confident, she might have been able to talk to Prince Philip about her fears, as he had suffered similar misgivings, but she did not.

On the day of the wedding, as she walked toward the altar of St Paul's Cathedral, she spotted Camilla in the congregation. "I was furious," Diana recalled. "I wanted to turn around and run." If she had had the courage, she said, she would have done what the girl played by Katharine Ross in the film *The Graduate* did, which was to hitch up her dress and bolt out of the church. The idea of becoming entangled in her long train as she attempted to make a run for it always made her laugh. There were several moments during the ceremony when she struggled to stop herself from giggling, at the sight of the ridiculous hats the women were wearing and when she blurted out Charles's names in the wrong order. "I had to see the funny side of it, otherwise I would have burst into tears," she said. "I felt like a sacrificial lamb."

Matters only got worse when, after their honeymoon on HMY *Britannia* in the Mediterranean, they traveled to Scotland. The Queen and Prince Philip, the Queen Mother, Princess Margaret and her children, David and Sarah, were all staying at Balmoral Castle along with Prince Andrew and Prince Edward. To begin with Charles and Diana stayed at Craigowan, a house on the estate, before they too moved into the castle. What was supposed to be a honeymoon turned into a family outing. The routine was formal and old-fashioned, and Diana loathed the long walks in the drizzle and the rain. The royal family never put the heating on, even when the weather turned cold, which it frequently does in Scotland. Everyone dressed for dinner, but all she wanted to do was pull on an extra jumper and sit in front of a fire. "And the minute you went out of a room there was always somebody switching off a light behind you," she recalled.

But when she found the restrictions of royal life difficult, it was Philip who helped her. Once she was married, she never sat next to her husband; she was always sat next to Philip at the endless black-tie dinners, and he took care of her. She never knew what to say. Her conversation, in line with her education, was severely limited, and she had yet to master the art of making royal small talk. She got away with a few witticisms and fluttering of her eyelashes to make sure she never had to get involved in any intellectual discussions with Prince Philip. She hadn't a clue about polo or carriage driving and would giggle at appropriate moments and hope he didn't notice that she had no idea what she was talking about. Instead she would watch him shovel food into his mouth at an alarming rate and try to think of a subject that would hold his attention before she was relieved by having to turn to talk to the person on the other side of her. Diana found the Balmoral dinners a massive strain and the atmosphere stifling. When the piper came around the table after dinner with his kilt swirling and pipes whining, she couldn't wait to leave the cold dining room.

The picnics were even worse. The focus of everything at Balmoral was picnics and barbecues. There were picnics every lunchtime, no matter how inclement the weather, and barbecues most evenings. It was simply not a choice to miss them; even the Queen Mother, in her ninth decade, continued to drag herself out on the hill wrapped in a tartan rug to join the others eating those chops and sausages Prince Philip took such pleasure in cooking. By the end of the first week of her extended honeymoon Diana was refusing to go.

If she made the picnic, she would excuse herself from the evening barbecue because she said she wasn't feeling well. The royal family went out barbecuing to give their staff the night off, but with Diana still in the house that was not possible. When the matter was raised with her, she said, "I'm only having baked beans." She failed to take into consideration that one of the kitchen staff had to stay on duty to cook them and someone had to bring them up to her room and wait around to clear up afterwards. It was, everyone agreed, "bad form" on Diana's part, and Prince Philip was not amused as he considered it an insult to his wife. Apart from supporting the Queen, Philip did not become involved with Charles and Diana's marriage until he had no choice.

Much later, when Philip realized that Diana's behavior was having a detrimental effect on the institute of the monarchy, he changed his tune and told her so in no uncertain terms. He tried not to take sides but to help her see the importance of her position and sympathize as he too had found it difficult when he was a newcomer. As things worsened, although he tried not to interfere, he became irritated with the Queen, whom he accused of "sitting on the fence" about the much-publicized unhappy marriage of their son.

Diana eventually came to dislike Prince Philip as she found him impossible to deal with. "He might be entertaining as a dinner guest," she explained, "but as a father-in-law he was far too judgemental." He could also be very unpleasant, especially when he felt she was letting down the family "firm." Philip did not hesitate to put his feelings into writing, and they were certainly straight to the point.

But by the summer of 1992 the Queen, encouraged by Prince Philip, was forced into action. She disliked any kind of moral confrontation and had always been gentle and understanding of Diana's despair and frequent tears over her unhappy marriage. But when the Andrew Morton book *Diana: Her True Story* began its serialization in the *Sunday Times* just before the start of Royal Ascot week, Prince Philip insisted they do something to avert the fallout of such a potentially catastrophic situation. Together they sat down with Charles and Diana in their private sitting room at Windsor Castle and discussed what could be done.

The meeting with her in-laws was worse than Diana had expected and left her shaken rigid. She claimed, with justification, that her husband's behavior was unreasonable, unjust, and unfair. Philip counseled them and told them to try to think of their children, the monarchy, and the country instead of their personal woes. He then accused Diana, correctly as it later emerged, of colluding with the book and, according to her, "was angry, raging and unpleasant." Charles remained virtually silent, much to Diana's disgust since they had discussed and agreed together they would plead for a trial separation.

The Queen and Philip decided they should all have a further meeting the following day, but although Diana agreed she failed to turn up. Prince Philip, always more explicit and gentler in letters than in person, then initiated a correspondence with his daughter-in-law that he hoped might prove useful. Depending on her mood, Diana could take the letters either way. Philip firmly told her she should not have missed the second meeting, for which he and the Queen had put time aside, and then gently reminded her there were always faults on both sides, although not for one minute did he condone his son's behavior.

He tried to make her face facts and deal with the problems within her marriage, explaining he knew firsthand the difficulties of marrying into the royal family. He signed the letters "Pa" and in the beginning was sympathetic, even saying Charles "was silly to risk everything with Camilla for a man in his position. We never dreamed he might feel like leaving you for her. I cannot imagine anyone in their right minds leaving you for Camilla. Such a prospect never even entered our heads."

On June 21, 1992, on Prince William's tenth birthday and five days after the publication of the Morton book (serialization June 7), Diana wrote to Prince Philip thanking him for a letter in which he offered to do what he could to help her.

> *Dearest Pa,*
> *I was so pleased to receive your letter, and particularly so to read that you are desperately anxious to help . . .*
> *Once again, Pa, I am very grateful to you for sending me such an honest and heartfelt letter. I hope you will read mine in the same spirit.*
> *With fondest love, from Diana.*

Four days later, on June 25, the duke replied by signed typewritten letter, as was his style, from Scotland, where he and the Queen

were in residence at the Palace of Holyroodhouse. That morning
the Queen and the duke had given a reception for delegates for the
Commonwealth Press Union conference.

*Thank you for taking the time to respond to my letter. I
hope this means that we can continue to make use of this
form of communication, since there appears to be very little
other opportunity to exchange views.*

Two days before her thirty-first birthday, on June 29, Diana replied.

Dear Pa,
*Thank you for responding to my long letter so speedily. I
agree this form of communication does seem to be the only
effective one in the present situation, but at least it's a start,
and I am grateful for it.*
 *I hope you don't find this letter overlong, but I was
so immensely relieved to receive such a thoughtful
letter as the one you sent me, showing such obvious
willingness to help.*
                        My fondest love, Diana.

On July 7, the duke replied to Diana.

Thank you for your very interesting letter.
 *I can only repeat what I have said before. If invited, I will
always do my utmost to help you and Charles to the best of
my ability. But I am quite ready to concede that I have no
talent as a marriage counsellor!*

On July 12, Diana replied.

Dearest Pa,
I was particularly touched by your most recent letter, which
proved to me, if I did not already know it, that you really do care.
*   You are very modest about your marriage guidance skills,*
and I disagree with you!
*   The last letter of yours showed great understanding and*
tact, and I hope to be able to draw on your advice in the
months ahead, whatever they may bring.
*   With my fondest love, Diana.*

On July 20, two days after Lady Helen Windsor's marriage to
Tim Taylor at St. George's Chapel, where Diana had been a guest
at the ceremony but declined the reception, the duke replied. The
Queen and Philip had returned from Windsor to take the salute at
a performance of the Royal Tournament, Earls Court, that night.

Phew, for the last days I had the feeling that I might have
overdone things in my last letter. It was good of you to be so
understanding and to reply.

Six days later, on July 26, it was the night before a lavish dinner
at Spencer House organized by Lord Callaghan to celebrate the
Queen's forty years as monarch and attended by five of the six surviving prime ministers who had served her during her reign. Diana
knew she would be seeing not only her husband but the duke and
the Queen, so she replied.

Dearest Pa,
Thank you again for such a thoughtful and revealing letter.
*   But even if you are unable to succeed in this, I would like*

you to know how much I admire you for the marvellous
way in which you have tried to come to terms with this
intensely difficult family problem.
                    With much love to you both, from Diana.

The next letter came after the royal family had returned from Balmoral in September and was from the duke to Diana, in which he said.

You will be relieved to see that this letter is rather shorter
than usual!!

On September 30, after a trip to Cornwall for her charities, Diana replied.

Dearest Pa.
Thank you so much for your letter.
    Thank you again for taking the trouble to write and
keep up our dialogue. It is good that our letters are getting
shorter. Perhaps it means that you and I are getting to
understand each other.
                        With much love from Diana.

Philip's missives were basically saying Charles was wrong to have returned to Camilla, but Diana too was wrong to take other lovers and asked her to reflect on why her husband had returned to his old flame. Unable to take criticism of any sort, Diana eventually decided she hated Prince Philip (that is what she told me) and his mission failed. Philip was troubled that Diana had lost sight of what being a consort to the Prince of Wales was about and reminded her it "involved much more than simply being a hero to the British people."

Philip also expressed concern about her bulimia and acknowledged it could have been responsible for some of her behavioral patterns. He also suggested to her things the couple could do together, listing common interests they shared, which is a tried and tested method favored by marriage counselors—not really Philip's style at all. He wrote a long and sympathetic letter to his son, in which he praised his "saint like fortitude."

The letters and their contents might never have come to public attention if it hadn't been for Diana's butler, Paul Burrell, publishing a book and the final lengthy inquest into Diana and Dodi's death in 2007 to 2008. Burrell acknowledged that "Prince Philip probably did more to save the marriage than Prince Charles," and his intentions were honorable, even if he "wore steelworkers gloves for a situation that required kid mittens."

On December 9, 1992, Prime Minister John Major announced in Parliament that the Prince and Princess of Wales were to separate, which was what they both wanted and the Queen and Prince Philip had finally agreed was the only way forward, although Philip guessed correctly the hostilities would continue. The Queen was more hopeful and clung to the idea that reconciliation with Charles was still possible. With this in mind, she insisted on inviting Diana to spend Christmas with the family at Sandringham. Philip was vehemently opposed to the idea but was overruled by his wife. There were no tearful scenes of the kind that had marred previous Christmases, but as a member of the household recalled, "that was about the best that could be said for it."

Diana arrived at 5 p.m. on Christmas Eve and was given her own suite. The following morning, she accompanied the sixteen-strong royal party to church wearing an eye-catching red coat with a black hat and veil tipped over one eye, which drew the cameras. Once again, she had stolen the show, but it was a show of family unity that pleased the Queen. No sooner was the service over, however, than

Diana left for London, telling the staff she had not been invited to lunch. She had, of course: the Queen, so keen to reunite the family, had invited her to stay as long as she wished.

As she drove out of the gates, Prince Philip turned to the Queen and said, "I told you so." He declared, "If she wants out, she can get out!" Diana, he pronounced, should henceforth be banned from every royal occasion. She should not be allowed to continue to play the royal princess at charity events and state banquets. But only the Queen could enforce such an order. And the Queen could not bring herself to do so.

In April 1993, a state banquet at Buckingham Palace was held in honor of President Soares of Portugal. All the royal family arrived, one after the other, to have drinks in the Audience Room. As they gathered together, who should come in but the Princess of Wales herself. None of them had realized she was going to arrive, except the Queen, who hadn't been able to bring herself to tell anyone, least of all Prince Philip. It was the Queen Mother who had the greatest shock and took the Queen to one side saying, "What is she doing here? Why have you allowed it? Why has Charles allowed it? Why didn't he stop her?" She told her daughter, "I am so cross with you all."

Prince Philip was furious and so were Princess Anne and Princess Margaret. They all thought the Queen was mad to have allowed her to come, but Diana had pleaded with the Queen, using tears to emphasize the drama of the situation. She reminded the monarch she was still the Princess of Wales and still married to the Prince of Wales. Faced with such desperation, the Queen, who has always disliked moral confrontation, especially when tears are involved, found herself unable to say no.

Prince Philip made it clear his wife had made a great mistake by not being stronger with Diana and claimed it put the whole unhappy situation backward instead of moving it forward. He is, of course, someone who believes once you have made up your mind to do something there should be no going back. The Queen, on the other hand, always looks for a compromise that will keep both sides happy—but in the case of Diana and Charles that didn't exist, as Philip realized only too well. He knew his son and daughter-in-law were in that stage of their marriage breakdown where they could not stand to be in the same room together. Diana had made it very clear to him and the Queen that she wanted out and wanted a separation. So, in his mind "out" she must go.

Prince Philip had spent his entire married life supporting the monarchy and defending the institution he had sacrificed so much to support. So, for one person to cast it into the waves was abhorrent to him. He raged at the Queen, "Lilibet, you have to do something." The Queen, seeing the wider picture, was reluctant because of Prince William and Prince Harry. She just didn't know what would happen to them under the influence of their mother, who was seemingly becoming unstable. The reason she allowed Diana to come to the banquet was not because she was married to the Prince of Wales, but because she was the mother of the princes who are the future.

The Queen felt trapped. Trapped by the princess's media power and her undiminished popularity. She felt there was nothing she could do without making matters worse. For once her mother did not agree with her and thought she should take a firm stand, regardless of the publicity. She told her daughter to make it clear to Diana she was no longer welcome as part of the family and just take the consequences for a few months and let it die down. Prince Philip, for once in accord with his forceful mother-in-law, agreed that if the Queen didn't do something, too much damage would be done. She should just take a gamble and tell Diana she had gone too far. She wasn't to use her boys as a pawn in the game and she just had to put up with her husband's behavior as generations of royal women had done before her.

Prince Philip's view was that Diana was in danger of bringing the royal family to its knees because of her huge popularity. If she wanted privacy and a private life, then she should stop throwing herself on the front page of every newspaper, upstaging the Queen and doing nothing to help the royal family, but only enhancing herself.

Diana had no intention of surrendering either the status or attention being royal had brought her, and despite the separation she continued to act as a magnet for the cameras. Her ability to outshine the family was given its most spectacular illustration on June 2, 1993, almost a year after the publication of the Morton book. It was the fortieth anniversary of the Queen's coronation. The Queen awoke that morning to find the morning newspapers dominated not by happy remembrances, but by her wayward daughter-in-law. The night before Diana had addressed a conference organized by the charity Turning Point. She had talked about the "desperation and loneliness" felt by so many women, of their "enormous courage" as they battled with postpartum depression or violence at home, "in a haze of exhaustion and stress," and how many "can't cope" and are forced to resort to tranquilizers and sleeping pills and antidepressants. Once again, the Queen, a pillar of doughty womanhood determinedly going about her duty with never a complaint, had been upstaged.

Philip was beside himself. But Diana dismissed the timing as unfortunate coincidence. To others it was nothing less than an exercise in the media power that Diana, free of any constitutional responsibility, had come to exercise. It was the apogee of a development that had begun innocently twelve years before. She was indeed, as Philip said, "a loose cannon."

Prince Philip laid much of the blame for this at Prince Charles's door. If only, he argued, his son had been possessed of either the strength of character or the emotional sensitivity to steer Diana out of her traumas, their tenuous marriage might have been saved and with it the reputation of the royal family. He had tried to talk to Charles about how his marital difficulties were bringing the institution he was born to head into disrepute, but because of the distant nature of their relationship his advice appeared to fall on deaf ears. Their conversations usually ended with Charles looking at his watch and making an excuse to leave the room, which irritated Philip further. Listening to his father was a task that proved beyond Charles, but they did agree on one thing: Diana was proving to be a woman beyond both their understanding.

The relationship that Prince Philip had worked so hard to establish with his daughter-in-law was at an end. Diana remained in two minds about what she had done. She insisted she was right to tell her story. On the one hand, she deeply regretted the unintentional hurt it had caused to people who had been her closest allies. She had permanently lost some good friends, and she had lost the goodwill of the Queen's husband, the one person who could have intervened when her royal denouement finally came. On balance, she admitted, telling her story was probably a silly thing to have done. It left her alone and isolated, a feeling magnified by the death three months earlier of her father, Earl Spencer. Her marriage was coming apart. and Diana had to deal with the fallout without her father or the irascible figure of Prince Philip for support.

When Prince Philip feels his advice is being ignored, he reverts to the cold man he is frequently portrayed as being. Diana had made the fatal mistake of alienating him and continued to do so, this time choosing the medium of television to launch a broadside against the palace and most damningly against her estranged husband.

On November 20, 1995, on Prince Philip and the Queen's forty-eighth wedding anniversary, Diana's interview for *Panorama* was broadcast to an audience of 23 million viewers. As head of state, the Queen relies on a secretariat of advisors whose integrity must be beyond question. Diana had portrayed them as conniving, under-handed intriguers who were conducting a personal vendetta against her. By direct implication Diana was attacking the sovereign. She also effectively said Charles was unfit to be king. Diana had thought that by telling the world how badly she had been treated she would somehow lure Charles back into the marriage. She had been very badly advised by the interviewer, Martin Bashir, who had cajoled Diana into saying a lot more than her normal discretion would have ever allowed.

Prince Philip was of the opinion Diana knew exactly the damage she had caused and was rightly extremely concerned about what she might do next. He understood how cunning but also unworldly she was. She had gone from schoolgirl to princess, a transformation at breathtaking speed that had deprived her of the chance to learn that human relations are all about compromise. She had overly romantic, unrealistic, almost childlike expectations of love and marriage, and in her naivete, she had wanted Charles to be something he wasn't.

The Queen, supported by Prince Philip, with whom she was now united in her views, took action. Her Majesty wrote to Prince Charles and Princess Diana to inform them, with the support of her husband, that an early divorce was now desirable. The full weight of Prince Philip's displeasure was witnessed when he proposed that as well as losing her rank as a Royal Highness, Diana should be downgraded from Princess of Wales to Duchess of Cornwall on the basis of his well-aired views that if she wanted out—she was out. But he did not push his point, and when Diana issued a statement saying she had agreed to the divorce and under pressure she would be giving up her HRH style, Buckingham Palace counteracted with

a strongly worded statement saying, "The decision to drop the title
is the Princess's and the Princess's alone. It is wrong that the Queen
or the Prince asked her. I can categorically say this is not true."

Prince Philip had said his piece and made up his mind. His characteristic coldness allowed him to shut down, and he refused to
have anything more to do with Diana. On the rare occasions she
appeared at Windsor Castle with William and Harry, he would
make himself scarce.

It was Prince Philip, not Diana, who first met the flamboyant figure
of Mohamed Al-Fayed, shortly after the controversial Egyptian
purchased the Knightsbridge store Harrods from House of Fraser
in 1985. Fayed immediately took over the House of Fraser's spon-
sorship of the Royal Windsor Horse Show's carriage-driving event,
which enabled him to seat himself in the royal box next to the Queen
on the final day of the show when she would present the prizes.

Prince Philip never liked Al-Fayed, and when he had to meet him
socially, he was brusque to the point of rudeness. On one occasion
in 1994, he was obliged to have a sponsors' lunch in the Harrods
dining room. He was in one of his "bloody Arabs" moods and froze
the atmosphere in the room. Afterward, he turned to his friend
General Sir Michael Hobbs, chairman of the Duke of Edinburgh
Award scheme, and said, "How did we do? Bloody awful wasn't it?"

When Diana met Al-Fayed through the English National Ballet,
of which she was patron, Prince Philip was unaware of their friendship, and if he did have an idea he cared even less. However, her relationship with Al-Fayed's son, Dodi Fayed, whom Philip was alleged
to have called an "oily bed hopper," was of concern. Al-Fayed was
one of the most contentious figures in British politics, whose bribery
of members of the British parliament contributed to the downfall of
John Major's Conservative government. He would have made a
highly dubious father-in-law to a British princess, just as Dodi, who

was a playboy with a history of alleged cocaine use, would have made a controversial stepfather for a future king.

As history relates, the matter was resolved with brutal finality when on the night of Sunday August 31, 1997, Diana's life ended in the crushed wreckage of a Mercedes in a Parisian underpass, with Dodi at her side. During the ensuing days, the royal family remained in the seclusion of Balmoral with Prince William and Prince Harry. And only when there was a disagreement about what role the boys should play in the funeral, if any, did Prince Philip intervene. The Queen's acting private secretary, Sir Robin Janvrin, was based at Balmoral and talking over the speakerphone to Buckingham Palace with the Spencer family representatives when Philip's voice came booming over the phone: "Stop telling us what to do with those boys! They've lost their mother! You're talking about them as if they were commodities. Have you any idea what they are going through?"

Prince Philip had lost his favorite sister, Cecile, when he was sixteen, so he knew to some extent what William and Harry were suffering. The princes both loved their grandpa and took no notice of his gruffness and acerbic comments. They just liked being around him and going shooting and duck flighting with him, and during that strange surreal week after their mother's death they were glad of his reassuring presence. So much so that, at Prince William's request, he walked with the fifteen-year-old behind his mother's coffin on the day of the funeral.

However tragic Diana's death was, Prince Philip was grateful for one thing—the hope he would never have to hear the name Mohamed Al-Fayed again. But he would not fade away. For years after the accident, Al-Fayed publicly stated his belief that a group, of which Prince Philip was the chief conspirator, had orchestrated the deaths. Early in the morning of February 18, 2008, an unusually large queue formed for tickets to the public gallery in courtroom 73 of the Royal Courts of Justice, where the inquest into the death of Diana was due to hear from its most eagerly anticipated witness. So great was the demand from both the public and the world's press for access to the court that an annex was set up in a marquee in the courtyard to house the overflow. On this day, there was not a spare seat in any section of the court because it was the day that Mohamed Al-Fayed was due to give his evidence at the inquest into the cause of the deaths of his son, Dodi Fayed, and Diana some ten years earlier in Paris. While Al-Fayed's testimony was expected to be controversial, it had not been anticipated that his evidence would be some of the most sensational ever heard in the long history of the law courts.

For his day in court, Al-Fayed arrived with four hefty security guards, who were required to wait outside the courtroom. He was dressed in a checked suit and a blue-and-green checked, open-necked silk shirt; this outlandish attire was in sharp contrast to the dark suit, white shirt, and smart tie he habitually wore when going about the business of Harrods.

Having sworn in the name of Allah to tell the truth, Al-Fayed first read a prepared statement in which he alleged that Princess Diana had told him that Prince Philip and Prince Charles wanted to get rid of her. He also claimed that Diana told him she was pregnant and was about to announce her engagement to be married to Dodi. He said that Prince Philip and Prince Charles plotted to assassinate Diana so that Charles could marry Camilla Parker Bowles, whom he described as Prince Charles's "crocodile wife." He stated that Prince Philip would never accept that his son, Dodi, could have anything to do with Prince William, the future king of England. Then Mr. Ian Burnett QC, counsel for the coroner, asked, "All this stems from your belief that Prince Philip is not only a racist but a Nazi as well?"

Al-Fayed replied: "That's right. It is time to send him back to

Germany where he came from. If you want to know his original name, it ends with Frankenstein." He started waving about a photograph taken in 1937 at the funeral of Prince Philip's sister Cecile. In this photograph, sixteen-year-old Prince Philip is seen walking through the street of Darmstadt, the Hesse family's hometown, which was festooned with swastikas, in the company of his brother-in-law Prince Christoph of Hesse in SS uniform and another family relative in a brown SA uniform. Prince Philip's uncle Lord Louis Mountbatten followed behind in British naval uniform. Al-Fayed added: "Prince Philip is a person who grew up with the Nazis, brought up by his auntie who married Hitler's general. This is the man who is in charge of the country, who can do anything, who manipulates." Al-Fayed expanded his theory to include a cover-up by the French police, the British CID, and the United States FBI, among others.

However, when at the end of the proceedings the coroner gave a detailed summing up of all the evidence, he told the jury there was "not a shred of evidence" in support of Al-Fayed's theory that Prince Philip had ordered MI6 to murder Diana, and he questioned Al-Fayed's credibility as a witness. He explained that he had made the decision not to hear evidence from Prince Philip, "in the light of all the evidence we have heard, which provided no evidence whatsoever for the suggestion that he was involved in killing his daughter-in-law and Dodi."

The inquest also shed new light on Prince Philip's relationship with Princess Diana when it demanded that their correspondence be made available, some of which had already appeared in her butler Paul Burrell's book. Philip was not happy about any of it, but there was little he could do. Once revealed, the letters in question, as we have seen, showed that he and Diana—at one time at least—had a very good relationship.

Simone Simmons was Diana's healer and knew her better than most. According to her, there were other letters that were written in quite a different tone. Prince Philip denied this and issued a statement through his office in Buckingham Palace saying so. He regarded the suggestion that he used derogatory terms to describe Diana as a "gross misrepresentation of his relations with his daughter-in-law and hurtful to his grandsons." Diana had always acknowledged that Prince Philip's letters were helpful in the beginning, but she also said that he had insisted that both William and Harry be subjected to DNA tests in the light of her affair with James Hewitt becoming public. There is nothing to prove this is correct, only the hearsay of others, but what was certain was that Prince Philip had moved to the top of Diana's hate list.

As far as Diana was concerned, things became so bad between them that she told her friend Roberto Devorik about her fears that Prince Philip was plotting to have her killed. Devorik repeated this under oath, adding that she once pointed to a picture of Prince Philip in a VIP lounge at an airport and said, "He really hates me and wants me to disappear." Her other great friend, the late American billionaire dealmaker Teddy Forstmann, said, "She hated Prince Philip."

She told me the same thing when I saw her at Kensington Palace shortly before her death. She explained that she had warned her boys, "Never, never shout at anyone the way Prince Philip does." Without doubt, having such details of the private lives of the royal family brought out in public—not to mention such outlandish accusations made against Prince Philip—was one of the more extraordinary episodes from the royal marriage.

"I don't spend a lot of time looking back," Prince Philip has frequently said. And on this occasion, he certainly meant it.

Chapter 18

TODAY AND YESTERDAY

At the beginning of the Golden Jubilee year in 2002, the Queen and Prince Philip gave a press reception in St. George's Hall at Windsor Castle. It was the kind of event that the duke disliked intensely, particularly as he blames many of the royal family's problems on the Murdoch press. "It's Murdoch's anti-establishment attitude which has really pulled the plug on an awful lot of things," he told TV presenter Jeremy Paxman. "He's succeeded in undermining them all. I think it gives a lot of tabloid journalists a tremendous buzz to feel that they can say whatever they like about people in public positions." And here he was with a whole hall full of them.

I was fortunate to be at the front, so that when the Queen and the Duke of Edinburgh entered, I was among the first people they met. The Queen was gracious but appeared bored, and Prince Philip was positively humming with indignation at having to be in such a place with what he considered such a desperate group of people. Stuck for something to say, I asked him what he was most looking forward to about the Golden Jubilee. It was, of course, one of those futile questions he hates, so not surprisingly he turned on his heel and growled at me, "When it's all over!"

I tell this story to illustrate the kind of things Prince Philip has had to endure since his wife ascended the throne in 1952. That is, fifty years of meaningless questions, so it is understandable, but not forgivable, if he gets irritated or is rude and irrational.

It was so different in the 1950s, at the beginning of the royal couple's first round-the-world tour, from November 1953 to May 1954, when Philip was the one who did the calming. He was eloquent and charming, and this did much to support his desperately shy young wife. He gave her much-needed courage when she was meeting the hundreds of people who were waiting for her. Sometimes he could be brusque, sometimes he made what later became known as his gaffes—but they were his way of relieving the tension. She was still only twenty-eight, in a distant land, and her children and family were half a world away. She had only been Queen for two years and the responsibility sometimes overwhelmed her. While traveling on board HMS *Gothic* to Fiji, Philip introduced the royal party to deck hockey minus the rules, and when they crossed the equator he flung himself with enthusiasm into the "Crossing the Line ceremony," part of which involves being covered in lather and dipped backwards into the swimming pool by Philip.

"Having been aghast at the idea of the ceremony," Pamela Mountbatten, who was then a lady-in-waiting to the Queen, recalled, "I ended up having enormous fun, but the Queen hated every minute of it because from where she was sitting it really did look as if we were all going to drown." As the tour continued to New Zealand and onward to Australia and back to England via Aden, Uganda, Malta, and Gibraltar, the Queen even developed big muscles in her arm as a result of waving, and her face ached from smiling. Prince Philip admitted he started to wake in the middle of the night feeling very cold on his right side, only to realize he had thrown back the bedclothes and had been waving to the crowds in his sleep. Occasionally, Philip would leave the Queen to enjoy her favorite sport while he pursued his, as he did when she was guest of honor at Australia's premier racetrack in Randwick, Sydney. Hating the idea of an afternoon at the races, he "sneaked off" to watch a match at Sydney Cricket Ground and have a few beers with cricket enthusiasts, spurning the royal box at the races in favor of the cricket pavilion.

In Colombo, when the royal couple were sat in an open-sided hall to open parliament, the sun caught the diamante-and-metalwork embroidery on the Queen's elaborate gown, and it became so hot, she was burned even through all her stiff petticoats. The climate, which veered from intense sun to torrential rain, was not always easy to deal with, and after one particularly rainy gathering, as the dark clouds hung over the governor's house, the royal party were diverted by a noise of bells, and a beaming Prince Philip arrived with nine elephants he had managed to waylay for the Queen to see and cheer everyone on. He always managed to make the Queen laugh as they faced the tedium, pitfalls, and difficulties of their royal duties together, overcoming the normal obstacles and challenges and occasional amusements that life in the public eye threw at them.

In Government House in Brisbane, on one of the rare days off, much to the Queen's delight they were introduced to a "talking horse" called Topsy. The horse managed to count the buttons on Pamela Mountbatten's dress by nodding, and it picked out the name Elizabeth from several others by pawing the ground. In spite of Prince Philip's attempts to get Topsy to give the wrong answer to the questions, which failed, they were fascinated with Topsy's expertise, which was light relief after the intensity of the fifty-thousand-strong crowd that had greeted them on their arrival.

"You won't remember this," the Prince said later. "But in the first years of the Queen's reign, the level of adulation—you wouldn't believe it. You really wouldn't. It could have been corroding. It would have been very easy to play to the gallery, but I took the conscious decision not to do that. Safer not to be too popular. You can't fall too far." He was being modest as, according to Pamela Mountbatten, "Prince Philip played an enormous part in the tour's success. I loved his mixture of teasing and humour with unexpected kindness and thoughtfulness. It was easy to see why he was so tremendously popular wherever we went. At a farewell party one of the local typists said, 'The best investment that the royal family has ever made in all its history is the Duke of Edinburgh.'"

Of course, it wasn't easy and occasionally tempers frayed. On the fifth week of the Australian tour, the Queen and Philip had a rare weekend off in a government chalet on the shores of the O'Shannassy Reservoir east of Melbourne. An Australian film crew recording the tour for Australia's first full-length color feature film, titled *The Queen in Australia*, were waiting outside for the royal couple to go off to look at some koalas, some of whom had been imported to enhance the photo shoot, when they heard the sound of arguing from within. Cameraman Frank Bagnall, who was fretting about the fading light, was positioned outside the door as instructed by press secretary Richard Colville. He was looking through the viewfinder when the door opened and Prince Philip literally charged out onto the patio followed by a flying pair of tennis shoes and a racket and a very angry Queen shouting for him to come back. Then the indignant Queen grabbed hold of her husband and dragged him back inside.

According to Dr. Jane Connors, who interviewed the director, Loch Townsend, forty years later, there was a moment of stunned silence when Townsend, Bagnall, and soundman Don Kennedy tried to assimilate what they had just seen before Richard Colville strode over to them in a state of high indignation and demanded they shut off their cameras immediately or they would be arrested. Of course they did, and Townsend removed the 300 feet (90 meters) of offending film from the back of the camera and gave it to Colville, who was able to take it to the Queen.

The Queen, always gracious, then came outside to meet the cameramen and thank them for the film. "I am sorry for that little interlude," Townsend recalled her saying, "but as you know it happens in every marriage. Now, what would you like me to do?"

Like most couples, the Queen and Prince Philip had many arguments throughout their marriage, and he could be very tough on her. He frequently called her a "bloody fool" and accused her of talking rubbish, but she seldom answered back, just changed the subject and started talking in riddles that would divert him as he tried to figure out what she was talking about. According to one courtier, "his mind runs on the lines of intellect and so, when she starts saying things that are non sequiturs, he's lost."

Dickie Mountbatten used to tell a story of when Philip was driving at his usual aggressive breakneck speed through Cowdray Park en route to a polo match. The Queen sitting beside him was sucking in her breath with fear when Philip shouted at her, "If you do that one more time, I shall put you out of the car." She didn't reply. When they arrived, a nervous Mountbatten asked the Queen why she hadn't stood up for herself. "But you heard what he said," the Queen replied, "and he meant it." As the years passed, the Queen gave as good as she got and used to tell him to shut up as he didn't know what he was talking about. Like all bullies he backed down. Occasionally, with the support of her friends, she prepared to face up to him, but they had to know their facts or he would trip them up and appear to be right after all.

Prince Philip hates being contradicted. On the occasion of the late Uffa Fox's memorial dinner on the Isle of Wight in 2016, he was sat next to Lord Beaverbrook's granddaughter, Laura Aitken, who was also one of Uffa Fox's godchildren. The first thing he said to her was, "I hated your grandfather," which indeed he did. The feeling was mutual: Beaverbrook was the newspaper baron who owned the *Daily Express*, and until his death in 1964 had waged a constant media campaign against Prince Philip, or Philip Mountbatten as he insisted on calling him, and even more vehemently against Lord Mountbatten, the latter of whom he called "the man who gave away India."

Through his senior journalists on both the *Daily Express* and *Evening Standard*, Beaverbrook was well informed about the "social misdemeanors" of both Edwina and Dickie Mountbatten, and Philip inevitably got caught in the cross fire. And even when Prince Philip and the Queen started holding occasional meet-the-people lunches at Buckingham Palace, Beaverbrook refused every invitation.

After Philip's scathing words of introduction, Laura decided to give him as good as she got. Philip had just been to Osborne House in East Cowes, Queen Victoria's favorite home, to see the refurbished Durbar wing and was obviously au fait with everything that was going on in the building. Laura lived in Cowes so had been there many times, but with a hazier memory. They embarked on a discussion about the nursery and how many cots it had. Laura swore it had four, and Prince Philip corrected her and said it only had three and a crib. Laura refused to agree with him and he refused to agree with her, sarcastically reminding her that his own relations had lived there so he should know. In the end, the disagreement got so heated, with neither side backing down, that Laura was asked by her horrified host to move further down the table. At ninety-five years old, Philip was not inhibited by anyone, even a guest, and was certainly not used to anyone crossing his path. For as long as he can remember no one has ever said to him, apart from the Queen, "That is not the way to behave."

*

In November 1997, the Queen famously said, Philip "is someone who doesn't take easily to compliments." This is because people come and talk to him because of who he is and not as a real person. He doesn't like compliments because he mistrusts their motive. He is the same when he is asked if he still likes doing things he has done for years. When asked by a charming lady if he still enjoyed carriage driving, he replied angrily, "Do I still enjoy breathing?" There is no answer for that.

Despite his brusque behavior, his so-called gaffes, and his prickly temper, Prince Philip has supported his wife and thereby the monarchy loyally throughout the decades. He has also visited many remote parts of the world on her behalf, but his approach to royal tours was very different when he was on his own. A briefing to South American embassies made in the 1960s gives an insight as to how he liked to have things done: "Formal functions had to be kept to a minimum and return hospitality should not be encouraged. All industrial visits should have a particular connection with Britain and HRH would like to play polo whenever there is an opportunity. Military events were extremely unwelcome. It is very much hoped that Service engagements are not included. In fact, HRH does not expect to take any uniforms with him."

During the 1990s, American financial advocate and fundraiser Charles Smithers, who was an international trustee of the Duke of Edinburgh's Award fellowship, and his wife, traveled on behalf of the award with Prince Philip and his then private secretary, Brigadier Sir Miles Hunt-Davis. Charles's wife Anne, a former French viscountess and journalist, was a very attractive, quick-witted redhead, and together with her affable husband, they made amusing companions.

"I enjoyed being with Prince Philip," Anne recalled. "Many people found him challenging but he was charismatic—a unique character, one of a kind. If you could hold your own, he was a great companion and always made an impact. He set the standard and expected you to meet that standard. He completely believed in the Duke of Edinburgh Award scheme as he felt he was giving young people an opportunity to succeed. Never once did I see him slip up, but you never knew what he was going to say. His mind was very quick and he enjoyed being around people who could keep up with him.

"When we were in New Zealand in 1997 at American fundraiser and socialite Barbara Wainscott's wedding to leading American lawyer David Berger, at Hapa Lodge in Christchurch [Prince Philip and Prince Edward served as groomsmen], a Maori tribesman in full tribal dress complete with a feather headdress ran by us on the riverbank. I said, 'He's probably the best man,' and quick as a flash Philip said, 'No, he was the bridesmaid!' "

From the early 1990s, as Philip toured the globe, Brigadier Sir Miles Hunt-Davies worked in tandem with the affable Brian McGrath, the duke's former private secretary and his lifetime friend. Sir Miles recalled one of his most memorable visits was to northern Siberia, where he stayed with the duke in a wooden house on the beach, but unfortunately, there are few noteworthy details of any of Prince Philip's solo visits. Over the years, Prince Philip has relied on a small team of loyal employees to accompany him on his extensive travels. As far as he was concerned, the fewer people around him the better, and if he could have, he would have done without his royal protection officers altogether. He frequently tried to get rid of them as he never liked having them around. Philip considered it an invasion of his privacy and an affront to his ability to look after himself.

Ken Wharfe, who worked in royalty protection for sixteen years, recalled a time he was in charge of royal protection for a week at Balmoral when Prince Philip and the Queen were in residence.

Prince Philip's valet telephoned Ken and said the duke wanted to go fishing with his friends the Gordon Lennoxes, who had beats on the Spey, and asked if Wharfe would provide a PPO (personal protection officer) to go with him. Knowing how difficult he could be, Ken found someone with experience and told him to be at the door of Balmoral Castle at 6:30 a.m., and he would be there to supervise the departure.

When Philip arrived at 6:30 a.m., according to Wharfe, he promptly made for the car and on seeing the PPO, he immediately told him to "bugger off," he didn't need him. Wharfe continued: "I signaled for him to stand his ground and grab the keys out of the ignition as soon as the duke looked away, which he managed to do. Unaware of this, the duke climbed into the driving seat then realized there were no keys and started shouting, 'Who's nicked the fucking keys!' I told the PPO just to get in the front passenger seat, and at that moment a window opens and the Queen leans out and says, 'What's the matter, Philip?'

"In a slightly calmer voice, he looked up at her and said, 'Someone nicked the fucking keys.' Eventually he cooled down and had to accept the police presence however much he disliked it, and they drove off."

Wharfe explained, "That is what went wrong when the duke had his accident in January 2019." The former royal protection officer said, "He was on the Sandringham estate, but it is crisscrossed with public roads and someone should have been protecting him. It would not have happened if he had a PPO with him, as it would have been another set of eyes. The royalty protection department is paid for by the taxpayer and he should understand that he can't keep avoiding them."

Philip has always loved speed, but he has too frequently failed to concentrate. In the 1990s, he crashed his Range Rover into the back of a Mercedes at a zebra crossing in London, and the driver of the

Mercedes ended up in a neck brace. He also had a couple of other near misses around Sandringham. He was once so busy chatting to his passenger ex-King Constantine of Greece, he drifted into the middle of a narrow road near Balmoral and the car coming the other way had to swerve hard to avoid hitting him head-on.

Doing things at double speed has not just applied to his driving but also to how he has lived his own life. He shovels his food into his mouth to get it down as quickly as possible and always has a shower instead of a bath. In his younger days, he would leap down steps two at a time and run along the Buckingham Palace corridors instead of walking.

He has always battled to find a way to maintain privacy, but at Balmoral in Scotland, where trespassing laws are different, it is impossible to stop the public from roaming over the land. Philip tried the usual "private property" notices, but nothing worked until he came up with the idea of signs saying "Beware of Adders," which to his delight was highly effective.

Prince Philip's love of travel lasted until he was well into his nineties, but then even he found the long-haul trips too tiring. His last trip on behalf of the Commonwealth was when he and the Queen traveled to Australia in October 2011. It was their sixteenth and last visit as Philip was ninety and the Queen was eighty-five. The short trips "down under," combined with the time change, were now too exhausting, and both the Queen and Prince Philip felt unwell afterward. Philip had celebrated his ninetieth birthday in June and although still remarkably active, they were not joking when they told friends another long-haul tour might finish them off.

The crowds might have been smaller than in the 1950s, but the welcome was just as enthusiastic, and when they took a trip up the Brisbane River huge numbers of people lined the banks cheering and waving. The Queen and Prince Philip were bowled over by their reception, and the usually unmoved prince found himself swept up by the atmosphere, rolling down the window of their official car to wave at the crowds. There were similar scenes in Melbourne, and by the time they had boarded a train for the short journey to their next destination, they were still waving enthusiastically. In Brisbane, they met koalas—for the umpteenth time—but the most significant moment of the tour was when the then Prime Minister David Cameron announced he had secured the agreement of the Commonwealth leaders for a change in the rules of succession so that daughters would have the same rights as sons, and heirs to the throne would no longer be forbidden to marry Roman Catholics.

At the Commonwealth Heads of Government Meeting in Perth at the end of the trip, the Queen quoted an Aboriginal proverb suggested by Prince Philip. "We are all visitors to this time, to this place. We are just passing through, our purpose here is to observe, to learn, to grow, to love . . . and then to return home."

Knowing how much her husband hates compliments, the Queen has praised him in public less than she would have liked. But three months after Diana's death in 1997, she had the opportunity to deliver an emotional tribute to her husband on their golden wedding anniversary at the Banqueting Hall in November.

"All too often, I fear, Prince Philip has had to listen to me speaking," she began. "Frequently, we have discussed my intended speech beforehand, and as you will imagine, his views have been expressed in a forthright manner. He has, quite simply, been my strength and stay all these years, and I, and his whole family and this and many other countries owe him a debt greater than he would ever claim, or we shall ever know."

In March 2012, she repeated the compliment in a Diamond Jubilee address to Parliament at Westminster Hall: "During these years as Queen, the support of my family has, across the generations, been beyond measure. Prince Philip is, I believe, well known for declining compliments of any kind. But throughout he has been a constant strength and guide."

When Philip had spoken at the Guildhall in 1997, he had been moved to say: "I think the main lesson we have learnt is that tolerance is the one essential ingredient in a happy marriage. It may not be quite so important when things are going well, but it is absolutely vital when the going gets difficult. You can take it from me, the Queen has the quality of tolerance in abundance."

Philip then recalled the early years of their marriage and the dramatic changes to their lives when his wife became Queen. Remarkably, he said, this had "less effect on their married life than he had anticipated. After an interval of ten hectic years, we had two more children and were more or less settled into our new way of life. Like all families we went through the full range of pleasures and tribulations of bringing up children. I am naturally somewhat biased, but I think our children have all done rather well under very difficult and demanding circumstances."

He also spoke of the lack of privacy endured by the royal family, adding those born into the monarchy "have to learn to accept certain constraints and to accommodate to that grey area of existence between official and what's left of a private life."

When Prince Philip celebrated his ninetieth birthday on June 10, 2011, among his gifts was a surprise from the Queen, when she made him lord high admiral, the titular head of the Royal Navy. She had held the title herself since 1964 but decided it would be appropriate to bestow it upon her husband to mark his landmark birthday. She broke the news to him over a private lunch at Buckingham Palace, but apart from that it was a normal working day. He hosted a centenary reception for the Royal Institute for Deaf People, of which he is patron, and was presented with a pair of ear protectors by the charity. As he looked at his gift, obviously unsure of what he would use them for, he joked, "Can you get Radio 3 on them?"

Although Prince Philip has frequently said he doesn't want any fuss and meant it, he wasn't going to be allowed to get away with it on his ninetieth birthday. Two days beforehand, Prime Minister David Cameron stood up in the House and paid a fulsome tribute to the duke, praising his many remarkable achievements. Cameron ended up by giving a rendition of his own favorite Philip "repost," which was: "After a long flight the umpteenth eager official asked him, 'How was your flight?' He replied, 'Have you been on a plane? Well you know how it goes up in the air and then comes back down again. Well it was just like that.'" It was Prince Philip in his best Tommy Cooper style, and Cameron's rendition brought gales of laughter from the House. A couple of weeks later, David and Samantha Cameron invited the Queen and Philip to 10 Downing Street, their first visit for nine years, for a special lunch of Philip's favorite Scottish beef followed by peaches and ice cream.

Most of the British royal family were at St. George's Chapel on June 12 for a service of celebration. Among the 750-strong congregation were King Constantine and Queen Anne Marie of the Hellenes, the Crown Princess of Romania and Prince Radu, and Prince Hassan of Jordan. Members of Prince Philip's extended family included the Margrave of Baden, his brother Prince Ludwig and sister Princess Margarita, nephews and nieces, and his great-nephew, Prince Philipp of Hohenlohe-Langenburg.

The dean of Windsor got a laugh when in his brief sermon he acknowledged that the duke "doesn't like to be praised." But he went on to insist that praise was due for the man who had been the Queen's tireless supporter for more than sixty years.

After the service there was a reception followed by a family lunch in the state apartments of Windsor Castle, where many of those who had worked for or with Prince Philip over the years were invited, including John Kent, his tailor for more than forty years. Kent, who has a small, bespoke business in Piccadilly, has claimed the duke has hardly changed shape over the years and he has never had to let out any of his clothes. Prince Philip's trim figure was put to the test that day: after the luncheon he was taken to dinner at one of the royal favorites, the Waterside Inn at Bray, by five of his grand-children. He and the Queen were entertained in the private dining room by the recently married Duke and Duchess of Cambridge, Princess Beatrice and Princess Eugenie, and Zara Tindall and her brother Peter Phillips as well his wife Autumn. The only one missing was Prince Harry, who was committed to a charity dinner. As far as Philip was concerned, the whole birthday was overplayed, but he was touched by the attention and put up with it, probably hoping he would never have to go through it again.

There are so many birthdays and anniversaries during the Queen and Prince Philips's year that if they chose to they could be com-memorating something almost every day. This is why they only celebrate decade birthdays and anniversaries, hence Prince Philip was in Argentina on his forty-fifth wedding anniversary on Novem-ber 20, 1992, when he received the news that the state apartments of Windsor Castle had been devastated by a serious fire. He im-mediately made plans to return, but it was a fourteen-hour flight, and by the time he landed at Heathrow and was taken to Windsor, the fire had been burning for fifteen hours. Thanks to the Duke of York being in the vicinity on the morning of the fire, almost all the valuables were saved—Andrew knew the castle better than anyone else, having explored all the hidden passages as a child.

The destruction to the state apartments of the ancient building was shocking, and as soon as he arrived, Prince Philip assessed the damage alongside the royal librarian Lady Roberts. "That was a traumatic event," she recalled. "And there were several hours when it looked as if the whole castle would go. He [Prince Philip] was there watching, he witnessed what the firemen did to save the castle and he wanted to pay tribute to them." His tribute was a chance for his passion for design to come to the fore, and he designed a stained-glass window for the new private chapel as the old Victorian one was burned to the ground. Sketching on a piece of graph paper, he drew a phoenix rising from the ashes to represent the saving of Windsor Castle and the subsequent restoration project and the good triumphing over evil of St. George slaying the dragon. The centerpiece is a fireman bravely wielding a hose and grappling with the flames.

Four days later on November 24, the Queen gave her famous "annus horribilis" speech at a luncheon at the Guildhall to mark the fortieth anniversary of her accession. She talked about the fire that had done so much damage to Windsor Castle the weekend before and reflected on the lessons learned over her last four decades. Her voice was stilted and husky because she had a terrible cold, but her delivery was moving and personal when she spoke of 1992 as "not a year I shall look back on with undiluted pleasure."

A touching footnote to the disaster was that the yeoman of the glass, Robert Hamilton, saved all the priceless crystal when the firemen kicked down the door to the glass pantry and discovered the glass was untouched, although the room was a sooty mess. Hamilton made sure not one glass from the set made for King George IV's coronation in 1821 was broken by carefully removing it all before the firemen could stop him. The Queen and Prince Philip were so grateful they had a special carriage clock made, inscribed on the back "Thank you for saving the glasses." At the Garter lunch, the only time the glasses have been used, the Queen had a little card made that read: "Robert Hamilton saved this glass during the fire at Windsor Castle. If it wasn't for him this collection would have been lost forever."

*

Almost exactly twenty-three years to the day after the Windsor fire, the Queen and Prince Philip returned to the Mediterranean island of Malta for their last-ever Commonwealth visit. From arriving at the ceremonial welcome in a 1950s Austin Princess, to a reception at the St. Anton Palace, it was a trip down memory lane. The Maltese had even found some faces from the 1950s, including eighty-one-year-old Freddie Mizzi, who had been a clarinetist with the Jimmy Dowling Band from the Phoenicia Hotel in Valetta. He reminded them he used to play their favorite song, "People Will Say We're in Love" from *Oklahoma*, when they danced. Another resident, eighty-seven-year-old Frank Attard, a photographer for the *Times of Malta* for fifty-five years, brought along some of his favorite photographs and was astounded when the eighty-three-year-old monarch laughingly said she could actually remember them being taken.

Opening the Commonwealth Heads of Government Meeting the next day, the Queen said she had cherished her time as head of the Commonwealth for more than six decades. She thanked her husband and, in perhaps a hint to the fifty-three leaders who will choose her successor when she dies, her eldest son the Prince of Wales for their support.

"Prince Philip and I first came to live here in 1949, the same year in which the Commonwealth was founded. I feel enormously proud of what the Commonwealth has achieved and all of it within my lifetime," she said. "For more than six decades of being Head of the Commonwealth—a responsibility I have cherished—I have had the fortune of the constancy of the Duke of Edinburgh. To that and to his many other Commonwealth associations, Prince Philip has brought boundless energy and commitment, for which I am indebted."

*

Prince Philip's boundless energy was an essential part of his character, as was his aggression, which doubled when he was distressed. It was seldom better illustrated than after Lord Mountbatten's murder at the hands of the IRA in August 1979. Prince Philip and Prince Charles, accompanied by Lord Rupert Nevill, then Prince Philip's treasurer and private secretary, traveled to Broadlands, the Mountbatten home. They were due to receive Lord Mountbatten's body at the nearby Eastleigh airport after it had been flown back from Ireland. It was decided they should eat a light lunch before leaving, and Prince Charles was so upset he could hardly speak, let alone eat. Irritated by his son's less than manly attitude, Philip was in no mood for lingering and was furious when, shortly before lunch was about to be served, Charles disappeared to a stretch of the river Test, where he used to fish with his great-uncle. Prince Philip sent John Barrett, Lord Mountbatten's private secretary, to fetch him, but when he saw Prince Charles silently standing by the river, he didn't have the nerve to disturb him.

When Charles eventually reappeared and sat down, Prince Philip started taunting his son, so much so Prince Charles got up and left the room. Prince Philip, covering his own distress by being curt and offhand, simply refused to countenance any display of emotion in his own son, and his method of dealing with it was to try to stiffen his backbone. Over the years Philip's attitude toward Charles has mellowed considerably, but despite Philip's respect for what Charles has achieved, their tastes and temperaments will always be completely different.

In spite of his doubts about the Duchess of Cornwall in the beginning, Philip has grown increasingly fond of her over the years. Since her own father, Major Bruce Shand, died in 2006, Camilla has taken great trouble with the duke and always manages to amuse him. She shares the same quick wit as he does and never asks what he considers inane questions. He can also see that she is the perfect spouse for his son because she is able to make Charles see the positive side of any situation and is able to laugh in the face of adversity.

One emotional moment the whole royal family shared was the decommissioning of HMY *Britannia* on December 11, 1997. When Prince Philip was asked how he felt about it later, he simply said, "sad." He was involved in the design of the vessel from the beginning, even down to the naming of the ship, which came about after endless discussions when both he and the Queen decided on *Britannia*. "*Britannia* was rather special as far as we were concerned," he said. "It conveyed something that people could understand."

Understanding Philip himself is far more complex. But like *Britannia* in her heyday, he has been a symbol of the monarchy. For seventy years, he supported his wife, always two steps behind. When he was taken into hospital after the river pageant for the Diamond Jubilee, suffering from a bladder infection, the Queen looked diminutive and lost at the service of thanksgiving two days later. She wasn't, and had even joked with Philip after he had been taken ill at Windsor Castle the previous day. As he was put into the ambulance to go to hospital, she waspishly said to him, "Don't die on me—not this week anyway." Whether it is an apocryphal story or not, it illustrates the bantering relationship they have always had and always will.

Always careful with his appearance and disliking any display of what he considered fragility, and despite the Queen's complaining he couldn't hear a thing, he refused to wear hearing aids in public until 2014. He eventually stopped wearing the heavy bearskin of the colonel of the Grenadier Guards, and for his final appearance at trooping the color in 2017 he wore a morning suit instead of his uniform for the first time since the 1950s.

Prince Philip has said many times he is a realist, but he finds the aging process of his razor-sharp mind "frustrating." His carefully timed retirement—it was exactly seventy years since he was created Duke of Edinburgh—did not mean he gave up work immediately. That same day he hosted a lunch at Buckingham Palace with the Queen for members of the Order of Merit, where mathematician Sir Michael Atiyah said he was sorry to hear he was standing down. Philip's quick retort was, "Well I can't stand up much longer."

When in 2011 the *Oldie* magazine awarded him the title "Consort of the Year," the duke wrote a wonderfully self-effacing letter on Sandringham House letterhead to the organizers regretting not being able to receive the award in person. "There is nothing like it for morale to be reminded that the years are passing—ever more quickly—and that bits are beginning to drop off the ancient frame," Philip wrote, "but it is nice to be remembered at all."

Chapter 19

WINDING DOWN

For a man of his advanced years, Prince Philip remained in remarkable shape throughout his late nineties. What he lacked in muscle power and vitality he made up for with sheer determination, cursing himself for his lack of dexterity, his aching joints, his arthritic hands, and his inability to hear. But he refused to give in, and when he was still accompanying the Queen to church ceremonies, the order of service was usefully highlighted so he could see when to stand up or sit down. What he lacked in cognitive ability he made up for with practical intelligence, and in spite of the Queen complaining that he couldn't hear a thing, he continued to listen to music and watch television with subtitles. He still painted when the mood took him, and although his eyesight was fading and he has always needed glasses, he wrote long letters and enjoyed reading. The extensive Sandringham library was a gold mine of biographies he wanted to read but had never had the time for. Philip has always enjoyed a curious mind, and although as he got older he forgot names, he retained the desire for self-improvement and made the effort to brush up his memory when he felt it was lapsing or he couldn't find the right word. He used all the recommended tools and refused to give in to brain fatigue. He also became more sensitive and therefore a little more tolerant but retained his acerbic opinions on events and people. One thing he couldn't improve was his increasing deafness, and despite multiple hearing aids, he has failed to remedy that particular affliction. His main irritation was the amount of time it took to prepare himself for the day, and each official engagement took more and more self-discipline. If, for instance, he had to be somewhere at 10 a.m., it would mean he had to start preparing himself several hours beforehand. With persuasion from his wife and members of his family, he eventually agreed it was time to step down, but even that took time.

"I reckon I've done my bit," he said on his ninetieth birthday, six years before he actually retired. "So, I want to enjoy myself a bit now, with less responsibility, less frantic rushing about, less preparation, less trying to think of something to say. On top of that, your memory's going. I can't remember names and things. It's better to get out before you reach your sell-by date."

Only he knew the right time. The 2012 Diamond Jubilee, the London Olympics, the 2015 milestone of the Queen becoming the longest-serving monarch, and her ninetieth birthday all came and went with Prince Philip at the center of national celebrations, beside his wife. Eventually, in May 2017, he announced his intentions a month before his ninety-sixth birthday, and before the autumn diaries were prepared and the invitations began to flood in. On August 2, 2017, almost seventy years after his first solo engagement, he made his final appearance in the forecourt of Buckingham Palace. His grand finale was appropriately enough in his role as captain general of the Royal Marines. It was raining heavily on the military parade in the forecourt of the palace, which marked the marines' finale of the 1664 Global Challenge. The challenge, which recognizes

1664 as the year when the corps was founded, involves Royal Marines from all over the world raising money for the Royal Marines Charity with a number of extreme feats, including a 1,664-mile (2,678-kilometer) trek and a 1,664-length underwater swim. Prince Philip, wearing a bowler hat and raincoat, inspected the guard of honor and met a group of hero commandos who had completed the extreme athletic feats. After hearing about their extraordinary exploits, he playfully told them, "You all should be locked up." He finally left the forecourt of Buckingham Palace raising his bowler hat in a salute while the Royal Marines Band played "For He's a Jolly Good Fellow" after a rousing three cheers for their captain general.

Philip's choice of the Royal Navy and Marine Corps engagement as his last was described as "an honor" and "brilliant" by Lt. Col. Gary Green, the commandant general of the Marines who devised the 1664 Global Challenge. Of having the duke as the head of the corps, he said: "It makes the Corps exceptional; it builds our Commando spirit and he's a wonderful figurehead for all Royal Marines to look up to."

Philip's association with the Royal Marines dated back appropriately sixty-four years to June 2, 1953, when he was appointed captain general in succession to the late kings George VI, Edward VIII, and George V. At that time, General Sir Leslie Hollis was commandant general of the Royal Marines. In his biography of Prince Philip, he recounted how he went to Buckingham Palace to meet Philip and discuss the appointment of a new captain general after the death of King George VI. Philip had assumed it would go to the Queen since the reigning monarchs had previously filled the position. However, Hollis invited Philip to take up the position, explaining that it might preferable to have Philip as captain general at the various dinners and mess nights when his presence was required. As Royal Navy men, they could all speak the same florid language and laugh at the same jokes that could not be uttered in the presence of the Queen. Philip's initial response was that it might be a little difficult, but he said, "Leave it with me and come back next week." He then suggested a gin and tonic, which he mixed himself in an adjoining room. A week later Hollis returned to Buckingham Palace. Philip shook hands with him and said: "You've got me. But I doubt whether the Queen will speak to me for a week. Now let's have the other half of the gin and tonic."

It might have been expected that after a lifetime of public service to Crown and country Philip could put his feet up and spend the rest of his days quietly enjoying simple pleasures at Wood Farm, a five-bedroom brick-built farmhouse on the Sandringham estate at Wolferton. Here his two pages, William Henderson and Stephen Niedojadlo, care for him; they take it in turns to spend a week with him. There is also a rota for a valet and on occasions a footman, and there is room for them all in the staff quarters at Wood Farm, except the housekeeper, who lives out. By royal standards it is very informal, and they all use the same kitchen that divides Prince Philip's dining room from the staff dining room. The secluded farmhouse has always been a favorite residence of the royal family and was once briefly the home of Prince John, the youngest son of George V and Queen Mary, who suffered from epilepsy and died in 1919 at just thirteen years old. During their Cambridge university days, both Prince Charles and later Prince Edward frequently used it at weekends, as did the princess royal and also Fergie when her daughters were staying at the big house over Christmas. When Sandringham House is open to the public, or it is more practical to use one of the smaller estate houses, the family always choose to use Wood Farm. The Queen often stays in the farmhouse and was in residence when John Major announced the Prince and Princess of Wales were to separate in on December 9, 1992. She did what she always does in tense situations: she put on her coat and took the dogs for a walk.

Wood Farm is near the local Church of St. Peter and is reached by a long tree-lined drive surrounded by arable farmland. Security is tight in the area, especially so when Prince Philip chose to use it as his retirement home. Until recently his Fell ponies and carriages were bought from Windsor and installed at the nearby stables so he could continue to enjoy carriage driving, which extraordinarily enough he did well into his ninety-eighth year, and if he is strong enough will continue to do.

Many years ago, Prince Philip oversaw the conversion of the farmhouse from a tenanted cottage to a small royal residence, and he has continued to enjoy planning improvements such as the beamed barn conversion with its solar-paneled heating and, most recently, installing a new kitchen. When he finally took up residence himself, he practiced his considerable cooking skills. Cooking is something he still enjoys, and he frequently experiments with some of the recipes he has seen on his favorite TV cooking programs. He grows black truffles, and in 2019, after twelve years of trying, he became the first person in Great Britain to cultivate a successful crop to create a truffière in the royal fruit farm at Sandringham. Years ago, he designed a picnic trailer for the Balmoral picnics that was meticulously crafted to be practical, efficient, and not rattle when it was driven over the moors. "When I first went to Balmoral all the picnics came out in baskets and it was a ghastly business trying to unpack them," he told Alan Harvey, the man responsible for looking after machinery on the Sandringham estate for more than thirty years. Philip delights in people like Harvey who are at the cutting edge of what they do, and in 2009 he held his staff Christmas party in Heston Blumenthal's restaurant, the Fat Duck, in Bray. He chose a menu of fish and chips and enthusiastically sprayed vinegar into the air from small bottles placed on each table supposedly to recreate the ambience of a local chippy.

However peaceful and idyllic Philip's retirement might appear, he has not totally disappeared. He still continues to attend occasional lunches and dinners. One such at Windsor Castle is the Order of Merit, established in 1902 by Edward VII to recognize distinguished service in the arts and sciences, literature, the military, and the promotion of culture; Prince Philip was appointed a member in 1968. In May 2019, just before his ninety-eighth birthday, two great champions of the future of our planet, Prince Philip and Sir David Attenborough, had a chance to converse before the annual lunch, this time at Windsor Castle. It was a fascinating gathering: among the guests were artist David Hockney, playwright Tom Stoppard, and Sir Tim Berners-Lee, inventor of the World Wide Web.

Despite the satisfaction of creating new enterprises and enjoying himself by doing as he wants, several significant events have caused him great personal distress and worry. One of Philip's pleasures in his retirement was driving at high speed around the Sandringham estate, and as the roads are private, he could dispense with the services of a chauffeur and private protection officer, whose presence in a car he has always resented. On January 17, 2019, Prince Philip was driving across the Sandringham estate, which is crisscrossed with public roads, when he came to a busy main road. When the then ninety-seven-year-old prince was turning onto the main road, blinded by the low winter sun, he failed to see an oncoming car. The Kia hit Prince Philip's Land Rover Freelander on the driver's side. The impact and the angle of the smaller Kia sent the heavy Land Rover spinning, ending up on the other side of the road after rolling over twice. A witness, seventy-five-year-old barrister Roy Warne, said Philip's car "came across the A149 like a somersault. It was turning on its side over and over." He described how first he had gone to help the passengers from the Kia, two women and a baby. With the engine still smoking from the impact, he lifted the baby from the back seat. He then helped Philip out of his vehicle, gently easing his trapped legs from under the steering wheel. "I couldn't see his face, but he kept saying 'my legs' so [I] put my hands under him and eased him out. He stood up and was unharmed but was obviously very shocked." Amazingly, once Prince Philip had steadied himself, he was able to walk away and check on the passengers of the other car himself, one of whom had a broken wrist.

Naturally, the accident caused a huge public outcry, and much to Philip's added distress, there were demands for him to cease driving and surrender his license. He was criticized for not having a protection officer in the car with him, as this would have provided another set of eyes and possibly prevented the accident. To compound the criticism, he was photographed at the wheel again only forty-eight hours later without a seat belt. He was not breaking the law—except that seat belts are mandatory—but having apparently admitted he had been a "fool" to turn on to a main road with the sun in his eyes, it was uncharacteristic of him to test his roadworthiness so soon after an accident in which he could have killed himself and the passengers in the other car. It was the apparent callousness of his getting behind the wheel again that stirred up more disapproval, especially when one of the passengers in the other car was still recovering from the shock and nursing a broken wrist, having not heard one word of apology. He did eventually write to the occupants of the car and apologized to Mrs. Fairweather, the passenger with the broken wrist, who gave several media interviews in which she excitedly showed his letter of apology.

"I have been across that crossing any number of times," Philip wrote. "I know very well the amount of traffic that uses that main road. It was a bright sunny day and at about three in the afternoon, the sun was low over the Wash. In other words, the sun was shining low over the main road. . . . I can only imagine that I failed to see the car coming, and I am very contrite about the consequences. . . . I was somewhat shaken after the accident, but I was greatly relieved that none of you were seriously injured. . . . I have since learned that you suffered a broken arm, I am deeply sorry about this injury."

Although he was thoroughly shaken and humiliated by the ordeal, which would most likely have killed a lesser man of his advanced age, he eventually bowed to public pressure—something that Philip has seldom done—and was persuaded to voluntarily surrender his license. The Queen had cannily enlisted the help of Countess Mountbatten of Burma (the former Penny Romsey), who visited Philip at Wood Farm and helped convince him he had to give up driving. He was reluctant as it meant giving up his independence to go where he wanted when he wanted, but eventually he agreed there was no alternative. Sometime later he pounced on the idea of resurrecting the late Queen Mother's golf buggy, which had been in the Sandringham museum for several years, since her death in 2001. Estate workers were instructed to hunt for the key so the duke could be at the wheel again, albeit at only at seventeen miles per hour. It was not speed but freedom that counted to Philip, whose nature is never to tell anyone what he is doing or intending to do. So, it suited him.

Another situation that has troubled Philip has been the behavior of his second son, the Duke of York. Throughout his married life, in addition to his unwavering support for the monarchy, Philip had dedicated himself to improving the standing and popularity of the royal family—his family—as a whole. His wife's favorite, their third child, named Andrew after his paternal grandfather, had a promising start as a young man, but later in his life he became something of a problem. Sandwiched between a bright and articulate sister and a brother who is heir to the throne, Andrew searched for a role after leaving the Royal Navy. A failed marriage to the girl-next-door Sarah Ferguson and a failed career as the UK's special envoy for overseas trade did little to help him. He could have taken heed from his father, who warned him of the dangers of being used, especially by what he described as "seedy billionaires" looking for a pet royal to elevate their own status. Andrew allowed himself to be seduced by the rich and powerful whose only interest was his royal connection and the doors it could open for them.

His ex-wife, Sarah, introduced him to the late Sir Robert Maxwell's daughter Ghislaine, and Andrew was fascinated by her worldly sophistication. Ghislaine, in turn, introduced the duke to a previously out-of-bounds, raunchy international lifestyle, and he was fascinated by it. It suited her to be able to produce Prince Andrew at parties, and she hosted dinners for him at her "sometime partner" the financier Jeffrey Epstein's Upper East Side apartment in New York. Ghislaine took Andrew wherever he was willing to go, but still naively the duke failed to see he was being used.

His continued association with Jeffrey Epstein, by now a convicted pedophile, led to a litany of well-publicized disasters that culminated after Epstein's death in prison in July 2019 and the duke's final downfall only months later. In a calamitous interview for BBC TV's *Panorama*, in which he failed to show regret or empathy for Epstein's young victims—one of whom has alleged she had sex with him—lost him any vestige of support he still had. It also turned him into a global figure of ridicule. He was seen as someone with immense privilege who took advantage of his position, and because of stupidity and immense arrogance simply couldn't be bothered to take care, when choosing his friends, to keep his nose clean. They saw the Swiss chalets, the holidays, the private jets, and the police protection officers following in his wake. They also saw a member of the royal family who appeared so arrogant he believed what he was saying.

The Duke of York is an emotionally battered figure. Having to step back from his royal duties and patronages and relinquish his military appointments for the foreseeable future has cost him his life as he knew it. It was a bitter pill for a man entering his sixties, and for Prince Philip and the Queen, their son's failure of judgment was a tragedy. Not only had he besmirched the reputation of the monarchy, but he had become involved in something extremely distasteful and far more serious. Since Philip's retirement, the Duke of York has been a staunch supporter at the Queen's side, accompanying her on occasional engagements and keeping her company at other times when she needed a family member to escort her. To see his son's demise through his own stupidity, arrogance, and sense of self-entitlement reminded Philip why he used to lose his temper with Andrew in the first place and tell him what a fool he was. As Fergie had defended her husband from Philip's vitriol, she later defended him from the global vitriol surrounding his association with Epstein. The Queen did what she could to dissuade Philip from upsetting himself and getting involved, but it would be difficult for any father to sit back while the press on both sides of the Atlantic hounds his son. Back in the 1990s, when the disasters that had befallen the younger royals had bought the royal family into disrepute—with Diana's separation from Charles and Andrew's impending divorce from Sarah Ferguson—Prince Philip was privately asked what he thought of it all and said at the time, "Everything I have worked for, for forty years has been in vain."

It wasn't, of course, and Philip carried on. As the longest-serving consort in British history and the oldest serving partner of a reigning monarch, he has a will of iron as well as an iron constitution. Over the past decade he has been admitted to hospital for abdominal surgery, a recurring bladder infection that saw him miss the service of thanksgiving for the Queen's Diamond Jubilee, and a blocked coronary artery, but it is his stubborn will that has served him best. At the beginning of April 2018, after weeks of pain, Prince Philip was admitted to the King Edward VII Hospital in London for a hip replacement. Renowned orthopedic surgeon Sarah Muirhead Allwood, who specializes in minimally invasive techniques, performed the operation. She also performed the Queen Mother's two hip replacements when she was ninety-five and ninety-seven. However successful the operation, elderly patients normally need several weeks of rehabilitation, moving with the aid of a stick or crutches as they learn to walk again on the new hip. Not so Prince Philip. He set his goal as attending Prince Harry's wedding to Meghan Markle but didn't confirm he would be there. Philip appeared at the Queen's side on May 19, walking with a straight back and without even a stick to assist him. Although he hates long sermons, he sat through the fourteen-minute sermon by Evangelical Bishop Michael Carey without wincing, and after the service took his place in the official photographs in the castle's green drawing room. He did not, however, attend the lunchtime reception given by the Queen for the newly ennobled Duke and Duchess of Sussex and six hundred guests in St. George's Hall, with Sir Elton John providing an exclusive surprise cabaret. Sir Elton sat himself at the Steinway grand piano and sang half a dozen of his own numbers using high-tech backing that made it sound as if he had an orchestra at his disposal. Luckily, Prince Philip couldn't hear it as Elton John's music is not among his favorites and he has been extremely rude to him over the years, albeit in a joking way.

Prince Philip has always got along well with his grandson Prince Harry, whose sporting abilities both with a gun and a polo pony he admired. Although he harbored doubts about his choice of bride, and later likened her to the Duchess of Windsor, he sincerely hoped their union would work. He knew Prince Harry had loved all things military since he was a child and was delighted when Harry was appointed captain general of the Royal Marines in his place on December 19, 2017. Prince Harry had a good relationship with the Royal

Marines, having fought alongside them in Afghanistan during his time as an Apache helicopter pilot. Harry, who joined the Blues and Royals in 2006 and served twice in Afghanistan—first as a forward air controller and then as an Apache pilot—left the army in 2015. Top brass viewed the appointment as a "brilliant move" that would attract young men and women to join the marines. Since taking up the post, Harry has visited the Commando Training Centre, joined them in action during war games in Norway, and spent a day with Special Boat Service (SBS) special forces in their base at Poole, Dorset. The marines were also part of the forces deployment that proudly lined the streets of Windsor for his May 2018 wedding.

Just before Christmas the following year, on December 20, 2019, Prince Philip was helicoptered from Sandringham to the King Edward VII Hospital in London, where he spent four nights for what was described as "observation and treatment for a pre-existing condition." His grandson Harry was on a six-week break in Canada with his wife and child, Archie Mountbatten-Windsor, but most of the rest of his family were waiting for him at Sandringham to celebrate Christmas together. Prince Philip returned by helicopter from London to Norfolk, having been released from hospital just in time for the Christmas Eve celebrations. It was just as well he was feeling stronger as only two weeks later, on January 8, Prince Harry and his wife, Meghan, made a surprise announcement on their new website that they intended to "step back as senior members of the royal family and balance their time between the United Kingdom and North America." The Queen and Prince Philip had known they were not happy but had thought they had agreed to wait for ongoing discussions about their future before making any kind of announcement. The Queen was informed ten minutes before the announcement went live on the website Sussex Royal. She was not amused. As Philip was in residence, he was also aware of the announcement and its implications.

It transpired that what the Duke and Duchess of Sussex wanted was to remain as part of the family but to relocate to North America, where they thought they would be able to escape from the intrusive European media and become financially independent through their own celebrity. In simple terms, they wanted to remain half in and half out of the royal family, which is impossible, as Prince Philip was so fond of reminding the Queen when Fergie and Diana wanted the same thirty years beforehand.

The Queen refused to allow their shenanigans to get to her husband. So, when she called an emergency summit at Sandringham on January 13, attended by her son the Prince of Wales and grandsons Prince William and Prince Harry, as well as their senior advisors, she asked one of her house guests, Countess Mountbatten, to drive Philip away from the house at least for the duration of the meeting. While they sat in the long library on the ground floor and thrashed out a solution that would allow Harry and Meghan their freedom without bringing the royal family and the Crown into disrepute, Philip remained out of the way. Buckingham Palace later released an unusually personal statement from the Queen saying that the family were entirely supportive of Harry and Meghan's desire to create a new life as a young family.

"Although we would have preferred them to remain full-time working members of the royal family, we respect their wish to live a more independent life as a family while remaining a valued part of my family." The underlying message being that the Queen wanted them to stay and do their duty as part of the firm, but she would not hold them to it against their wishes.

Ten days later, on January 18, a further personal statement was issued confirming arrangements for their new life without public funding or official royal duties on behalf of the Queen, to come into effect in the spring of 2020. It was decided that Harry, who holds the rank of major in the army, would lose his position as captain general of the Royal Marines, but the title would remain in abeyance, with no one else being appointed in his place until April 2021, when there is an agreed review of the situation.

It must have come as a heavy blow for Prince Philip to know that his grandson would be more or less giving up his homeland and everything he cared about for a life of self-centered celebrity in North America. Philip knew leaving was not a decision that Harry made lightly and could not grasp exactly what it was about the family firm that made his grandson's life so unbearable. As far as Philip was concerned, Harry and Meghan had everything going for them: a beautiful home at Frogmore, their healthy son, Archie Mountbatten-Windsor—his eighth great-grandchild—and a unique opportunity to make a global impact with their charity work. For Philip, whose entire existence has been based on a devotion to doing his duty, it appeared that his grandson had abdicated his for the sake of his marriage to an American divorcee in much the same way as Edward VIII gave up his crown to marry Wallace Simpson in 1936.

Whatever discomfort Prince Philip's ailments may be causing him as he enters his centennial year, they pale into insignificance compared with the disappointment and dismay his grandson Harry's dereliction of duty and his son Andrew's antics with Epstein must be causing him. He was also saddened by the breakdown of the marriage of his eldest grandchild, Peter Phillips, to the Canadian Autumn Kelly, but it didn't have the same shock effect as Harry's and Andrew's imprudent behavior. Peter and Autumn's twelve-year marriage, which produced two daughters, Savannah, born in December 2010, and Isla, born in March 2012, had appeared to be happy, but that obviously was not the case. Philip comes from the generation that puts up and shuts up, and to his mind and that of the Queen's it has always been that divorce is the very last resort.

Having cautioned the couple to try to make it work for a two-year period, when it eventually fell apart, he knew there was nothing more to do except tell them to just get on with it.

Philip's dotage is not lonely. He is his own master almost for the first time since he took command of his ship in the Royal Navy in 1950. He can keep his own timetable and get up to what he wants without an equerry or a private secretary telling him he has to be somewhere. He enjoys his own company and, as he hates throwing things away, spends a lot of time sorting through his papers and old correspondence. He has a horror of getting rid of anything that might be of historical importance, like Princess Margaret did with many of the Queen Mother's letters. Philip's archivist, the late Dame Anne Griffiths, who had worked at Buckingham Palace on and off since the 1950s, had ensured everything was neatly filed, so it was easily moved to Wood Farm. Anne Griffiths was an important part of Philip's life, having been one of the two lady clerks to accompany him and Mike Parker on HMY *Britannia* on the 1956–57 trip to the South Atlantic and the Melbourne Olympic Games. After the death of her husband in 1982, she returned to work at Buckingham Palace, and Philip eventually put her in charge of his personal archive, working three days a week right up until the last few weeks of her life. Such was the respect he had for her that he attended her memorial service in 2017 accompanied by members of the royal household including some of the Queen's ladies-in-waiting and the Lord Chamberlain, the Earl Peel, at St. Mark's Church in Primrose Hill, London.

Inevitably, Prince Philip has outlived most of his friends and contemporaries, but he still socializes locally in Norfolk and travels to Windsor for the occasional weekend or wedding. The most recent wedding trip was in May 2019 for Prince and Princess Michael's daughter Lady Gabriella Windsor's marriage to Thomas Kingston, which was attended by much of the nobility of Europe, including some of Philip's relations. A month short of his ninety-eighth birthday Philip appeared in buoyant form as he stood outside the chapel, joking with the new father, Prince Harry, and other members of the family. He even stayed for part of the reception at Frogmore House after the official photographs were taken in the Duchess of Kent's drawing room.

The divorces of three out of four of his children, the divorce of his first grandson, and the problems with his grandson Prince Harry and, more poignantly, his own son Prince Andrew make a depressing appraisal. Prince Philip knows the methods by which they were raised, which seemed so right at the time, appear to have turned out to be woefully inadequate for the demands and pressures of the modern age. The art of being royal, the Queen has said, is a matter of practice. Prince Philip believes it is a sense of duty, which in the all-consuming royal sense puts public performance before the needs of the individual. This obligation and sense of responsibility is a way of royal life that is coming to an end. Prince Philip has done his bit, and now it is up to his descendants to face the challenge of sustaining the existence of the monarchy of the future.

Chapter 20

CONCLUSION

Prince Philip never accepted anything as fact until he had thoroughly examined it to his own satisfaction. He would never agree with someone else's point of view just for the sake of it, and when in an argument he would never admit he had been convinced by it even if he had. His grandson the Duke of Cambridge has described him as "a legend," which he certainly is, but he has also been described as a person who is ultimately "unknowable," which I would agree with. His achievements are easier to assess than his complex personality.

"He knows an incredible amount, but doesn't like being contradicted," Lord Patrick Beresford once observed.

If helping support the Queen in her role as monarch had been his only attribute, it would be enough, but through his vision and wisdom he has helped her guide the monarchy through the twentieth century into the twenty-first century. He was always there in the background of the foreground, offering his strident opinions, but only when required. When the Queen said, "We owed him a debt greater than he would ever claim, or we shall ever know," she said it all.

More than fifty years ago, when Prince Philip was asked what his proudest achievements were, something that he would like to be remembered for, he replied, "I doubt whether I've achieved anything likely to be remembered." If asked the same question today, he would probably give the same answer. "I couldn't care less," he said, when asked in a BBC interview for his ninetieth birthday if he thought he had been successful in his role.

"Who cares what I think about it?" he grumpily told TV presenter Fiona Bruce. "I mean it's ridiculous." He has always disliked talking about himself and the creative role he played in the setting up of the organization that bears his name, namely the highly successful Duke of Edinburgh Awards scheme. Philip has always said it was Kurt Hahn's brainchild. It is ironic that Philip takes no credit for what is arguably his greatest achievement of lasting value.

"It would never have started but for Kurt Hahn," he said. "He suggested I ought to do it and I fought against it for quite a long time. I said, 'I am not going to stick my neck out and do anything as stupid as that.'"

"I've no reason to be proud," Philip said in 2010. "It's satisfying that we have set up a formula that works, but I don't run it. I didn't want my name attached to it. That was against my better judgement, I tried to avoid it, but I was overridden."

This self-effacing assessment does not take account of Philip's contribution to the scheme. Without the Duke's name attached to it and his annual presentation of the gold awards, it is most unlikely that it would have achieved its current level of success, where more than 8 million young people have taken part in the scheme since its foundation in 1956. Now Prince Edward, his youngest son and the one who is eventually expected to take the title Duke of Edinburgh, has taken on his father's responsibilities and the award in all its various connotations is the main focus of his work. Edward has explained that his father's reluctance to speak about all aspects of his life is due to modesty.

"My father plain and simply is very modest about himself and doesn't believe in talking about himself. One of his best pieces of advice he gives to everybody, is talk about everything else, don't talk about yourself—nobody's interested in you."

Philip provided his own job description when he said that his job—first, second, and last—was to never let the Queen down. His greatest achievement is to have performed his duties as consort faultlessly for almost seventy years, thus becoming the world's longest-serving consort of a reigning monarch. In the early days, when the young Queen was shy and unsure of herself, Philip helped build her self-confidence as she slipped her arm through his. He shared the duties of hundreds of overseas tours with the Queen and in their early days got her to relax in front of the television cameras. Although always in a subordinate position to the monarch, Philip took part in the ceremonies of state such as trooping the color and the state opening of Parliament. He helped receive foreign heads of state on official state visits and seldom put a foot wrong when he appeared in public with the Queen.

"He has been the most incredible support to her," Prince William said. "I don't know how anyone coming from the background he came from, who was going places, hugely promotable, a strong personality—could go from that and then take a sidestep or even a backstep and be the support he has to the Queen. It's a real eye opener to us all."

As Philip would put it, he's just the Duke of Edinburgh and she's the Queen. But it is largely thanks to Philip that the monarchy is so popular in the twenty-first century. When the Queen acceded the throne in February 1952, Philip came into Buckingham Palace like a new broom, bringing in time and motion studies to update the workings of the palace and getting rid of old arcane practices. He understood the importance of public relations for the family firm and made sure the royal press office did so too, although he never agreed with image-making, saying, "I am doubtful of the whole concept of trying to create an image." He has always claimed the monarchy exists in the interests of the people. "If at any time any nation decides that the system is unacceptable, then it is up to them to change it."

In addition to his appearances as consort, Philip has undertaken thousands of solo engagements and tours. The figures speak for themselves. When he retired from public life in 2017, shortly after his ninety-sixth birthday, Buckingham Palace announced that he had undertaken 22,219 solo engagements and 637 overseas tours since 1952. During that time, he gave 5,496 speeches, mostly written by himself, and wrote fourteen books.

Philip's first public appearance was on March 2, 1948, a few months after his marriage, when he attended the London Federation of Boys' Club Boxing finals at the Royal Albert Hall. The Court Circular recorded that the duke, then aged twenty-six, presented the prizes. His final solo appearance was as captain general of the Royal Marines at the age of ninety-six, when he attended a parade at Buckingham Palace in 2017 to mark the finale of the 1664 Global Challenge. As he left the forecourt of Buckingham Palace, the Royal Marines Band played "For He's a Jolly Good Fellow," expressing their sense of gratitude towards the prince as he entered a well-earned retirement.

Before Philip started to slow down and pass on some of his duties to the younger generation, he was president, patron, or member of some 785 organizations, for many of which he was a low-key but tireless fundraiser. His interests have always been in the future generation and the well-being of the individual, and in addition to the Duke of Edinburgh Awards scheme, Philip has been president of the National Playing Fields Association since 1949. Within a few years, with the help of funds raised by Philip, playing fields were opening at the rate of two hundred a year across the country. One of the last events he organized before his retirement was a reception in the gardens of Buckingham Palace in May 2017 to celebrate his seventy years as patron of London Youth, formerly the Association of London Boys' Clubs, now a collection of more than three hundred clubs for boys and girls. They were full of admiration for him and praised his involvement at all levels. "You would think he is cut from a different cloth," their spokesperson said, "but he understands what they are going through, from poverty to problems at home." Philip must be dismayed at the current increase in knife crime and gang warfare among young people in many cities across the UK.

As one of the world's foremost conservationists, Philip has been vociferous in expressing the threats posed by man to the natural world. He has long argued that the "greenhouse effect" and global warming are threats to the future of mankind and has stated that the greatest threat the world faces is the "colossal increase in the human population . . . which is reaching plague proportions." Over the years he has continually asserted that one of the biggest problems facing the world today is the population explosion. It is a subject he goes back to time and time again.

As discussed previously, one of the voices who have supported Philip is Sir David Attenborough. He is patron of Population Matters, a charity set up in 1991 with the purpose of influencing policymakers to make positive changes for a sustainable human population.

Attenborough, who was ninety-four in May 2020, has spoken

with Prince Philip, Prince Charles, and Philip's grandsons Prince William and Prince Harry frequently on this subject. Even the opinionated Harry agrees with him and has stated he will only have two children.

Harry made the revelation in a candid interview with conservationist Dr. Jane Goodall as part of his wife's 2019 edition of British *Vogue*. Discussing the "terrifying" effects of climate change, he assured her that he and the duchess were planning on having only one more child after the birth of their son, Archie. He said becoming a father has made him see the world differently and the couple only want "two maximum" to help protect the environment.

Prince Philip has always believed that science is able to elucidate any problem, and he is certain the difficulty of feeding the increasing population, with more than three hundred thousand children being born every day, can be resolved by producing food under controlled scientific conditions. This is already happening, but in order to make it work on a global scale it needs water, and that, according to Prince Philip and countless others, is our next global obstacle, as there will simply not be enough.

As the world population continues to expand at an ever-increasing rate and global warming becomes an ever more dangerous reality, Philip's concerns seem to be well founded. "If we've got this extraordinary diversity on this globe, it seems awfully silly for us to destroy it. All these other creatures have an equal right to exist here, we have no prior rights to the earth than anybody else and if they're here let's give them a chance to survive."

However, he has refused to describe himself as "green." "I think that there's a difference between being concerned for the conservation of nature and being a bunny hugger . . . people who simply love animals," he said. "People can't get their heads round the idea of a species surviving, you know, they're more concerned about how you treat a donkey in Sicily or something."

Philip's ability to always be able to speak his mind coherently has been both an advantage and a disadvantage, as the late Countess Mountbatten accurately observed. "He always speaks his mind, sometimes not necessarily with a high degree of tact," she said. "But on the other hand, I think that people have come to expect that of him, and they really rather enjoy it and they think how nice to hear somebody actually say what they think."

As he approached retirement in his nineties, Philip talked about having "done his bit" and the need to slow down. But, before he did so, at the age of ninety-four, he gave one last interview to Radio 4, in which he talked about his favorite subject—engineering. He criticized the "curious" lack of a Nobel Prize for engineering and said that "everything not invented by God was invented by an engineer." He added that engineers hold the key to humanity and its ability to thrive on this planet.

Philip has always put engineering as being of critical importance to humanity. In 1976, he was responsible for creating the National Fellowship of Engineering to advance and promote excellence in engineering for the benefit of society. This led to the formation of the Royal Academy of Engineering of which he is the senior fellow. The academy's objective is to make the UK the leading nation for engineering innovation and businesses. Throughout his working life, Philip has blown the trumpet for British science and engineering. One of his early achievements was the speech he gave in 1951 as president of the British Association for the Advancement of Science in which he detailed scientific progress in the UK since the Great Exhibition of 1851. This speech was remarkable not only for its length and content but also for the fact that he wrote the speech in his cabin while an active officer in the Royal Navy. Philip was also instrumental in the setting up of the Queen Elizabeth Prize for Engineering, which is a £1 million global engineering prize that rewards and celebrates the engineers responsible for a ground-breaking innovation in engineering that has been of global benefit to humanity.

As a keen sportsman, Philip excelled at yachting, polo, and carriage driving. It was the latter two sports that led to his becoming president of the Fédération Equestre Internationale (FEI), the governing body of equestrian sports. Philip served as president for twenty-two years, until his daughter, the princess royal, took over in 1986. During his presidency, Philip set up the World Equestrian Games that are held every four years, served as a judge of dressage and show jumping at several Olympic games, and rewrote the rules for carriage driving, which he still enjoyed in his ninety-eighth year.

Philip is a man of many interests and many parts. Few people have enjoyed a working life for as long as he has. From the time he was forced to leave the life he loved in the Royal Navy until he stepped down in his ninety-sixth year, he worked for the good of the monarchy, for the good of the United Kingdom, and for the good of mankind. Even as a member of the royal family, he was not always successful. When he was president of the Automobile Association for ten years, he failed to persuade successive ministers of transport that all buses and lorries should have their exhaust pipes mounted vertically at roof height in order to keep the diesel fumes away from pedestrians.

Shortly before he died in 2001, Mike Parker talked about Philip's work ethic, saying: "I don't think he has let up. I've watched it over the years. And he keeps up this incredible pace. I've actually said to him from time to time 'it's time you eased up somewhat' and you know he grins a bit and he says, 'Well what would I do? Sit around and knit?' I only hope the United Kingdom shows its gratitude for what he has done, for the constant flogging up hill and down dale and around the world . . . and never really stopping. They're the most extraordinarily lucky country to have him."

The many speeches Prince Philip has given are intelligent, articulate, and usually entertaining. He loves a discussion but can't stand losing an argument. In his view he is always right. Visiting the Chelsea Flower Show in 2008, he commented that he liked the tree fern in the Australian garden. When he was told that it was not in fact a tree fern and was told its proper Latin name, he said as he walked away, "I didn't want a bloody lecture." He dislikes questions about himself almost as much as he dislikes the press. On more than one occasion he has been asked if he still flies planes or still enjoys carriage driving, reasonable questions for someone in their nineties. He frequently puts his questioner down with his favorite riposte: "I can still breathe, still drink a glass of water, and I am still here." Guests at Buckingham Palace luncheons are advised not to ask him personal questions and let him do the talking.

He has written several slim volumes of philosophical musings on the meaning of life. These books are largely forgotten and out of print. However, collections of Philip's so-called gaffes can be found in any bookshop, usually classed as wit and wisdom. From any of these collections, it can be seen that when Philip was young his politically incorrect gaffes were on the whole inoffensive and amusing asides to break the ice in formal situations. As he got older, he became more openly aggressive and even sometimes appeared racist, although he doesn't have a racist bone in his body. His worst barbs were uttered when he was in his seventies and later. Age has not softened him; he has become cantankerous, brusque, and on occasion offensive. Regrettably, his rudeness has made him something of a folk hero to many people. His insults have been described as "glorious gaffes." The press are always repeating and recycling and, in some cases, inventing his gaffes.

*

When Philip's great-grandson Prince George is King George VII, what might the history books show as Philip's achievements? Prince Albert, Philip's predecessor as consort, has left a lasting memorial in the many institutions that have been established in his name in London. Albert died at the young age of forty-two and did not live to see the fruits of his cultural dreams come true. Philip has said he never saw being consort as a role, more a way of life, and he never visualized himself as playing a part. In terms of physical achievements of a lasting nature, Philip has been instrumental in setting up many things—one example is the Queen's Gallery in what was once the bombed chapel at Buckingham Palace—but most of Philip's achievements are of a different nature. He has undoubtedly done much to improve the lives of young people and he has performed his duties to the Queen in an exemplary manner. Will he be remembered for the immense amount of good that he has done in many fields during his long life, most of which don't bear his name, or for his so-called gaffes? Will he be remembered for his contribution to conservation, or for the number of game birds and stags he has shot? I think he will be remembered for the former. He is an integral part of the second Elizabethan age and an important figure in its history.

"It is with deep sorrow that Her Majesty the Queen announces the death of her beloved husband, His Royal Highness Prince Philip, Duke of Edinburgh. His Royal Highness passed away peacefully this morning at Windsor Castle."

When the news came on the morning of Friday, April 9, 2021, for that moment the world seemed to stand still. The man who had spent his long life supporting the Queen, always two steps behind, was no longer. It was the sixteenth anniversary of the Prince of Wales and the Duchess of Cornwall's wedding and, poignantly for the Queen, the anniversary of Queen Elizabeth the Queen Mother's funeral in 2002. The Duke wanted as little fuss as possible, and because of the restrictions surrounding the COVID-19 pandemic, Operation Forth Bridge, the code name for the Duke's funeral, was exactly as he would have liked. The service held at St George's Chapel was attended by those who meant the most to him, and after the service he was placed in the royal vault.

Prince Philip's passing, just two months short of his one hundredth birthday, followed a lengthy stay in hospital and several weeks of illness at Windsor Castle. His death brought to an end the longest love affair in British royal history. He and Queen Elizabeth had been married for nearly seventy-four years. In the time that they had known each other, they had seen the Second World War come to an end and the Cold War come and go. They had welcomed countless presidents and heads of states into their homes and seen the world change unimaginably from their own childhoods.

Prince Philip died with his "darling Lilibet" at his side in his private apartments, having refused to return to hospital. His family and the nation and the world mourned the passing of a man whose life exemplified service and a sense of duty, above all to his wife, all of it performed with good humor and grace. As one well-wisher who placed flowers at the gates of Buckingham Palace said, he brought "the kind of stability that's so old-fashioned, it's difficult to comprehend. He was a rock who brought integrity."

Acknowledgments

I would like to thank Nick Cowan for his invaluable help with this book. He is more used to writing about rockers than royalty, but his assistance on every aspect in writing this book was second to none. I would also like to thank *Majesty* magazine's managing editor Joe Little for casting his forensic eye over the manuscript in the little time he had to do it. Once again, the back copies of *Majesty* magazine, which was first published forty years ago, in 1980, were absolutely invaluable and are without doubt some of the few available printed records of royal tours and visits.

At my publishers Simon & Schuster I would like to thank my editor Ian Marshall for his hard work and faith in my idea and also Louise Davies and Theresa Bebbington.

I would also like to thank my agent from Sheil Land, Piers Blofeld.

My grateful thanks to Dr. Peter Collett for his fascinating insight into the character of Prince Philip and to those who helped me understand him, including Lord Patrick Beresford, John Kidd, Anne de Richmond Smithers, Ken Wharfe, Alan Titchmarsh, Christopher Wilson, Simone Simmons, General Sir Michael Hobbs, Marina Mowatt, Eileen Parker, David Muir, Brian McGrath, James Edwards, Ronald Ferguson, Betty Parsons, Sir John Peel, James Thomas, and many more over the years I have been writing about Prince Philip.

Prince Philip's Extended Family

Prince Philip and his extended family, showing his connection to Queen Victoria and the royal family, to the tsars of Russia, to the throne of Denmark, and to German aristocracy.

Philip—Prince Philip Duke of Edinburgh, born 1921, formerly Lieutenant Mountbatten R.N., formerly Prince Philip of Greece and Denmark

Alice—Princess Andrew of Greece, 1885–1969, Philip's mother, formerly Alice of Battenberg, great-granddaughter of Queen Victoria

Andreas—Prince Andrew of Greece and Denmark, 1882–1944, Philip's father, son of King George I of Greece and Grand Duchess Olga of Russia

Margarita—Princess of Greece and Denmark, 1905–1981, Philip's sister, wife of Prince Gottfried of Hohenlohe-Langenburg

Theodora—Princess of Greece and Denmark, 1906–1969, Philip's sister, wife of Berthold Margrave of Baden

Cecile—Princess of Greece and Denmark, 1911–1937, Philip's sister, wife of George Donatus Hereditary Grand Duke of Hesse and by Rhine

Sophie—Princess of Greece and Denmark, 1914–2001, Philip's sister, wife of (1) Prince Christoph of Hesse (2) Prince Georg of Hanover

George I—King of Greece, Philip's paternal grandfather, 1845–1913, formerly Prince William, son of King Christian IX of Denmark

Olga—Grand Duchess of Russia 1851–1926, Philip's paternal grandmother, wife of King George I of Greece

Louis of Battenberg—1st Marquess of Milford Haven, 1854–1921, Philip's maternal grandfather, husband of Princess Victoria

Victoria—Princess Victoria, Dowager Marchioness of Milford Haven, 1863–1950, Philip's maternal grandmother, granddaughter of Queen Victoria

George Mountbatten—2nd Marquess of Milford Haven, 1892–1938, Philip's uncle and guardian

"Nada"—Marchioness of Milford Haven, 1896–1963, Philip's aunt, formerly Countess Nadejda Torby, wife of George Mountbatten

"Dickie" Mountbatten—Lord Louis Earl Mountbatten of Burma, 1900–1979, Philip's uncle, brother of Alice, George Milford Haven, and Louise Queen of Sweden

Edwina—Countess Mountbatten of Burma, 1901–1960, Philip's aunt, formerly Edwina Ashley, granddaughter of Sir Ernest Cassel

Constantine I—King of Greece, 1868–1923, Philip's uncle, husband of Sophia of Prussia

"Big" George—Prince of Greece and Denmark, 1869–1957, Philip's uncle, husband of author and psychoanalyst Marie Bonaparte

Nicholas—Prince of Greece and Denmark, 1872–1938, Philip's uncle, husband of Grand Duchess Elena of Russia, father of Marina Duchess of Kent

Christopher—Prince of Greece and Denmark, Philip's uncle, 1888–1940, husband of (1) "Nancy" Leeds (2) Princess Françoise of France

Christian IX—King of Denmark, 1818–1906, Philip's great-grandfather, father of Alexandra Queen of England, George I King of Greece, and Dagmar Tsarina of Russia

Louis IV—Grand Duke of Hesse 1837–1892, Philip's great-grandfather, husband of Queen Victoria's daughter Princess Alice

Maria Feodorovna—formerly Princess Dagmar of Denmark, 1847–1928, Philip's great-aunt, wife of Tsar Alexander III of Russia, mother of Tsar Nicholas II

George V—King of United Kingdom, 1865–1936, first cousin of Philip's father Andreas

Ernest Ludwig—"Uncle Ernie," Grand Duke of Hesse and by Rhine, 1868–1937, Philip's great-uncle, father-in-law of Philip's sister Cecile, grandson of Queen Victoria, brother of Philip's grandmother Victoria

Louise Mountbatten—formerly Princess Louise of Battenberg, 1889–1965, Philip's aunt, married to King Gustaf VI Adolf of Sweden

Alexandra—Queen of England, 1844–1925, Philip's great-aunt, wife of King Edward VII, daughter of King Christian IX of Denmark

Alexandra—Empress of Russia, 1872–1918, Philip's great-aunt, wife of Tsar Nicholas II, formerly Princess Alix of Hesse, granddaughter of Queen Victoria

Alexandra—Queen of Yugoslavia, 1921–1993, Philip's second cousin and biographer, formerly Princess Alexandra of Greece

Alexandra—Princess Alexandra, Lady Ogilvy, born 1936, Philip's confidante, daughter of the Duke of Kent and Marina Duchess of Kent

Bibliography

Airlie, Mabell, Countess of. *Thatched with Gold: The Memoirs of Mabell, Countess of Airlie*. London: Hutchinson of London, 1962.

Alexandra, Queen of Yugoslavia. *Prince Philip: A Family Portrait*. London: Hodder & Stoughton, 1960.

Benson, Ross. *Charles: The Untold Story*. London: Victor Gollancz, 1993.

Bertin, Celia. *Marie Bonaparte: A Life*. New York: Harcourt Brace Jovanovich, 1982.

Boothroyd, Basil. *Philip: An Informal Biography*. London: Longman, 1971.

Bradford, Sarah. *Elizabeth: A Biography of Her Majesty the Queen*. Portsmouth, NH: Heinemann, 1996.

Brandreth, Gyles. *Philip and Elizabeth: Portrait of a Marriage*. New York: Century, 2004.

Butt, Anthony A. *The Wisdom of Prince Philip*. London: Hardie Grant Books, 2015.

Channon, Henry and Robert James, ed. *Chips: The Diaries of Sir Henry Channon*. London: Weidenfeld & Nicolson, 1967.

Corbitt, F. J. *My Twenty Years in Buckingham Palace*. Philadelphia: David McKay Co., 1956.

Cordet, Hélène. *Born Bewildered*. London: Peter Davies, 1961.

Crawford, Marion. *The Little Princesses*. London: Cassell & Co., 1950.

Dampier, Phil, and Ashley Walton. *Prince Philip: A Lifetime of Wit and Wisdom*. Barzipan Publishing, 2017.

Dean, John. *HRH Prince Philip, Duke of Edinburgh: A Portrait by his Valet*. London: Robert Hale, 1954.

De Courcy, Anne. *Snowdon: The Biography*. London: Weidenfeld & Nicholson, 2008.

Dimbleby, Jonathan. *The Prince of Wales: A Biography*. New York: Little, Brown, 1994.

Farnes, Norma. *Spike Milligan: Man of Letters*. New York: Penguin Books, 2014.

Ferguson, Ronald. *The Galloping Major: My Life and Singular Times*. New York: Macmillan, 1994.

Gathorne-Hardy, Jonathan. *The Rise and Fall of the British Nanny*. London: Hodder & Stoughton, 1972.

Gibson, John, and Valerie Carroll. *From Belfast's Sandy Row to Buckingham Palace*. Cork, Ireland: Mercier Press, 1994.

Hall, Unity. *Philip: The Man Behind the Monarchy*. London: Michael O'Mara Books, 1987.

Hardman, Robert. *Our Queen*. London: Hutchinson, 2011.

Hardman, Robert. *Queen of the World: Elizabeth II: Sovereign and Stateswoman*. New York: Century, 2018.

Hart-Davis, Duff. *King's Counsellor*. London: Weidenfeld & Nicholson, 2006.

Hartley, John. *Accession: The Making of a Queen*. London: Quartet Books, 1992.

Heald, Tim. *The Duke: A Portrait of Prince Philip*. London: Hodder & Stoughton, 1991.

Hicks, Pamela. *Daughter of Empire: My Life as a Mountbatten*. London: Weidenfeld & Nicholson, 2012.

Hoey, Brian. *The Royal Yacht* Britannia: *Inside the Queen's Floating Palace*. Somerset, UK: Patrick Stephens Ltd., 1995.

Hollis, General Sir Leslie. *The Captain General: A Life of HRH Prince Philip*. London: Herbert Jenkins Ltd., 1961.

Judd, Denis. *Prince Philip: A Biography*. London: Michael Joseph, 1980.

Kirkwood, Pat. *The Time of My Life*. London: Robert Hale, 1999.

Lacey, Robert. *Royal: Her Majesty Queen Elizabeth II.* New York: Little, Brown, 2002.

Mann, the Rt. Rev. Michael. *Some Windsor Sermons.* Norfolk, UK: Michael Russell Publishing Ltd., 1968.

Marco, Earl Mountbatten of Burma. *An Introduction to Polo.* UK: Royal Naval Saddle Club, 1982.

Oliver, Charles. *Dinner at Buckingham Palace.* Upper Saddle River, NJ: Prentice Hall, Inc., 1972.

Parker, Eileen. *Step Aside for Royalty: Treasured Memories of the Royal Household.* London: Bachman & Turner, 1982.

Parker, John. *Prince Philip: A Critical Biography.* London: Sidgwick & Jackson, 1990.

Philip, HRH Prince. *Birds from Britannia,* Harlow, Essex, UK: Longmans Green & Co. Ltd., 1962.

———. *Down to Earth.* Glasgow, Scotland: William Collins & Sons, 1988.

———. *Driving & Judging Dressage.* Wiltshire, UK: J. A. Allen, 1996.

———. *Men, Machines and Sacred Cows.* London: Hamish Hamilton, 1984.

———. *Prince Philip Speaks: Selected Speeches 1956–1959.* London: Collins, 1960.

———. *A Question of Balance.* Norfolk, UK: Michael Russell Publishing Ltd., 1982.

———. *Selected Speeches 1948–1955.* Oxford, UK: Oxford University Press, 1957.

———. *30 Years On and Off the Box Seat,* Wiltshire, UK: J. A. Allen, 2004.

Philip, HRH Prince, and James Fisher. *Wildlife Crisis.* London: Hamish Hamilton Ltd., 1970.

Philip, HRH Prince, and the Rt Rev. Michael Mann. *A Windsor Correspondence.* Norfolk, UK: Michael Russell Publishing Ltd., 1984.

———. *Survival or Extinction: A Christian Attitude to the Environment.* Norfolk, UK: Michael Russell Publishing Ltd., 1989.

Pimlott, Ben. *The Queen: Elizabeth II and the Monarchy.* New York: HarperCollins, 1996.

Pope-Hennessy, James. *The Quest for Queen Mary*. London: Hodder & Stoughton, 2018.

Scarfe, Rory. *Do You Still Throw Spears at Each Other?* New York: Simon & Schuster, 2011.

Seward, Ingrid. *The Last Great Edwardian Lady*. London: Century, 1999.

———. *My Husband and I: The Inside Story of 70 Years of the Royal Marriage*. New York: Simon & Schuster, 2017.

———. *Prince Edward: A Biography*. London: Century, 1995.

———. *The Queen and Di: The Untold Story*. New York: HarperCollins, 2000.

———. *The Queen's Speech: An Intimate Portrait of the Queen in Her Own Words*. New York: Simon & Schuster, 2015.

———. *Royal Children of the Twentieth Century*. New York: HarperCollins, 1993.

———. *Royalty Revealed*. London: Sidgwick & Jackson, 1989.

———. *Sarah: The Life of a Duchess*. New York: HarperCollins, 1991.

Shawcross, William. *Queen Elizabeth: The Queen Mother*. New York: Macmillan, 2009.

Sherbrook-Walker, Eric. *Treetops Hotel*. London: Robert Hale, 1962.

Taylor, Jimmy. *Growing Up at Cheam School 1922–1934*. Woodville, MA: The Friends of Whitehall, 2011.

Townsend, Peter. *Time and Chance: An Autobiography*. London: Collins, 1978.

Turner, Graham. *Elizabeth: The Woman and the Queen*. Macmillan, 2002

Vickers, Hugo. *Alice: Princess Andrew of Greece*, New York: Viking, 2000.

Warwick, Christopher. *Princess Margaret: A Life of Contrasts*. London: André Deutsch, 2000.

Zeepvat, Charlotte. *From Cradle to Crown: British Nannies and Governesses at the World's Royal Courts*. Gloucestershire, UK: Sutton Publishing Ltd., 2006.

Ziegler, Philip, ed. *Personal Diary of Admiral the Lord Louis Mountbatten 1943–1946*. London: Collins, 1988.

Index